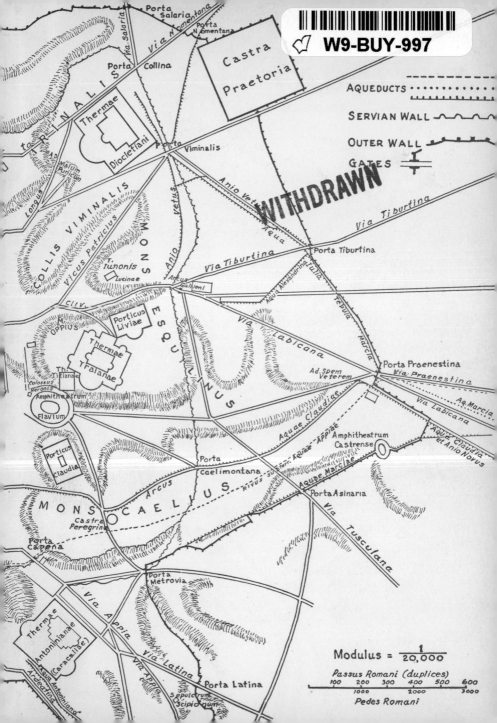

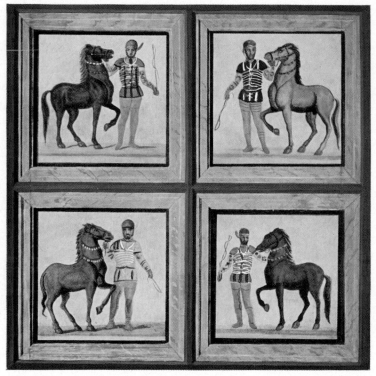

A MOSAIC SHOWING AURĪGAE WEARING THE COLORS OF THE
FOUR FACTIŌNĒS

This mosaic was found in a villa near Rome.

𝕺𝖍𝖊 𝕷𝖆𝖐𝖊 𝕮𝖑𝖆𝖘𝖘𝖎𝖈𝖆𝖑 𝕾𝖊𝖗𝖎𝖊𝖘

THE PRIVATE LIFE OF THE ROMANS

BY

HAROLD WHETSTONE JOHNSTON

*Sometime Professor of Latin in
Indiana University*

REVISED BY

MARY JOHNSTON

MacMurray College

SCOTT, FORESMAN AND COMPANY
CHICAGO   ATLANTA   DALLAS   NEW YORK

PREFACE TO THE ORIGINAL EDITION

In preparing this book I have had in mind the needs of three classes of students.

It is intended in the first place for seniors in high schools and freshmen in colleges, and is meant to give such an account of the Private Life of the Romans in the later Republic and earlier Empire as will enable them to understand the countless references to it in the Latin texts which they read in the classroom. It is hoped that the book contains all that they will need for this purpose and nothing that is beyond their comprehension.

It is intended in the second place for more advanced college students who may be taking lectures on the subjects of which it treats. The work of both teacher and student will be made less irksome and more effective if the student is aided in the taking of notes by even so general a knowledge of the subject (previously announced to the class) as is here given. This I know from actual experience with my own classes.

In the third place it is intended for readers and students of Roman history, who are engaged chiefly with important political and constitutional questions, and often feel the need of a simple and compact description of domestic life, to give more reality to the shadowy forms whose public careers they are following. Such students will find the Index especially useful.

The book is written as far as possible in English: that is, no great knowledge of Latin is presumed on the part of the reader. I have tried not to crowd the text with Latin

1

words, even when they are immediately explained, and those given will usually be found worth remembering. Quotations from Latin authors are very few, and the references to their works, fewer still, are made to well-known passages only.

To every chapter are prefixed references to the standard secondary authorities in English and German. Primary sources are not indicated: they would be above the heads of the less advanced students, and to the more advanced the lecturer will prefer to indicate the sources on which his views are based. It is certain, however, that all these sources are indicated in the authorities named, and the teacher himself may occasionally find the references helpful.

The illustrations are numerous and are intended to illustrate. Many others are referred to in the text, which limited space kept me from using, and I hope that Schreiber's *Atlas*, at least, if not Baumeister's *Denkmaeler*, may be within the reach of students in classroom or library.

It goes without saying that there must be many errors in a book like this, although I have done my best to make it accurate. When these errors are due to relaxed attention or to ignorance, I shall be grateful to the person who will point them out. When they are due to mistaken judgment, the teacher will find in the references, I hope, sufficient authorities to convince his pupils that he is right and I am wrong.

H. W. JOHNSTON

INDIANA UNIVERSITY
February, 1903

PREFACE TO THE REVISED EDITION

For twenty-nine years *The Private Life of the Romans* has been the standard work on this subject in classroom and library. It now appears in a new and enlarged edition.

While keeping all the advantage of Dr. Johnston's ripe scholarship and charm of style, the reviser has simplified some difficulties and added a considerable body of new information not available at the time when the original edition was brought out. Much of this is due to recent excavations at Pompeii and elsewhere.

Special attention is called to the following features of the revised book: (1) There are two bibliographies: The one in the Introduction (pp. 23-26) gives complete information about general works of an encyclopedic nature; the other, at the back of the book (pp. 409-412), includes all the volumes referred to in the text.

(2) Except in the Index, the vowel quantities of all Latin words are marked, regardless of whether they are so indicated in books referred to. This has been done for the convenience of students who are accustomed to marked vowels.

(3) No pains have been spared to make it more attractive in every mechanical way. Especially noteworthy are the numerous illustrations, all of which are taken from classical sources.

The author of this edition is grateful to the Keystone View Company for the use of the following pictures: the stove on page 206, the carriage on 306, and the bridge on 310.

To Professor Selatie E. Stout, who commented on the manuscript, to Mr. H. F. Scott, who kindly read proof of the book in its entirety, and to Dr. Charles Knapp, who has, with his usual painstaking care and scholarly accuracy, gone over text and bibliographies, the author extends her warmest thanks.

MARY JOHNSTON

MacMurray College
Feb. 1, 1932

CONTENTS

4

LIST OF ILLUSTRATIONS

THE PRIVATE LIFE OF THE ROMANS

INTRODUCTION

1. The topics that are discussed in this book have to do
with the everyday life of the Roman people. Such things
will be considered as the family, the Roman name, marriage
and the position of women, children and education, slaves,
clients, the house and its furniture, clothing, food and meals,
amusements, travel and correspondence, religion, funeral
ceremonies and burial customs. These things are of interest
to us in the case of any ancient or foreign people; in the case
of the Romans they are of especial importance, because they
help to explain the powerful influence which that nation
exerted over the old world, and make it easier to understand
why that influence is still felt in some degree today.

2. Public and Private Antiquities. The subjects that
have been named above belong to what is called Classical
Antiquities, taking their place in the subdivision of Roman
Antiquities as opposed to Greek Antiquities. They are
grouped loosely together as Private Antiquities, in opposition
to what we call Public Antiquities.[1] Under the latter head
we consider the Roman as a citizen, and we examine the
several classes of citizens, their obligations, and their privileges; we study the form of their government, its officers and
machinery, its legislative, judicial, and executive procedure,
its revenues and expenditures, etc. It is evident that no

---

[1] "Private" in such usage is equivalent to Latin *prīvātus*, "public" to Latin *pūblicus*.

hard and fast line can be drawn between the two branches of the subject; they cross each other at every turn. One scarcely knows, for example, under which head to put the religion of the Romans, or their games in the *circus*.

Fig. 1
A ROMAN MAN AND WIFE
From a tombstone now in the Vatican Museum, Rome.

3. In the same way, the daily employment of a slave, his keep, his punishments, his rewards are properly considered under the head of Private Antiquities. But the State undertook sometimes to regulate by law the number of slaves that a master might have, and the State regulated the manumission of the slave and gave him certain rights as a freedman. All such matters belong to Public Antiquities. So, too, a man might or might not be eligible to certain priestly offices, according to the particular ceremony used at the marriage of his parents. It will be found, therefore, that the study of Private Antiquities cannot be completely separated from its complement, though in this book the dividing line will be crossed as seldom as possible.[1]

4. Antiquities and History. It is just as impossible to draw the boundary line between the subjects of Antiquities and History. Formerly, it is true, histories were concerned little with the private life of the people, but dealt almost solely with the rise and fall of dynasties. They told us of kings and generals, of the wars they waged, the victories they

Fig. 2
RUINS OF THE AQUA CLAUDIA
An aqueduct near Rome (*see* §§ 219, 500).

won, and the conquests they made. Then, in course of time, institutions took the place of dynasties and parties the place of heroes, and history traced the growth of great political ideas; such masterpieces as Thirlwall's and Grote's histories of Greece are largely constitutional histories. But changes in international relations affect the private life of a people as surely, if not as speedily, as they affect the machinery of government.

---

[1] Students in secondary schools will find useful for preliminary reading the outline of the Roman Constitution in the Introduction to Johnston-Kingery, *Selected Orations and Letters of Cicero*. For more advanced students the following will be found useful: Abbott, *Roman Political Institutions*, and *Roman Politics*; Granrud, *Roman Constitutional History*; Greenidge, *Roman Public Life*.

5. You cannot bring into contact, friendly or unfriendly, two different civilizations without affecting the peoples concerned, without altering their occupations, their ways of living, their very ideas of life and its purposes. These changes react in turn upon the temper and character of a people; they affect its capacity for self-government and the government of others, and in the course of time they bring about the movements of which even the older histories took notice. Hence our more recent histories give more and more space to the life of the common people, to the very matters, that is, that were mentioned as belonging to Private Antiquities (§§ 1-2).

6. On the other hand, it is equally true that a knowledge of political history is necessary for the study of Private Antiquities. We shall find the Romans giving up certain ways of living and habits of thinking that seemed to have become fixed and characteristic. These changes we could not explain at all if political history did not inform us that just before they took place the Romans had come into contact with the widely different ideas and different civilizations of other nations. The most important event of this sort was the spread of Greek culture after the First Punic War, and to this we shall have to refer again and again. It follows from all this that students who have had even the most elementary course in Roman history have already some knowledge of Private Antiquities, and that those who have not studied the history of Rome at all will find very helpful the reading of even the briefest of our school histories of Rome.[1]

7. Antiquities and Philology. The subject of Classical Antiquities has always been regarded as a branch ("discipline" is the technical word) of Classical Philology since Friedrich August Wolf (1759-1824) made Philology a science.

---

[1]Among such short histories are: Abbott, *A Short History of Rome;* Frank, *A History of Rome;* Boak, *A History of Rome.*

It is quite true that Philology, in the common acceptation of the word, is merely the science of language, but even here Antiquities has an important part to play. It is impossible to read understandingly an ode of Horace or an oration of Cicero if one is ignorant of the social life and the political institutions of Rome. But Classical Philology is much more than the science of understanding and interpreting the classical languages. It claims for itself the

FIG. 3
A ROMAN TEMPLE IN FRANCE
This building is now used as a Museum of Numismatics in Nîmes
(Nemausus), France.

investigation of Greek and Roman life in all its aspects, social, intellectual, and political, so far as it has become known to us from the surviving literary, monumental, and epigraphic records. Whitney puts it thus: "Philology deals with human speech and with all that speech discloses as to the nature and history of man." If it is hard to remember the definitions, one can hardly forget the epigram of Benoist: "Philology is the geology of the intellectual world." Under this, the only scientific conception of Philology, the study of Antiquities takes at once a higher place.   It becomes the end, with linguistics the means, and this is the true relation between them.

8. But it happens that the study of the languages in which the records of classical antiquity are preserved must first occupy the investigator, and that the study of language as mere language—of its origin, its growth, its decay—is in itself very interesting and profitable.   It happens that the languages of Greece and Rome cannot be studied apart from literatures of singular richness, beauty, and power, and the study of literature has always been one of the most attractive and absorbing to cultivated men.   It is not hard to understand, therefore, why the study of Antiquities has not been more prominent in connection with philological training.   Such study was the end to which only the few pressed on.   It was reserved, at least in systematic form, for the trained scholar in the university.   From the courses in Greek and in Latin conducted in our colleges it was crowded out by the more obvious, but not more essential or interesting, subjects of linguistics and literary criticism, or it was presented in those courses at best in the form of scrappy notes on the authors read in the classroom or in the dismembered alphabetical arrangement of a dictionary.

9. Within more recent years, however, a change has been taking place, a change due to several causes.   In the first place, the literary criticism which was once taught exclusively in connection with classical authors and which claimed so large a part of the time allotted to classical study has found a place in the departments of English.   Secondly, a shift of emphasis has relieved college courses of much elementary linguistic drill that was formerly considered necessary.   In the third place, the last seventy-five years have seen a very great advance in the knowledge of Classical Antiquities; it is possible to present in positive dogmatic form much in fields wherein, at one time, guesswork and speculation played a large part.

10. Finally, modern theories of education, which have narrowed the stream of classical instruction only to deepen its channel and quicken its current, have caused more stress to be laid upon the points of contact between the ancient and the modern world. The teacher of the classics has come to realize that the obligations of the present to the past are not to be so clearly presented and so vividly ap-

Fig. 4
A ROMAN BRIDGE NEAR SEGOVIA, SPAIN
This bridge is still in use.

preciated in connection with the formal study of art and literature as in the investigation of the great social, political, and religious problems which throughout all the ages have engaged the thought of cultivated men.

11. Sources. It has been already remarked (§ 7) that Classical Philology draws its knowledge from three sources, the literary, monumental, and epigraphic remains of Greece and Rome. It is necessary that we should understand at the outset precisely what is meant by each of these. By literary evidence we mean the formal writings of the Greeks and Romans, that is, the books which they published that have come down to us. The form of these books, the way they were published and have been preserved, will be considered later. For the present it is sufficient to say that only a mere fraction of these writings has come down to our day, and that of the surviving works we possess no originals, but merely more or less imperfect copies. It is true, nevertheless, that these form as a whole the most important of our sources of information, largely because they have been most carefully studied and are best understood.

FIG. 5
A ROMAN AMPHITHEATER IN AFRICA
These remains are near El Djem.

12. By monumental evidence we mean all the things actually made by the Greeks and Romans that have come down to us. These things are collectively very numerous and of very many kinds: coins, medals, pieces of jewelry, armor, pottery, statues, paintings, bridges, aqueducts, fortifications, ruins of cities, etc. It is impossible to enumerate them all. It is upon such remains as these that most of the surviving inscriptions (§ 13) are preserved. Of the first importance for the study of the private life of the Romans are the ruins of the city of Pompeii, preserved to us by the protection of the ashes that buried it at the time of the eruption of Vesuvius in the year 79 A.D.

13. By epigraphic evidence we mean the words that were

written, scratched, cut, or stamped on hard materials, such as metal, stone, or wood, usually without thought of literary finish. These vary from single words to records of very considerable extent, and are briefly called "inscriptions." The student may get a good idea of the most ancient and curious by merely turning over a few pages of Ritschl's *Priscae Latinitatis Monumenta Epigraphica* or of Egbert's *Latin Inscriptions*. The legends stamped on coins and medals are of

Fig. 6
ROMAN POTTERY FOUND IN BRITAIN
Large jars for household use, now in the Toronto Museum.

great historical importance; many of these coins are now to be found in American collections. With modern inscriptions on similar materials and for similar purposes every student is, of course, familiar.

14. It will be seen at once that the importance of these sources will vary with the nature of the subject we are studying and the fullness of their preservation. For example, we may read in a Roman poet a description of an ornament worn by a bride. A painting of a bride wearing such an ornament would make the description clearer, but any doubt that might remain would be removed if there should be found in the ruins of Pompeii (§ 12) a similar ornament with its character proved by an inscription upon it. In this case all three sources would have contributed to our knowledge.

15. For other matters, especially intangible things, we may have to rely solely upon descriptions, that is, upon literary sources. But it may well happen that no Roman wrote a set description of the particular thing that we are studying, or that, if he did, his writings have been lost, so that we may be forced to build up our knowledge bit by bit, by putting together laboriously the scraps of information, mere hints perhaps, that we find scattered here and there in the works of different authors—authors, it may be, of very different times. It is not hard to understand, therefore, that our knowledge of some things pertaining to Roman Antiquities may be fairly complete, while of others we may have no knowledge at all. It may be worth remarking of literary sources that the more common and familiar a thing was to the ancients, the less likely is it that we shall find a description of it in ancient literature.

16. Reference Books. The collecting and arranging of the information gleaned from these sources has been the task of scholars from very early times, but so much has been added to our knowledge by recent discoveries that all but the later books may be neglected by the student. A convenient list of reference works in English is Professor McDaniel's *Guide for the Study of English Books on Roman Private Life.* A list giving selections from the constantly increasing number of books treating of Roman Antiquities will be found on pages 409-412 of this book; at the head of Chapters I-XVI there will be given passages to be consulted in certain standard works. These works have been arranged in two classes, systematic treatises and encyclopedic works, a list of which will be found on pages 23-26. The student who lacks time to consult all these books should select one at least of the better and larger works in each class for regular and methodical study. The student should be warned not to neglect a book merely because it happens to be written in a language that he does not read fluently; the very part that he wants may happen to be easy to read, and many of these works contain illustrations that tell their own stories independently of the letterpress that accompanies them.

Systematic Treatises[1]

1. Marquardt, Joachim, *Das Privatleben der Römer*, second edition, by August Mau (Leipzig, Hirzel, 1886). This is the seventh volume of the *Handbuch der römischen Altertümer*, by Joachim Marquardt and Theodor Mommsen. It is a full and authoritative treatise, with a few illustrations. [Marquardt.]

2. Blümner, Hugo, *Die römischen Privataltertümer*, third edition (Munich, Beck, 1911). This is a part of the fourth volume of the *Handbuch der klassischen Altertumswissenschaft*, edited by Iwan von Müller (known now, however, as *Handbuch der Altertumswissenschaft*, edited by Walter Otto). It is the latest elaborate work on the subject, especially rich in the citation of authorities, and has some illustrations. [Blümner.]

3. Becker, Wilhelm Adolph, *Gallus oder römischen Scenen aus der Zeit Augusts*, second edition, by Hermann Göll, three volumes (Berlin, Calvary, 1880, 1881, 1882). This is a standard authority in the form of a novel. The story is of no particular interest, but the notes and "Excursuses" are of importance. There is an English translation of the first edition, by Frederick Metcalfe, which is entitled *Gallus, or Roman Scenes of the Time of Augustus* (ninth edition, London, Longmans, 1888). If it is used with caution, this translation will help those who do not read German. [Becker-Göll: the references in this book are all to the German original.]

4. Friedländer, Ludwig, *Darstellungen aus der Sittengeschichte Roms in der Zeit von August bis zum Ausgang der Antonine*, in four volumes, ninth and tenth editions, by Georg Wissowa (Leipzig, Hirzel, 1919, 1922, 1920, 1921). This is the great authority for the time it covers. It gives, in effect, the history from the earliest times of all the matters which

---

[1] At the close of each item will be given in square brackets [ ] the abbreviation by which the particular work will be named in references to it in this book.

it treats. There is an English translation of the seventh edition, in four volumes, with the title *Roman Life and Manners under the Early Empire* (New York, Dutton, undated). References in this book following the name Friedländer will be to this English translation. [Friedländer.]

5. Sandys, Sir John Edwin, *A Companion to Latin Studies*, third edition (Cambridge: At the University Press, 1921). This is a convenient handbook. [Sandys, *Companion.*]

6. Jones, H. Stuart, *A Companion to Roman History* (Oxford: At the Clarendon Press, 1912). This is excellent for those subjects which it treats. [Jones.]

7. Cagnat, René, and Chapot, V., *Manuel d'archéologie romaine* (Paris, Picard, Volume I, 1916; Volume II, 1920). This is a very valuable work. Volume I deals with "Les Monuments, Décoration des Monuments, Sculpture"; Volume II deals with "Peinture et Mosaique, Instruments de Vie Publique et Privée." [Cagnat-Chapot.]

8. McDaniel, Walton Brooks, *Roman Private Life and Its Survivals*, in the series entitled "Our Debt to Greece and Rome" (Boston, Marshall Jones Company, 1924; now published by Longmans, New York). This is a compact and interesting book. [McDaniel.]

9. Blümner, Hugo, *Technologie und Terminologie der Gewerbe und Künste bei Griechen und Römern*, in four volumes (1875-1887). The first volume appeared in a new edition in 1912, by H. Blümner (Leipzig, Teubner). This is the best description of the arts and industries of ancient Greece and Rome. [Blümner, *Technologie.*]

Encyclopedic Works

1. Pauly-Wissowa, *Real-Encyclopädie der classischen Altertumswissenschaft*. This is a monumental work, destined to be for many years the great authority upon the subject. Unfortunately it has appeared very slowly and is not yet (1932) complete (it was begun in 1894). Volumes I-XV

(First Half), covering the articles *Aal* to *Mesyros*, and Second Series, Volumes I-IV (First Half), covering the articles *Ra* to *Symposion*, have appeared. [Pauly-Wissowa.]

2. Daremberg, Charles Victor, and Saglio, Edmond, *Dictionnaire des antiquités grecques et romaines d'après les textes et les monuments* (Paris, Hachette, 1877-1918). This is a standard and authoritative work, with many illustrations. [Daremberg-Saglio.]

3. Smith, William, *A Dictionary of Greek and Roman Antiquities*, third edition, by W. Wayte and G. E. Marindin, two volumes (London, Murray, 1890, 1891). This is the best work of the sort in English. [Smith.]

4. Baumeister, August, *Denkmäler des klassischen Altertums*, in three volumes. (Munich and Leipzig, Oldenbourg, 1889). This work deals with Greek and Roman religion, art, and customs. It is richly illustrated. [Baumeister.]

5. *Harper's Dictionary of Classical Literature and Antiquities*, Edited by Harry Thurston Peck, second edition (New York, American Book Company, 1897). [Harper's.]

6. Schreiber, T., *Atlas of Classical Antiquities*, Edited, for English Use, by W. C. F. Anderson (London, Macmillan, 1895). This gives a copious collection of illustrations bearing on Greek and Roman life, with explanatory text. [Schreiber.]

7. Rich, Anthony, *A Dictionary of Roman and Greek Antiquities*, fifth edition (London, Longmans, 1884). This is a convenient manual with many illustrations. [Rich.]

8. Walters, H. B., *A Classical Dictionary of Greek and Roman Antiquities, Biography, Geography, and Mythology* (Cambridge: At the University Press, 1916). [Walters.]

Other Books

Besides the systematic treatises and encyclopedic works, there may be listed five books which treat the discoveries at

Pompeii, the importance of which has been mentioned (§ 12), and one book on Ostia.

1. Overbeck, Johannes, *Pompeii, in seinen Gebäuden, Alterthümern, und Kunstwerken,* fourth edition, by August Mau (Leipzig, Engelmann, 1884). This is the standard popular work upon the subject, richly supplied with illustrations. [Overbeck.]

2. Mau, August, *Pompeii, Its Life and Art,* translated by Francis W. Kelsey, second edition (New York, Macmillan, 1902). This is the best account of the treasures of the buried city that has appeared in English. It is at once interesting and scholarly. [Mau-Kelsey.]

3. Gusman, Pierre, *Pompeii, the City, Its Life and Art,* translated by Florence Simmonds and M. Jourdain (London, Heinemann, 1900). This gives the very best collection of illustrations, but is not so trustworthy in letterpress. [Gusman.]

4. Engelmann, Wilhelm, *Neue Führer durch Pompeii* (Leipzig, Engelmann, 1925). An English version of this work, entitled *A New Guide to Pompeii,* appeared in 1925 (Leipzig, Engelmann). [Engelmann.]

5. Calza, Guido, *Ostia: Historical Guide to the Monuments,* translated by R. Weeden-Cooke (Milan and Rome, Bestetti and Tuminelli, 1926). [Calza.]

CHAPTER I

THE FAMILY

REFERENCES: Marquardt, 1-6; Blümner, 301-302; Becker-Göll, II, 1-4, 61-65, 187; Pauly-Wissowa, under *adfīnitās, agnātiō, cognātiō, familia, gēns;* Daremberg-Saglio, under *adoptiō, adrogātiō, affīnitās, agnātiō, cognātī, cognātiō, familia, gēns, patria potestās;* Walters, under *adoptiō, cognātiō;* McDaniel, 23-26; Showerman, 66-68. Look up the word *familia,* in Harpers' *Latin Dictionary,* and notice carefully its range of meanings. See, also, Sherman, II, 44-116, and the article "Roman Law" in the *Encyclopaedia Britannica,* eleventh edition, XXIII, 529-531, 540-542, 565, 566, 573, fourteenth edition, XIX, 451-452.

17. The Household. If by our word "family" we understand a group consisting of husband, wife, and children, we may acknowledge at once that it does not correspond exactly to any of the meanings of the Latin *familia,* varied as the dictionaries show these to be. Husband, wife, and children did not necessarily constitute an independent family among the Romans, and were not necessarily members even of the same family. The Roman *familia,* in the sense nearest to that of the English word "family," was made up of those persons who were subject to the authority of the same Head of the House (*pater familiās*). These persons might make a host in themselves: wife, unmarried daughters, sons, adopted sons, married or unmarried, with their wives, sons, unmarried daughters, and even remoter descendants (always through males), yet they made but one *familia* in the eyes of the Romans. The Head of such a *familia*—"household" or "house" is the nearest English word—was always *suī iūris* ("his own master," "independent"), while the others were *aliēno iūrī subiectī* ("subject to another's authority," "dependent").

27

18. Other Meanings of *Familia*. The word *familia* was also very commonly used in a slightly wider sense to include, in addition to the persons named above (§ 17), all the slaves and clients (§§ 176-182) and all the property real and per-

FIG. 7
SOME MEMBERS OF THE FAMILY OF AUGUSTUS
Part of a relief from the Ara Pacis of Augustus, now in the Uffizi
Gallery, Florence.

sonal belonging to the *pater familiās*, or acquired and used by the persons under his *potestās*. The word was also used of the slaves alone, and, rarely, of the property alone. In a still wider and more important sense the word was applied to a larger group of related persons, the *gēns*, consisting of all the "households" (*familiae* in the sense of § 17) that derived their descent through males from a common ancestor. This remote ancestor, could his life have lasted through all the intervening centuries, would have been the *pater familiās* of all the persons included in the *gēns*, and all would have been subject to his *potestās*. Membership in the *gēns* was proved by the possession of the *nōmen* (§§ 46-47), the second of the three names that every citizen of the Republic regularly had (§ 38).

19. Theoretically this *gēns* had been in prehistoric times one of the *familiae*, "households," whose union for political purposes had formed the State. Theoretically its *pater familiās* had been one of the Heads of Houses from whom, in the days of the kings, had been chosen the *patrēs*, or assembly cf old men (*senātus*). The splitting up of this prehistoric household in the manner explained in § 27, a process repeated generation after generation, was believed to account for the numerous *familiae* that, in later times, claimed connection with the great *gentēs*. There came to be, of course, *gentēs* of later origin that imitated the organization of the older *gentēs*. The *gēns* had an organization of which little is known. It passed resolutions binding upon its members; it furnished guardians for minor children, and curators for the insane and for spendthrifts. When a member died without leaving heirs, the *gēns* succeeded to such property as he did not dispose of by will and administered it for the common good of all its members. These members were called *gentīlēs*, were bound to take part in the religious services of the *gēns* (*sacra gentīlīcia*), had a claim to the common property, and might, if they chose, be laid to rest in a common burial ground, if the *gēns* maintained one.

Finally, the word *familia* was often applied to certain branches of a *gēns* whose members had the same *cognōmen* (§§ 48-50), the last of the three names mentioned in § 38. For this sense of *familia* a more accurate word is *stirps*.

20. *Patria Potestās*. The authority of the *pater familiās* over his descendants was called usually *patria potestās*, but also *patria maiestās*, *patrium iūs*, and *imperium paternum*.

It was carried to a greater length by the Romans than by any other people, so that, in its original and unmodified form, the *patria potestās* seems to us excessive and cruel. As they understood it, the *pater familiās*, in theory, had absolute power over his children and other agnatic descendants (§ 30). He decided whether or not the newborn child should be reared; he punished what he regarded as misconduct with penalties as severe as banishment, slavery, and death; he alone could own and exchange property—all that those subject to him earned or acquired in any way was his; according to the letter of the law they were little better than his chattels. If his right to one of them was disputed, he vindicated it by the same form of action that he used in order to maintain his right to a house or a horse; if one of them was stolen, he proceeded against the abductor by the ordinary action for theft; if for any reason he wished to transfer one of them to a third person, it was done by the same form of conveyance that he employed to transfer inanimate things. The jurists boasted that these powers were enjoyed by Roman citizens only.

FIG. 8
PORTRAIT BUST OF A CHILD
(First Century A.D.)
Now in the Boston Museum of
Fine Arts.

21. Limitations. But however stern this authority was theoretically, it was greatly modified in practice, under the Republic by custom, under the Empire by law. King Romulus was said to have ordained that all sons and all first-born daughters should be reared, and that no child should be put to death until its third year, unless it was grievously deformed. This at least secured life for the child, though the *pater familiās* still decided whether it should be admitted to his household, with the resultant social and religious privileges, or be disowned and become an outcast. King Numa was said to have forbidden the sale into slavery of a son who had married with the consent of his father. But of much greater importance was the check put by custom upon arbitrary and cruel punishments. Custom, not law, obliged the *pater familiās* to call a council of relatives and friends (*iūdicium domesticum*) when he contemplated inflicting severe punishment upon his children, and public opinion obliged him to abide by its verdict. Even in the comparatively few cases where tradition tells us that the death penalty was actually inflicted, we usually find that the father acted in the capacity of a magistrate happening to be in office when the offense was committed, or that the penalties of the ordinary law were merely anticipated, perhaps to avoid the disgrace of a public trial and execution.

22. So, too, in regard to the ownership of property the conditions were not really so hard as the strict letter of the law makes them appear to us. It was customary for the Head of the House to assign to his children property, *peculium* ("cattle of their own"), for them to manage for their own benefit. Furthermore, although the *pater familiās* theoretically held legal title to all their acquisitions (§ 20), yet practically all property was acquired for and belonged to the household as a whole, and the *pater familiās* was, in effect, little more than a trustee to hold and administer it for the common benefit. This is shown by the fact that there was no graver offense against public morals, no fouler blot on private character, than to prove untrue to this trust (*patrimōnium prōfundere*). Besides this, the long continuance of the *potestās* is in itself a proof that its rigor was more apparent than real.

23. Manus. The subject of marriage will be considered later; at this point it is necessary only to define the power over the wife possessed by the husband in its most extreme form, called by the Romans *manus*. By the oldest and most solemn form of marriage the wife was separated entirely from her father's family (§ 35) and passed into her husband's power or "hand" (*conventiō in manum*). This assumes, of course, that he was *suī iūris;* if he was not, then she was,

FIG. 9
SOME ROMANS OF THE SECOND CENTURY A.D.
From a relief, now in the Museo Laterano, Rome.

though nominally in his "hand," really subject, as he was, to his *pater familiās*. Any property she had of her own—and to have had any she must have been independent before her marriage—passed to her husband's father as a matter of course. If she had none, her *pater familiās* furnished a dowry (*dōs*), which shared the same fate, though it must be returned if she should be divorced. Whatever she acquired by her industry or otherwise while the marriage lasted also became her husband's (subject to the *patria potestās* under which he lived). So far, therefore, as property rights were concerned, *manus* differed in no respect from the *patria potestās:* the wife was *in locō fīliae*, and on the husband's death took a daughter's share in his estate.

24. In other respects *manus* conferred more limited powers. The husband was required by law, not merely obliged by custom, to refer alleged misconduct of his wife to the *iūdicium domesticum* (§ 21), and this was composed in part of her cognates (§ 32). He could put her away for certain grave offenses only; Romulus was said to have ordained that, if he divorced her without good cause, he should be punished with the loss of all his property. He could not sell her at all. In short, public opinion and custom operated even more strongly for her protection than for that of her children. It must be noticed, therefore, that the chief distinction between *manus* and *patria potestās* lay in the fact that the former was a legal relationship based upon the consent of the weaker party, while the latter was a natural relationship independent of all law and choice.

25. *Dominica Potestās.* Whereas the authority of the *pater familiās* over his descendants was called *patria potestās*, his authority over his chattels was called *dominica potestās*. So long as he lived and retained his citizenship, these powers could be terminated only by his own deliberate act. He could dispose of his property by gift or sale as freely as we do now. He might "emancipate" his sons, a very formal proceeding (*ēmancipātiō*) by which they became each the Head of a new House, even if they were childless themselves or unmarried or mere children. He might also emancipate an unmarried daughter, who thus in her own self became an independent *familia*, or he might give her in marriage to another Roman citizen, an act by which she passed, according to early usage (§§ 23, 35, 62), into the House of which her husband was Head, if he was *suī iūris* (§ 17), or into that of which he was a member, if he was still *aliēnō iūrī subiectus*. It must be noticed, on the other hand, that the marriage of a son did not make him a *pater familiās* or relieve him in any degree from the *patria potestās*: he and his wife and their children were subject to the Head of his House as he had been before his marriage. On the other hand, the Head of the House could not number in his *familia* his daughter's children; legitimate children were under the same *patria potestās* as their father, while an illegitimate child was from the moment of birth in himself or herself an independent *familia*.

26. The right of a *pater familiās* to ownership in his property (*dominica potestās*) was complete and absolute. This ownership included slaves as well as inanimate things, for slaves, as well as inanimate things, were mere chattels

in the eyes of the law. The influence of custom and public opinion, so far as these tended to mitigate the horrors of their condition, will be discussed later (§§ 156-158, 162-163). It will be sufficient to say here that, until imperial times, there was nothing to which the slave could appeal from the judgment of his master. That judgment was final and absolute.

Fig. 10
PORTRAIT BUST OF A ROMAN BOY
(Second Century A.D.)
Now in the Vatican Museum, Rome.

27. The Splitting Up of a House. Emancipation was not very common, and it usually happened that the household was dissolved only by the death of its Head. When this occurred, as many new households were formed as there were persons directly subject to his *potestās* at the moment of his death: wife, sons, unmarried daughters, widowed daughters-in-law, and children of a deceased son. The children of a surviving son, it must be noticed, merely passed from the *potestās* of their grandfather to that of their father.

A son under age or an unmarried daughter was put under the care of a guardian (*tūtor*), selected from the same *gēns*, very often an older brother, if there was one. The following diagram[1] will make this clearer:

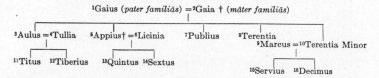

28. It is assumed that Gaius was a widower who had had five children, three sons and two daughters. Of the sons, Aulus and Appius had married and each had two children; Appius then died. Of the daughters, Terentia Minor had married Marcus and become the mother of two children. When Gaius died, Publius and Terentia were unmarried. Gaius had emancipated none of his children. The following points should be noticed:

(1) The living descendants of Gaius were ten (3, 7, 8, 10, 11, 12, 13, 14, 15, 16); his son Appius was dead.

(2) Subject to his *potestās* were nine (3, 4, 6, 7, 8, 11, 12, 13, 14).

(3) His daughter Terentia Minor (10) had passed out of his *potestās* by her marriage with Marcus (9), and her children (15, 16) alone out of all the descendants of Gaius had not been subject to him.

(4) At his death were formed six independent *familiae*, one consisting of four persons (3, 4, 11, 12), the others of one person each (6, 7, 8, 13, 14).

(5) Titus and Tiberius (11, 12) merely passed out of the *potestās* of their grandfather, Gaius, to come under that of their father, Aulus.

(6) If Quintus (13) and Sextus (14) were minors, guardians were appointed for them, as stated above (§ 27).

---

[1] The sign = means "married"; the sign † means "deceased."

29. Extinction of the *Potestās*. The *patria potestās* was extinguished in various ways:

(1) By the death of the *pater familiās*, as has been explained in § 27.

(2) By the emancipation of a son or a daughter.

(3) By the loss of citizenship by either father or son.

(4) If the son became a *Flāmen Diālis* or the daughter a *virgō vestālis*.

(5) If either father or child was adopted by a third party.

(6) If the daughter passed by formal marriage into the power (*in manum*) of a husband, though this did not essentially change her dependent condition (§§ 23, 35).

(7) If the son became a public magistrate. In this case the *potestās* was suspended during the period of office, but, after it expired, the father might hold the son accountable for his acts, public and private, while he held the magistracy.

30. *Agnātī*. It has been remarked (§ 25) that the children of a daughter could not be included in the *familia* of her father, and (§ 18) that membership in the larger organization known as the *gēns* was limited to those who could trace their descent through males to a common ancestor, in whose *potestās* they would be were he alive. All persons related to one another by such descent were called *agnātī*, "agnates." *Agnātiō* was the closest tie of relationship known to the Romans. In the list of *agnātī* were included two classes of persons who would seem by the definition to be excluded. These were (1) the wife, who passed by *manus* into the family of her husband (§§ 23, 25), becoming by law his agnate and the agnate of all his agnates, and (2) the adopted son. On the other hand a son who had been emancipated (§ 25) was excluded from *agnātiō* with his father and his father's agnates, and could have no agnates of his own until he married or was adopted into another *familia*. The following diagram will make this clear:

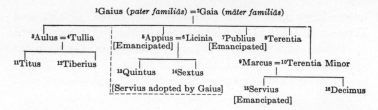

31. It is supposed that Gaius and Gaia have five children (Aulus, Appius, Publius, Terentia, and Terentia Minor), and six grandsons (Titus and Tiberius, the sons of Aulus, Quintus and Sextus, the sons of Appius, and Servius and Decimus, the sons of Terentia Minor). Gaius has emancipated two of his sons, Appius and Publius, and has adopted his grandson Servius, who had previously been emancipated by his father, Marcus. There are four sets of *agnātī:*

(1) Gaius, his wife, and those whose *pater familiās* he is: Aulus, Tullia, the wife of Aulus, Terentia, Titus, Tiberius, and Servius, a son by adoption (1, 2, 3, 4, 8, 11, 12, 15).

(2) Appius, his wife, and their two sons (5, 6, 13, 14).

(3) Publius, who is himself a *pater familiās*, but has no *agnātī* at all.

(4) Marcus, his wife, Terentia Minor, and their child Decimus (9, 10, 16). Notice that the other child, Servius (15), having been emancipated by Marcus, is no longer agnate to his father, mother, or brother, but has become one of the group of *agnātī* mentioned above, under (1).

32. Cognātī. *Cognātī*, on the other hand, were what we call blood relations, no matter whether they traced their relationship through males or through females, and regardless of what *potestās* had been over them. The only barrier in the eyes of the law was loss of citizenship (§ 29), and even this was not always regarded. Thus, in the table last given, Gaius, Aulus, Appius, Publius, Terentia, Terentia Minor, Titus, Tiberius, Quintus, Sextus, Servius, and Decimus are all cognates with one another. So, too, is Gaia with all her descendants mentioned. So also are Tullia, Titus, and Tiberius; Licinia, Quintus, and Sextus; Marcus, Servius, and Decimus. But husband and wife (Gaius and Gaia, Aulus and Tullia, Appius and Licinia, Marcus and Terentia Minor) are not cognates by virtue of their marriage, though that

FIG. 11
MAN AND WIFE
From a grave relief, now in the Metropolitan Museum of Art, New York.

made them agnates. Public opinion strongly discountenanced the marriage of cognates within the sixth (later the fourth) degree, and persons within this degree were said to have the *iūs ōscul*ī, "the right to kiss." The degree was calculated by counting from one of the interested parties through the common kinsman to the other. The matter may be understood from the table in Smith's *Dictionary of Antiquities* under *cognātī*, or from the one given here (Fig. 12). Cognates did not form an organic body in the State as the agnates formed the *gēns* (§§ 18-19), but the twenty-second of February was set aside to commemorate the tie of blood (*cāra cog-*

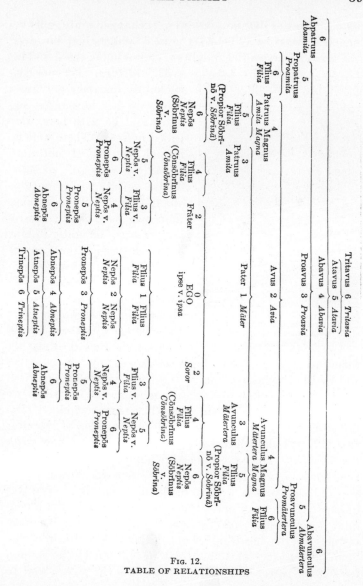

Fig. 12.
TABLE OF RELATIONSHIPS

nātiō). On this day presents were exchanged and family re-unions were probably held. It must be understood, however, that *cognātiō* gave no legal rights or claims under the Republic.

FIG. 13
PORTRAIT BUST
OF A ROMAN MATRON
Now in the Vatican Museum, Rome.

33. *Adfīnēs*. Persons connected by marriage only, as a wife with her husband's cognates and he with hers, were called *adfīnēs*. There were no formal degrees of *adfīnitās*, as there were of *cognātiō*. Those *adfīnēs* for whom distinctive names were in common use were *gener*, son-in-law; *nurus*, daughter-in-law; *socer*, father-in-law; *socrus*, mother-in-law; *prīvignus*, *prī-vigna*, step-son, step-daughter; *vitricus*, step-father; *noverca*, step-mother. If we compare these names with the awkward compounds that do duty for them in English, we shall have additional proof of the stress laid by the Romans on family ties; two women who married brothers were called *iānitrīcēs*, a relationship for which we do not have even a compound. The names of blood relations tell the same story; a glance at the table of cognates (Fig. 12) will show how strong the Latin is here, how weak the English. We have "uncle," "aunt," and "cousin," but between *avunculus* and *patruus*, *mātertera* and *amita*, *patru-ēlis* and *cōnsōbrīnus* we can distinguish only by descriptive phrases. For *atavus* and *tritavus* we have merely the indefinite "forefathers." In the same way the Latin language testifies to the headship of the father. We speak of the "mother-country" and "mother-tongue," but to the Roman these were *patria* and *sermō patrius*. As the *pater* stood to the *fīlius,* so stood the *patrōnus* to the *cliēns* (§§ 175, 177-180), the *patriciī* to the *plēbēiī,* the *patrēs* (senators) to the rest of the citizens, and *Iuppiter* (Jove the Father) to the other gods.

34. The Family Cult. It has been said (§ 30) that *agnātiō* was the closest tie known to the Romans. The importance they attached to the agnatic group is largely explained by their ideas of the future life. They believed that the souls of men had an existence apart from the body, but they did not originally think that the souls were in a separate spirit-land. They conceived of the soul as hovering around the place of burial and requiring for its peace and happiness that offerings of food and drink be made to it regularly. Should the offerings be discontinued, the soul, they thought, would cease to be happy, and might even become a spirit of evil to bring harm upon those who had neglected the proper rites. The maintenance of these rites and ceremonies devolved naturally upon the descendants from generation to generation, whom the spirits in turn would guide and guard. Contact with Etruscan and Greek art and myth later brought in such ideas of a place of torment or possible happiness as Vergil gathers up in Book VI of the *Aeneid.*

35. The Roman was bound, therefore, to perform these acts of affection and piety so long as he himself lived, and was bound no less to provide for their performance after his death by perpetuating his race and the family cult. A curse was believed to rest upon the childless man. Marriage was, therefore, a solemn religious duty, entered into only with the approval of the gods, ascertained by the auspices. In taking a wife to himself the Roman made her a partaker of his family mysteries, a service that brooked no divided allegiance. He therefore separated her entirely from her father's family, and was ready in turn to surrender his daughter without reserve to the husband with whom she was to minister at another altar (§§ 23, 25, 62). The *pater familiās* was the priest of the household; those subject to his *potestās* assisted in the prayers and offerings, the *sacra familiāria*.

36. But it might be that a marriage was fruitless, or that

FIG. 14
PORTRAIT BUST OF A
ROMAN LADY
(Second Century A.D.)
Now in the Boston Museum of Fine Arts.

the Head of the House saw his sons die before him. In this case he had to face the prospect of the extinction of his family, and his own descent to the grave with no posterity to make him blessed. One of two alternatives was open to him to avert such a calamity. He might give himself in adoption and pass into another family in which the perpetuation of the family cult seemed certain, or he might adopt a son and thus perpetuate his own family. He usually followed the latter course, because it secured peace for the souls of his ancestors no less than for his own.

37. Adoption. The person adopted was sometimes a *pater familiās* himself; more usually he was a *fīlius familiās*. In the case of the latter the process was called *adoptiō* and was a somewhat complicated proceeding by which the natural parent conveyed his son to the adopter, the effect being to transfer the adopted person from one family to the other. The adoption of a *pater familiās* was a much more serious matter, for it involved the extinction of one family (§ 36) in order to prevent the extinction of another. This was called *adrogātiō* and was an affair of state. It had to be sanctioned by the *pontificēs*, the highest officers of religion, who had probably to make sure that the *adrogātus* had brothers enough to attend to the interests of the ancestors whose cult he was renouncing. If the *pontificēs* gave their consent, the *adrogātiō* had still to be sanctioned by the *comitia cūriāta*, as the act might deprive the *gēns* of its succession to the property of the childless man (§ 19). If the *comitia* gave consent, the *adrogātus* sank from the position of Head of a House to that of a *fīlius familiās* in the household of his adoptive father. If he had a wife and children, they passed with him into the new family, and so did all his property. Over him the adoptive father had *potestās* as over a son of his own, and looked upon him as flesh of his flesh and bone of his bone. We can have at best only a feeble and inadequate notion of what adoption meant to the Romans.

Fig. 15
A YOUNG ROMAN

CHAPTER II

ROMAN NAMES

REFERENCES: Marquardt, 7-27; Pauly-Wissowa, under *cognō-men;* Smith, Daremberg-Saglio, Harper's, Walters, under *nōmen;* Sandys, *Companion*, 174-175. See, also, Egbert, 82-113; Cagnat, *Cours d'Epigraphie Latine*, 37-87; Sandys, *Latin Epigraphy*, 207-221; Showerman, 91-92.

38. The Threefold Name. Nothing is more familiar to the student of Latin than the fact that the Romans whose works he reads first have each a threefold name, Caius Julius Caesar, Marcus Tullius Cicero, Publius Vergilius Maro. This was the system that prevailed in the best days of the Republic, but it was itself a development, starting in earlier times with a more simple form, and ending, under the Empire, in utter confusion. The earliest legends of Rome show us single names, Romulus, Remus, Faustulus; but side by side with these we find also double names, Numa Pompilius, Ancus Marcius, Tullus Hostilius. It is possible that single names were the original fashion, but in early inscriptions we find two names, the second of which, in the genitive case, represented the father or the Head of the House: *Mārcus Mārcī, Caecilia Metellī.* A little later such a genitive was followed by the letter *f* (for *fīlius* or *fīlia*) or *uxor*, to denote the relationship. Later still, but very anciently nevertheless, we find the free-born man in possession of the three names with which we are familiar, the *nōmen* to mark his clan (*gēns*), the *cognōmen* to mark his family, and the *praenōmen* to mark him as individual. The regular order of the three names is *praenōmen, nōmen, cognōmen*, although in poetry the order is often changed to adapt the name as a whole to the meter.

39. Great formality required even more than the three names. In official documents and in the state records it was usual to insert between a man's *nōmen* and *cognōmen* the *praenōmina* of his father, grandfather, and great-grandfather, and sometimes even the name of the tribe in which he was registered as a citizen. So Cicero might have written his name as *M. Tullius M. f. M. n. M. pr. Cor. Cicero*, that is, Marcus Tullius Cicero, son (*fīlius*) of Marcus, grandson (*nepōs*) of Marcus, great-grandson (*pronepōs*) of Marcus, of the tribe Cornelia.

Fig. 16

M. TULLIUS M. f. M. n. M. pr. Cor. CICERO

A bust in the Vatican Museum, Rome.

40. On the other hand, even the threefold name was too long for ordinary use. Children, slaves, and intimate friends addressed the father, master, friend, and citizen by his *praenōmen* only. Ordinary acquaintances used the *cognōmen*, with the *praenōmen* prefixed for emphatic address. In earnest appeals we find the *nōmen* also used, with sometimes the *praenōmen* or the possessive *mī* prefixed. When two only of the three names are thus used in familiar intercourse, the order varies. If the *praenōmen* is one of the two, it always stands first, except in the poets, for metrical reasons, and in a few places in prose where the text is uncertain. If the *praenōmen* is omitted, the arrangement varies; the older writers regularly put the *cognōmen* first. Cicero usually follows this practice: cf. *Ahāla Servīlius, (Milo 3, 8)*; contrast *C. Servīlius Ahāla, (Cat. I, 1, 3)*. Caesar puts the *nōmen* first;

Horace, Livy, and Tacitus have both arrangements, while
Pliny the Younger adheres to Caesar's usage.

41. The *Praenōmen*. The number of names in actual use
as *praenōmina* seems to us preposterously small as compared
with our Christian names, to which they in some measure
correspond. It was never much in excess of thirty, and in
Sulla's time had dwindled to eighteen. The following are all
that are often found in the authors read in school and in college: *Aulus (A), Decimus (D), Gāïus (C),*[1] *Gnaeus (CN),*[1] *Kae-
sō (K), Lūcius (L), Mānius (M'), Mārcus (M), Pūblius (P),
Quīntus (Q), Servius (SER), Sextus (SEX), Spurius (S),
Tiberius (TI),* and *Titus (T)*. The abbreviations of these
names vary: for *Aulus* we find regularly *A*, but also *AV*
and *AVL;* for *Sextus* we find *SEXT* and *S* as well as
SEX. Similar variations are found in the case of other
praenōmina.

42. But small as this list seems to us, the natural con-
servatism of the Romans found in it a chance to display
itself, and the great families repeated the *praenōmina* of their
children from generation to generation in such a way as to
make the identification of individuals often very difficult in
modern times. Thus the Aemilii contented themselves
with seven of these *praenōmina, Gāïus, Gnaeus, Lūcius,
Mānius, Mārcus, Quīntus,* and *Tiberius,* but used in addition one that is not found in any other *gēns, Māmercus
(MAM)*. The Claudii used only six, *Gāïus, Decimus, Lūcius,
Pūblius, Tiberius,* and *Quīntus,* with the additional name
Appius (APP), of Sabine origin, which they brought to
Rome. The Cornelii used only seven, *Aulus, Gnaeus, Lūcius,
Mārcus, Pūblius, Servius,* and *Tiberius*. A still smaller
number sufficed for the Julian *gēns, Gāïus, Lūcius,* and
Sextus, with the *praenōmen, Vopiscus,* which went out of use
in very early times. And even these selections were subject

---

[1]C originally had the value of G and retains it in the abbreviations *C* and *Cn.* for
Gaïus and *Gnaeus*. See Cagnat, 39, and Egbert, 25, 85. When they are Anglicized,
these *praenōmina* are often written with the C.

to further limitations. Thus, of the *gēns Claudia* only one branch (*stirps*), known as the *Claudiī Nerōnēs*, used the *praenōmina Decimus* and *Tiberius*, and out of the seven *praenōmina* used in the *gēns Cornēlia* the branch of the Scipios (*Cornēliī Scīpiōnēs*) used only *Gnaeus*, *Lūcius*, and *Pūblius*. Even after a *praenōmen* had found a place in a given family, it might be deliberately discarded: the senate decreed that no Antonius should have the *praenōmen Mārcus* after the downfall of the famous triumvir, Marcus Antonius.

43. From the list of *praenōmina* usual in his family the father gave one to his son on the ninth day after his birth, the *diēs lūstricus*. It was a custom then, one that seems natural enough in our own times, for the father to give his own *praenōmen* to his first-born son; Cicero's name (§ 39) shows the *praenōmen Mārcus* four times repeated. When these *praenōmina* were first given, they must have been chosen with due regard to their etymological meaning (§ 44) and have had some relation to the circumstances attending the birth of the child.

Fig. 17
C. JULIUS CAESAR
A statue in the Capitoline Museum, Rome.

44. So, *Lūcius* meant originally "born by day," *Mānius* "born in the morning"; *Quīntus, Sextus, Decimus, Postumus,* etc., indicated the succession in the family; *Servius* was connected, perhaps, with *servāre*, *Gāius* with *gaudēre*. Others are associated with the name of some divinity, as *Mārcus* and *Māmercus* with Mars, and *Tiberius* with the river god Tiberis. But these meanings in the course of time were

forgotten as completely as we have forgotten the meanings
of our Christian names, and even the numerals were employed with no reference to their proper force: Cicero's
only brother was called *Quīntus*.

45. The abbreviation of the *praenōmen* was not a matter
of mere caprice, as is the writing of initials with us, but was
an established custom, indicating, perhaps, Roman citizenship. The *praenōmen* was written out in full only when it
was used by itself or when it belonged to a person in one of
the lower classes of society. When Roman *praenōmina* are
carried over into English, they should always be written
out in full and pronounced accordingly. In the same way,
when we read a Latin author and find a *praenōmen* abbreviated, the full name should always be pronounced if we read
aloud or translate.

46. The *Nōmen*. The *nōmen*, the all-important name, is
called for greater precision the *nōmen gentīle* and the *nōmen
gentīlicium*. The child inherited it, as one inherits one's sur-
name now, and there was, therefore, no choice or selection
about it. The *nōmen* ended originally in *-ius*, and this ending
was sacredly preserved by the patrician families; the endings
-eius, *-aius*, *-aeus*, and *-eüs* are merely variations from it.
Other endings point to a non-Latin origin of the *gēns*.
Names in *-ācus* (*Avidiācus*) are Gallic; those in *-na* (*Caecīna*)
are Etruscan; those in *-ēnus* or *-iēnus* (*Salvidiēnus*) are
Umbrian or Picene.

47. The *nōmen* belonged by custom to all connected with
the *gēns*, to the plebeian as well as the patrician branches,
to men, women, clients, and freedmen, without distinction.
It was perhaps the natural desire to separate themselves from
the more humble bearers of their *nōmen* that led patrician
families to use a limited number of *praenōmina*, avoiding
those used by their clansmen of inferior social standing. At
any rate, it is noticeable that the plebeian families, as soon as
political nobility and the busts in their halls (§§ 107, 200)

gave them a standing above their fellows, showed the same exclusiveness in the selection of names for their children that the patricians had displayed before them (§ 42).

48. The *Cognōmen*. Besides the individual name and the name that marked his *gēns*, the Roman had often a third name, called the *cognōmen*, that served to indicate the family or branch of the *gēns* to which he belonged (§§ 18-19). Almost all the great *gentēs* were thus divided, some of them into numerous branches. The Cornelian *gēns*, for example, included the plebeian Dolabellae, Lentuli, Cethegi, and Cinnae, in addition to the patrician Scipiones, Maluginenses, Rufini, etc.

49. From the fact that in the official name (§§ 38-39) the *cognōmen* followed the name of the tribe, it is generally believed that the oldest of the *cognōmina* did not go back beyond the time of the division of the people into tribes. It is also generally believed that the *cognōmen* was originally a nickname, bestowed on account of some personal peculiarity or characteristic, sometimes as a compliment, sometimes in derision. So we find many pointing at physical traits, such as *Albus, Barbātus, Cincinnātus, Claudus, Longus* (all originally adjectives), and *Nāsō* and *Capitō* (nouns: "the man with a nose," "the man with a head"); others, such as *Benignus, Blandus, Catō, Serēnus, Sevērus*, refer to the temperament; still others, such as *Gallus, Ligus, Sabīnus, Siculus, Tuscus*, denote origin. These *cognōmina*, it must be remembered, descended from father to son; they would naturally lose their appropriateness as they passed along, until in the course of time their meanings were entirely lost sight of, as were those of the *praenōmina* (§ 44).

50. Under the Republic the patricians had almost without exception this third or family name; we are told of but one man, Caius Marcius, who lacked it. With the plebeians the *cognōmen* was not so common; perhaps its possession was the exception. The great families of the Marii, Mummii, and Sertorii had none, although the plebeian branches of the Cornelian *gēns* (§ 48), the Tullian *gēns*, and others, did. The *cognōmen* came, therefore, to be prized as an indication of ancient lineage, and individuals whose nobility was new were anxious to acquire one to transmit to their children.

Fig. 18
C. OCTAVIUS CAEPIAS
A bust now in the Vatican
Museum, Rome.

Hence many assumed *cognōmina* of their own selection. Some of these were conceded to them by public opinion as their due, as in the case of Cnaeus Pompeius, who took *Magnus* as his *cognōmen*. Other *cognōmina* were given in derision, as we deride the made-to-order coat of arms of some upstart in our own times. It is probable, however, that only patricians ventured to assume *cognōmina* under the Republic, though under the Empire their possession was hardly more than the badge of freedom.

51. Additional Names. Besides the three names already described, we find not infrequently, even in Republican times, a fourth or a fifth. These also were called *cognōmina* by a loose extension of the word, until in the fourth century of our era the name *agnōmina* was given them by the grammarians. They may be conveniently considered under four heads.

52. In the first place, the process that divided the *gēns* into branches might be continued even further. That is, as the *gēns* became extensive enough to throw off a *stirps* (§ 19), so the *stirps* in process of time might throw off a branch of itself, for which there is no better name than the vague *familia*. This actually happened very frequently: the *gēns* *Cornēlia*, for example, threw off the *stirps* of the *Scīpiōnēs*, and this in turn the family or "house" of the *Nāsīcae*. So we find the fourfold name *Pūblius Cornēlius Scīpiō Nāsīca*, in which the last name was probably given very much in the same way as the third had been given before the division took place.

53. In the second place, when a man passed from one family to another by adoption (§ 37), he regularly took the three names of his adoptive father and added his own *nōmen gentīle* modified by the suffix -*ānus*. Thus, Lucius Aemilius Paulus, the son of Lucius Aemilius Paulus Macedonicus (*see* § 54 for *Macedonicus*), was adopted by Publius Cornelius Scipio, and took as his new name *Pūblius Cornēlius Scīpiō Aemiliānus*. In the same way, when Caius Octavius

Fig. 19
C. JULIUS CAESAR
OCTAVIANUS
A statue found in Prima Porta, now in the Vatican Museum, Rome.

Caepias (Fig. 18) was adopted by Caius Julius Caesar, he became *Gāïus Iūlius Caesar Octāviānus* (Fig. 19), and hence is variously styled "Octavius" and "Octavianus" in the histories.

54. In the third place, an additional name, sometimes called *cognōmen ex virtūte*, was often given by acclamation to a great statesman or victorious general, and was put after his *cognōmen*. A well-known example is in the name of Publius Cornelius Scipio Africanus; the title *Āfricānus* was given him after his defeat of Hannibal. In the same way, his grandson by adoption, the Publius Cornelius Scipio Aemilianus mentioned above (§ 53), received the same honorable title after he had destroyed Carthage, and was called *Pūblius Cornēlius Scīpiō Aemiliānus Āfricānus*. Other

examples are *Macedonicus*, given to Lucius Aemilius Paulus
for his defeat of Perseus, and the title *Augustus*, given by
the senate to Octavianus. It is not certainly known whether
or not these names passed by inheritance to the descendants of those who originally earned them, but it is probable
that the eldest son only was strictly entitled to take his
father's title of honor.

55. In the fourth place, the fact that a man had inherited
a nickname from his ancestors in the form of a *cognōmen*
(§ 49) did not prevent his receiving another from some
personal characteristic, especially as the inherited name had
often no application, as we have seen (§ 49), to its later
possessor. To some ancient Publius Cornelius was given the
nickname *Scīpiō* (§ 49); in the course of time this title was
taken by all his descendants, without thought of its appropriateness, and it became a *cognōmen*. Then, to one of these
descendants another nickname, *Nāsīca*, was given for personal reasons, which in course of time lost its individuality
and became the name of a whole family (§ 50); then, in
precisely the same way a member of this family became
prominent enough to need a separate name and was called
Corculum, his full name being *Pūblius Cornēlius Scīpiō
Nāsīca Corculum*. It is evident that there is no reason why
the expansion should not have continued indefinitely. It is
also evident that we cannot always distinguish between a
mere nickname, one applied merely to an individual and not
passing to his descendants, and the additional *cognōmen* that
marked the family off from the rest of the *stirps* (§ 19) to
which it belonged.

56. Confusion of Names. A system so elaborate as that
described was almost sure to be misunderstood or misap-
plied, and in the later days of the Republic and under the Empire we find all law and order in names disregarded. Confusion was caused by the misuse of the *praenōmen*. Sometimes two are found in one name, e.g., *Pūblius Aēlius*

Aliēnus Archelāus Mārcus. The familiar *Gāius* must have been a *nōmen* in very ancient times. Like irregularities occur in the use of the *nōmen.* Two in a name were not uncommon, one being derived, perhaps, from the family of the mother; occasionally three or four are used, and fourteen are found in the name of one of the consuls of the year 169 A.D. By another change, a word might go out of use as a *praenōmen* and appear as a *nōmen:* Cicero's enemy *Lūcius Sergius Catilīna* had for his *nōmen gentīle Sergius,* which had once been a *praenōmen* (§ 41). The *cognōmen* was similarly abused. It ceased to denote the whole family and came to distinguish members of the same family, as the *praenōmina* originally had done: thus the three sons of Marcus Annaeus Seneca, for example, were called, respectively, *Mārcus Annaeus Novātus, Lūcius Annaeus Seneca,* and *Lūcius Annaeus Mela.* Again, a name might be arranged differently at different times: in the consular lists we find the same man called *Lūcius Lucrētius Tricipitīnus Flāvus* and *Lūcius Lucrētius Flāvus Tricipitīnus.*

57. There is even greater variation in the names of persons who had passed from one family into another by adoption. Some took the additional name (§§ 51-55) from the *cognōmen* instead of from the *nōmen.* Some used more than one *nōmen.* Finally, it may be noticed that late in the Empire we find a man struggling under the load of forty names.

58. Names of Women. No very satisfactory account of the names of women can be given, because it is impossible to discover any system in the choice and arrangement of those that have come down to us. It may be said that the three-fold name for women was unknown in the best days of the Republic; *praenōmina* for women were rare and when used were not abbreviated. More common were the adjectives *Maxima* and *Minor,* and the numerals *Secunda* and *Tertia,* but these, unlike the corresponding names of men (§ 44), seem always to have denoted the place of the bearer among a group of sisters. It was more usual for the unmarried woman to be called by her father's *nōmen* in its feminine form, with the addition of her father's *cognōmen* in the genitive case, followed later by the letter *f* (*fīlia*) to mark the relationship. An example is *Caecilia Metellī*. Caesar's daughter was called *Iūlia*, Cicero's *Tullia*. Sometimes a woman used her mother's *nōmen* after her father's. The married woman, if she passed into her husband's "hand" (*manus*, § 23) by the ancient patrician ceremony, originally took his *nōmen*, just as an adopted son took the name of the family into which he passed, but it cannot be shown that the rule was universally or even usually observed. Under the later forms of marriage the wife retained her maiden name. In the time of the Empire we find the threefold name for women in general use, with the same riotous confusion in selection and arrangement as prevailed in the case of the names of men at the same time.

59. Names of Slaves. Slaves had no more right to names of their own than they had to other property, but took such as their masters were pleased to give them, and even these did not descend to their children. In the simpler life of early times the slave was called *puer*, just as the word "boy" was once used in this country for slaves of any age. Until late in the Republic the slave was known only by this name, corrupted to *por* and affixed to the genitive of his master's *praenōmen: Mārcipor* (*Mārcī puer*), "Marcus's slave," *Ōlipor* (*Aulī puer*), "Aulus's slave." When slaves became numerous, this simple form no longer sufficed to distinguish them, and they received individual names. These were usually foreign names, and often denoted the nationality of the slave; sometimes, in mockery perhaps, they were the high-sounding appellations of eastern potentates, such as Afer, Eleutheros, Pharnaces. By this time, too, the word *servus* had supplanted *puer*. We find, therefore, that toward the end of the Republic the full name of a slave consisted of his individual name followed by the *nōmen* and *praenōmen* (the order is important) of his master and by the word *servus: Pharnacēs Egnātiī Pūbliī servus.* When a slave passed from one master to another, he took the *nōmen* of the new master and added to it the *cognōmen* of the old modified by the suffix -*ānus:* when Anna, the slave of Maecenas, became the property of Livia, she was called *Anna Līviae serva Maecēnātiāna.*

Fig. 20
TOMB OF THE JULII AT SAINT-REMY, FRANCE

60. Names of Freedmen. The freedman regularly kept the individual name which he had had as a slave, and received the *nōmen* of his master with any *praenōmen* the latter assigned him, the individual name coming last as a sort of *cognōmen.* It happened naturally that the master's *praenōmen* was often given, especially to a favorite slave. The freedman of a woman took the name of her father, e.g., *Mārcus Līvius Augustae l Ismarus;* the letter *l* stood for *lībertus,* and was inserted in all formal documents. Of course the master might disregard the regular form and give the freedman any name he pleased. Thus, when Cicero manumitted his slaves Tiro and Dionysius, he called the former, in strict accord with custom, *Mārcus Tullius Tīrō,* but to the latter he gave his own *praenōmen* and the *nōmen* of his friend Titus Pomponius Atticus, the new name being *Mārcus Pompōnius Dionȳsius.* The individual names (Pharnaces, Dionysius, etc.) were dropped by the descendants of freedmen, who were, with good reason, anxious to hide all traces of their mean descent.

61. Naturalized Citizens. When a foreigner received the right of citizenship, he took a new name, which was arranged on much the same principles as have been explained in the cases of freedmen. His original name was retained as a sort of *cognōmen,* and before it were written the *praenōmen* that suited his fancy and the *nōmen* of the person, always a Roman citizen, to whom he owed his citizenship. The most familiar example is that of the Greek poet Archias, whom Cicero, in the well-known oration, defended; his name was *Aulus Licinius Archiās.* He had long been attached to the family of the Luculli, and, when he was made a citizen, he took as his *nōmen* that of his distinguished patron Lucius Licinius Lucullus; we do not know why he selected the *praenōmen* Aulus. Another example is that of the Gaul mentioned by Caesar (*B. G.,* I, 47), *Gāius Valerius Cabūrus.* He took his name from Caius Valerius Flaccus, the governor of Gaul at the time that he received his citizenship. To this custom of taking the names of governors and generals is due the frequent occurrence of the name "Julius" in Gaul, "Pompeius" in Spain, and "Cornelius" in Sicily.

Fig. 21
A ROMAN PILASTER
(First Century A. D.)
From a relief now in the Metropolitan
Museum of Art, New York.

CHAPTER III

MARRIAGE AND THE POSITION OF WOMEN

REFERENCES: Marquardt, 28-80; Becker-Göll, II, 5-60; Friedländer, I, 228-267; Smith, under *mātrimōnium;* Baumeister, 696-698; Harper's, under *cōnūbium, mātrimōnium;* Pauly-Wissowa, under *coēmptiō, cōnfarreātiō, cōnūbium;* Walters, under *marriage;* Daremberg-Saglio, under *mātrimōnium, manus, gynaecēum;* Sandys, *Companion,* 175-179, 184-190; McDaniel, 41-59; Showerman, 112-123. See, also, Fowler, *Social Life,* 135-167; Abbott, *Society and Politics,* 41-99.

62. Early Forms of Marriage. Polygamy was never sanctioned at Rome, and we are told that for five centuries after the founding of the city divorce was entirely unknown. Up to the time of the Servian constitution (traditional date, sixth century B.C.) patricians were the only citizens and intermarried only with patricians and with members of surrounding communities having like social standing. The only form of marriage known to them was the stately religious ceremonial called *cōnfarreātiō.* With the direct consent of the gods, while

FIG. 22
A ROMAN GIRL
(First Century A. D.)
A bust now in the Museo
Nazionale, Rome.

the *pontificēs* celebrated the solemn rites, in the presence of the accredited representatives of his *gēns,* the patrician took his wife from her father's family into his own (§ 35), to be a *māter familiās,* to bear him children who should conserve the family mysteries, perpetuate his ancient race, and extend the power of Rome. By this, the one legal

57

form of marriage of the time, the wife passed *in manum virī*, and the husband acquired over her practically the same rights as he would have over his own children (§§ 23-24) and other dependent members of his family. Such a marriage was said to be *cum conventiōne uxōris in manum virī* (§ 23).

63. During this period, too, the free non-citizens, the plebeians (§§ 177-178), had been busy in marrying and giving in marriage. There is little doubt

FIG. 23
A ROMAN MATRON
(Second Century A. D.)
A bust now in the Vatican
Museum, Rome.

that their unions had been as sacred in their eyes, their family ties as strictly regarded and as pure as those of the patricians, but these unions were unhallowed by the national gods and unrecognized by the civil law, simply because the plebeians were not yet citizens. Their form of marriage, called *ūsus*, consisted essentially in the living together continuously of the man and woman as husband and wife, though there were, probably, conventional forms and observances, about which we know absolutely nothing. The plebeian husband might acquire the same rights over the person and property of his wife as the patrician, but the form of marriage did not in itself involve *manus*. The wife might remain a member of her father's family and retain such property as he allowed her (§ 22) by merely absenting herself from her husband for the space of a *trinoctium*, that is, three nights in succession, *each year*.[1] If she did this, the marriage was

---

[1] In Roman law unbroken possession (*ūsus*) of movable things for one year gave full title to ownership of them. If the possession was broken (interrupted), the time of the *ūsus* had to begin to run afresh (i.e., the previous possession, or *ūsus*, was regarded as canceled).

sine conventiōne in manum, and the husband had no control over her property; if she did not, the marriage, like that of the patricians, was *cum conventiōne in manum*.

64. Another Roman form of marriage goes at least as far back as the time of Servius. This was also plebeian, though not so ancient as *ūsus*. It was called *coēmptiō* and was a fictitious sale, by which the *pater familiās* of the woman, or her *tūtor*, if she was subject to one (§ 27), transferred her to the man *mātrimōniī causā*. This form must have been a survival of the old custom of purchase and sale of wives, but we do not know when it was introduced among the Romans. It carried *manus* with it as a matter of course, and seems to have been regarded socially as better form than *ūsus*. The two existed for centuries side by side, but *coēmptiō* survived *ūsus* as a form of marriage *cum conventiōne in manum*.

65. *Iūs Cōnūbiī.* Though the Servian constitution made the plebeians citizens and thereby legalized their forms of marriage, it did not give them the right of intermarriage with the patricians. Many of the plebeian families were hardly less ancient than the patricians, many were rich and powerful, but it was not until 445 b.c. that marriages between the two Orders were formally sanctioned by the civil law. The objection on the part of the patricians was largely a religious one: the gods of the State were gods of the patricians, the auspices could be taken by patricians only, the marriages of patricians only were sanctioned by heaven. Their orators protested that the unions of the plebeians were not marriages at all, not *iūstae nūptiae* (§ 68); the plebeian wife, they insisted, was only taken *in mātrimōnium:* she was at best only an *uxor*, not a *māter familiās;* her offspring were "mother's children," not *patriciī*.

66. Much of this was class exaggeration, but it is true that for a long time the *gēns* was not so highly valued by the plebeians as by the patricians, and that the plebeians assigned to cognates certain duties and privileges that devolved upon the patrician *gentīlēs*. With the extension of the *iūs cōnūbiī* many of these points of difference disappeared. New conditions were fixed for *iūstae nūptiae; coēmptiō* by a sort of compromise became the usual form of marriage when one of the parties was a plebeian; and the stigma disappeared from the word *mātrimōnium*. On the other hand, patrician women learned to understand the advantages of a marriage *sine conventiōne in manum,* and marriage with *manus* grew less frequent, the taking of the auspices before the ceremony came to be considered a mere form, and marriage began to lose its sacramental character. With these changes came later the laxness in the marital relation and the freedom of divorce that seemed in the time of Augustus to threaten the very life of the commonwealth.

FIG. 24
A ROMAN MATRON
A statue in the Uffizi Gallery, Florence.

67. It is probable that by the time of Cicero marriage with *manus* was uncommon, and consequently that *cōnfarreātiō* and *coēmptiō* had gone out of general use. To a limited extent, however, the former was retained into Christian times, because certain priestly offices (those of the *flāminēs maiōrēs* and the *rēgēs sacrōrum*) could be filled only by persons whose parents had been married by the confarreate ceremony (§§ 81-82), the sacramental form, and who had themselves been married by the same form. Augustus offered exemption from *manus* to mothers of three children, but this was not enough, for so great became the reluctance of women to submit to *manus* that in order to fill even these few priestly offices it was found necessary under Tiberius to eliminate *manus* from the confarreate ceremony.

68. *Iūstae Nūptiae.* There were certain conditions that had to be satisfied before a legal marriage could be contracted even by citizens.   The requirements were as follows:

(1) The consent of both parties should be given, or that of the *pater familiās* if one or both were *in patriā potestāte*. Under Augustus it was provided that the *pater familiās* should not withhold his consent unless he could show valid reasons for doing so.

(2) Both of the parties should be *pūberēs;* there could be no marriage between children.   Although no precise age was fixed by law, it is probable that fourteen and twelve were the lowest limit for the man and the woman respectively.

(3) Both man and woman should be unmarried.   Polygamy was never sanctioned at Rome (§ 62).

(4) The parties should not be nearly related.   The restrictions in this direction were fixed by public opinion rather than by law and varied greatly at different times, becoming gradually less severe.   In general it may be said that marriage was absolutely forbidden between ascendants and descendants, between other cognates within the sixth (later the fourth) degree (§ 32), and between the nearer *adfīnēs* (§ 33).

If the parties could satisfy these conditions, they might be legally married, but distinctions were still made that affected the civil status of the children, although no doubt was cast upon their legitimacy or upon the moral character of their parents.

69. If the conditions named in § 68 were fulfilled and the husband and wife were both Roman citizens, their marriage was called *iūstae nūptiae*, which we may translate by "regular marriage." The children of such a marriage were *iūstī liberī* and were by birth *cīvēs optimō iūre*, "possessed of all civil rights."

If one of the parties was a Roman citizen and the other a member of a community having the *iūs cōnūbiī* but not full Roman *cīvitās*, the marriage was still called *iūstae nūptiae*, but the children took the civil standing of the father. This means that, if the father was a citizen and the mother a foreigner, the children were citizens, but, if the father was a foreigner and the mother a citizen, the children were foreigners (*peregrīnī*), as was their father.

But if either of the parties was without the *iūs cōnūbiī*, the marriage, though still legal, was called *iniūstae nūptiae* or *iniūstum mātrimōnium*, "an irregular marriage," and the children, though legitimate, took the civil position of the parent of lower degree. We seem to have something analogous to this today in the loss of social standing which usually follows the marriage of one person with another of distinctly inferior position.

70. Betrothals. Formal betrothal (*spōnsālia*) as a preliminary to marriage was considered good form but was not legally necessary and carried with it no obligations that could be enforced by law. In the *spōnsālia* the maiden was promised to the man as his bride with "words of style," that is, in solemn form. The promise was made, not by the maiden herself, but by her *pater familiās*, or by her *tūtor* (§ 27) if she was not *in patriā potestāte*. In the same way, the promise was made to the man directly only in case he was *suī iūris* (§ 17); otherwise it was made to the Head of his House, who had asked for him the maiden in marriage. The "words of style" were probably something like this:

"*Spondēsne Gāiam, tuam fīliam* (or, if she was a ward, *Gāiam, Lūciī fīliam*), *mihi* (or *fīliō meō*) *uxōrem darī?*"

"*Dī bene vortant! Spondeō.*"

"*Dī bene vortant!*"

71. At any rate, the word *spondeō* was technically used of the promise, and the maiden was henceforth *spōnsa*. The person who made the promise had always the right to cancel it. This was usually done through an intermediary (*nūntius*); hence the formal expression for breaking an engagement was *repudium renūntiāre*, or simply *renūntiāre*. While the contract was entirely one-sided, it should be noticed that a man was liable to *īnfāmia* if he formed two engagements at the same time, and that he could not recover any presents made with a view to a future marriage if he himself broke the engagement. Such presents were almost always made. Though we find that articles for personal use, the toilet, etc., were common, a ring was usually given. The ring was worn on the third finger of the left hand, because it was believed that a nerve (or sinew) ran directly from this finger to the heart. It was also usual for the *spōnsa* to make a present to her betrothed.

72. The Dowry. It was a point of honor with the Romans, as it is now with some European peoples, for the bride to bring to her husband a dowry (*dōs*, Modern French *dot*). In the case of a girl *in patriā potestāte* this would be furnished by the Head of her House; in the case of one *suī iūris* it was furnished from her own property, or, if she had none, was contributed by her relatives. It seems that if they were reluctant she might by process of law compel her ascendants at least to furnish it. In early times, when marriage *cum conventiōne* prevailed, all the property brought by the bride became the property of her husband, or of his *pater familiās* (§ 23), but in later times, when *manus* was less common, and especially after divorce had become of frequent occurrence, a distinction was made. A part of the bride's possessions was reserved for her own exclusive use, and a part was made over to the groom under the technical name of *dōs*. The relative proportions varied, of course, with circumstances.

73. Essential Forms. There were really no legal forms

necessary for the solemnization of a marriage; there was no
license to be procured from the civil authorities; the ceremonies, simple or elaborate, did not have to be performed by

persons authorized
by the State. The
one thing necessary
was the consent of
both parties, if they
were *suī iūris*, or of
their *patrēs fami-
liās*, if they were *in
patriā potestāte*. It
has been remarked
[§ 68, (1)] that the
pater familiās could
refuse his consent
for valid reasons
only; on the other
hand, he could
command the con-
sent of persons sub-
ject to him. Pa-
rental and filial af-
fection (*pietās*) made

Fig. 25
DEXTRĀRUM IŪNCTIŌ
From a sarcophagus in the British Museum, London.

this hardship much less rigorous than it now seems to us
(§§ 21-22).

74. But, though this consent was the only condition for
a legal marriage, it had to be shown by some act of personal
union between the parties, that is, the marriage could not
be entered into by letter or by messenger or by proxy. Such
a public act was the joining of hands (*dextrārum iūnctiō*)
in the presence of witnesses, or the bride's act in letting
herself be escorted to her husband's house, never omitted
when the parties had any social standing, or, in later times,
the signing of the marriage contract. It was never neces-

sary to a valid marriage that the parties should live together
as man and wife, though, as we have seen (§ 63), this living
together of itself constituted a legal marriage.

75. The Wedding Day. It will be noticed that super-
stition played an important part in the arrangements for a
wedding two thousand years ago, as it does now. Especial
pains had to be taken to secure a lucky day. The Kalends,
Nones, and Ides of each month, and the day following each
of them, were unlucky. So was all of May and the first half
of June, on account of certain religious ceremonies observed
in these months, in May the Argean offerings and the
Lemūria, in June the *diēs religiōsī* connected with Vesta.
Besides these, the *diēs parentālēs,* February 13-21, and the
days when the entrance to the lower world was supposed to
be open, August 24, October 5, and November 8, were carefully avoided. One-third of the year, therefore, was absolutely barred. The great holidays, too, and these were
legion, were avoided, not because they were unlucky, but
because on these days friends and relatives were sure to have
other engagements. Women being married for the second
time chose these very holidays to make their weddings less
conspicuous.

76. The Wedding Garments. On the eve of her wedding
day the bride dedicated to the *Larēs* of her father's house her
bulla (§ 99) and *toga praetexta* (§ 246), which married women
did not wear, and also, if she was not much over twelve years
of age, her childish playthings. For the sake of the omen
she put on before going to sleep the *tunica rēcta,* or *tunica
rēgilla,* woven in one piece and falling to the feet. It was said
to have derived the name *rēcta* from being woven in the old-
fashioned way at an upright loom, though some authorities
have thought it so called because it hung straight, not
being bloused over at the belt. This same tunic was
worn at the wedding.

77. On the morning of the wedding day the bride was

dressed for the ceremony by her mother. Roman poets show unusual tenderness as they describe the mother's solicitude. A wall painting of such a scene is reproduced in Figure 26. The chief article of dress was the *tunica rēcta* already mentioned (§ 76), which was fastened around the

FIG. 26
DRESSING THE BRIDE
From a wall painting found at Pompeii, now
in the Museo Nazionale, Naples.

waist with a band of wool tied in the knot of Hercules (*nōdus Herculāneus*), probably because Hercules was the guardian of wedded life. This knot the husband only was privileged to untie. Over the tunic was worn the bridal veil, the flame-colored veil (*flammeum*), shown in Figure 27. So important was the veil of the bride that *nūbere*, "to veil oneself," is the word regularly used for the marriage of a woman.

78. Especial attention was given to the arrangement of the hair. It was divided into six locks by the point of a spear, or comb of that shape, a practice surviving, probably, from ancient marriage by capture (§ 86); these locks, perhaps braided, were kept in position by ribbons (*vittae*). As the Vestals wore the hair thus arranged, it must have been an extremely early fashion, at any rate. The bride had also a wreath of flowers and sacred plants gathered by herself. The groom wore, of course, the toga and had a similar wreath of flowers on his head. He was accompanied to the home of the bride at the proper time by relatives, friends, and clients (§§ 176-180), who were bound to do him every honor on his wedding day.

79. The Ceremony. In connection with the marriage ceremonies it must be remembered that only the consent was necessary (§§ 73-74), with the act expressing the consent, and that all other forms and ceremonies were nonessential and variable. Something depended upon the particular form used, but more upon the wealth and social position of the families interested. It is probable that most weddings were a good deal simpler than those described by our chief authorities. The house of the bride's father, where the ceremony was performed, was decked with flowers, boughs of trees, bands of wool, and tapestries. The guests arrived before the hour of sunrise, but even then the omens had been already taken. In the ancient confarreate ceremony these were taken by the public augur, but in later times, no matter what the ceremony, the haruspices merely consulted the entrails of a sheep which had been killed in sacrifice.

Fig. 27
THE
FLAMMEUM

80. After the omens had been pronounced favorable, the bride and groom appeared in the atrium (§ 198), the public room of the house, and the wedding began. This consisted of two parts:

(1) The ceremony proper, varying according to the form used (*cōnfarreātiō*, *coēmptiō*, or *ūsus*), the essential part being the consent before witnesses (§§ 73-74).

(2) The festivities, including the feast at the bride's home, the taking of the bride with a show of force from her mother's arms, the escorting of the bride to her new home (the essential part), and her reception there.

81. The confarreate ceremony began with the *dextrārum iūnctiō* (§ 74). The bride and groom were brought together by the *prōnuba,* a matron but once married and living with her husband in undisturbed wedlock. They joined hands in the presence of ten witnesses representing the ten *gentēs* of the *cūria.* These are shown on an ancient sarcophagus found at Naples (Fig. 28). Then followed the words of consent spoken by the bride: *Quandō tū Gāius, ego Gāia.* The words mean, "When (and where) you are Gaius, then (and there) I am Gaia," i.e., "I am bone of your bone, flesh of your flesh." The formula was unchanged, no matter what the names of the bride and groom, and goes back to a

FIG. 28
A MARRIAGE SCENE
From a sarcophagus found at Naples.

time when *Gāius* was a *nōmen,* not a *praenōmen* (§ 56). It implied that the bride was actually entering the *gēns* of the groom (§§ 23, 25, 30, 35), and was probably chosen for the lucky meaning (§ 44) of the names *Gāius* and *Gāia.* Even in marriages *sine conventiōne* the old formula came to be used, its import having been lost in lapse of time. The bride and groom then took their places side by side at the left of the altar and facing it, sitting on stools covered with the pelt of the sheep slain for the sacrifice (§ 79).

82. A bloodless offering was made to Jupiter by the *Ponti-*

fex Maximus and the *Flāmen Diālis*, consisting of the cake of spelt (*farreum lībum*) from which the ceremony got the name *cōnfarreātiō*. Then the cake was eaten by the bride and groom. With the offering to Jupiter a prayer was recited by the Flamen to Juno as the goddess of marriage, and to Tellus, Picumnus, and Pilumnus, deities of the country and its fruits. The utensils necessary for the offering were carried in a covered basket (*cumera*) by a boy called *camillus* (Fig. 29), whose parents must both be living at the time (i.e., he must be *patrīmus et mātrīmus*). Then followed the congratulations, the guests using the word *fēlīciter*.

FIG. 29

A CAMILLUS

(*See also* Figures 127 and 128.)

83. The *coēmptiō* began with the fictitious sale, carried out in the presence of no fewer than five witnesses. The purchase money, represented by a single coin, was laid in the scales held by a *lībripēns*. The scales, scaleholder, coin, and witnesses were all necessary for this kind of marriage. Then followed the *dextrārum iūnctiō* and the words of consent (§ 81), borrowed, as has been said, from the confarreate ceremony. Originally the groom had asked the bride *an sibi māter familiās esse vellet*. She assented, and put to him a similar question, *an sibi pater familiās esse vellet*. To this he too gave an affirmative answer. A prayer was then recited and sometimes, perhaps, a sacrifice was offered, after which came the congratulations, as in the other and more elaborate ceremony.

84. The third form, that is, the ceremonies preliminary to *ūsus*, probably admitted of more variation than either of the others, but no description has come down to us. We may be sure that the hands were clasped, the words of consent spoken (§ 81), and congratulations offered, but we know of no special customs or usages. It was almost inevitable that the three forms should become more or less alike in the course of time, though the cake of spelt (§ 82) could not be borrowed from the confarreate ceremony by either of the others, or the scales and their holder (§ 83) from the ceremony of *coēmptiō*.

85. The Wedding Feast. After the conclusion of the ceremony came the wedding feast (*cēna nūptiālis*), lasting in early times until evening. There can be no doubt that this was regularly given at the house of the bride's father and that the few cases when, as we know, it was given at the groom's house were exceptional and due to special circumstances which might cause a similar change today. The feast seems to have concluded with the distribution among the guests of pieces of the wedding cake (*mustā-ceum*[1]). There came to be so much extravagance at these feasts and at the *repōtia* mentioned in § 89 that under Augustus it was proposed to limit their cost by law to one thousand sesterces (fifty dollars). His efforts to limit such expenditures were, however, fruitless.

Fig. 30
A ROMAN LADY OF THE THIRD
CENTURY A.D.
A bust now in the Metropolitan Museum of Art, New York.

86. The Bridal Procession. After the wedding feast the bride was formally taken to her husband's house. This ceremony was called *dēductiō*, and, since it was essential to the

---

[1] Cato gives the recipe for this cake: "Sprinkle a peck of flour with must ‹§ 296›. Add anise, cumin, bay leaves, two pounds of lard, and a pound of cheese. Knead well and bake on bay leaves."

validity of the marriage (§ 74), it was never omitted. It was a public function, that is, anyone might join the procession and take part in the merriment that distinguished it; we are told that persons of rank did not scruple to wait in the street to see a bride. As evening approached, the procession was formed before the bride's house with torch-bearers and flute-players at its head. When all was ready, the marriage hymn (*hymenaeus*) was sung and the groom took the bride with a show of force from the arms of her mother. The Romans saw in this custom a reminiscence of the rape of the Sabines, but it probably goes far back beyond the founding of Rome to the custom of marriage by capture that prevailed among many peoples (§ 78). The bride then took her place in the procession. She was attended by three boys, *patrīmī et mātrīmī* (§ 82); two of these walked beside her, each holding one of her hands, while the other carried before her the wedding torch of white thorn (*spīna alba*). Behind the bride were carried the distaff and spindle, emblems of domestic life. The *camillus* with his *cumera* (§ 82) also walked in the procession.

87. During the march were sung the *versūs Fescennīnī*, abounding in coarse jests and personalities. The crowd also shouted the ancient marriage cry, the significance of which the Romans themselves did not understand. We find it in at least five forms, all variations of Talassius or Talassio, the name, probably, of a Sabine divinity, whose functions, however, are unknown. Livy derives it from the supposed name of a senator in the time of Romulus. On the way the bride, by dropping one of three coins which she carried, made an offering to the *Larēs Compitālēs*, the gods of the crossroads (§ 490); of the other two she gave one to the groom as an emblem of the dowry she brought him, and one to the *Larēs* of his house. The groom meanwhile scattered nuts through the crowd. This is explained by Catullus that the groom had become a man and had put away childish things (§§ 99,

103), but the nuts were rather a symbol of fruitfulness. The custom survives in the throwing of rice in modern times.

88. When the procession reached the groom's house, the bride wound the door posts with bands of wool, probably a symbol of her own work as mistress of the household, and anointed the door with oil and fat, emblems of plenty. She was then lifted carefully over the threshold, in order, some say, to avoid the chance of so bad an omen as a slip of the foot on entering the house for the first time. Others, however, see in the custom another survival of marriage by capture (§ 78). She then pronounced again the words of consent: *Ubi tū Gāius, ego Gāia* (§ 81), and the doors were closed against the general crowd; only the invited guests entered with the newly-married pair.

89. The husband[1] met his wife in the atrium and offered her fire and water in token of the life they were to live together and of her part in the home. Upon the hearth was ready the wood for a fire; this the bride kindled with the marriage torch, which had been carried before her. The torch was afterwards thrown among the guests to be scrambled for as a lucky possession. A prayer was then recited by the bride and she was placed by the *prōnuba* on the *lectus geniālis,* which always stood in the atrium on the wedding night. Here it afterwards remained as a piece of ornamental furniture only. On the next day there was given in the new home the second wedding feast (*repōtia:* § 85) to the friends and relatives, and at this feast the bride made her first offering to the gods as a *mātrōna.* A series of feasts followed, given in honor of the newly-wedded pair by those in whose social circles they moved.

90. The Position of Women. With her marriage the Roman woman reached a position not attained by the women of any other nation in the ancient world. No other people

---

[1]The husband had at some point slipped away from the procession and gone to his home, there to await the coming of the bride.

held its women in such high respect; nowhere else did women exert so strong and beneficent an influence. In her own house the Roman matron was absolute mistress. She directed its economy and supervised the tasks of the household slaves, but did no menial work herself. She was her children's nurse, and conducted their early training and education. Her daughters were fitted under their mother's eye to be mistresses of similar homes, and remained her closest companions until
she herself had dressed them for
their bridal and their husbands had
torn them from her arms. She was
her husband's helpmeet in business
as well as in household matters, and
he often consulted her on affairs of
state. She was not confined at home
to a set of so-called women's apartments, as were her sisters in Greece;
the whole house was open to her.
She received her husband's guests
and sat at table with them. Even

Fig. 31
HAND SPINNING

when she was subject to the *manus* of her husband, the restraint was so tempered by law and custom (§ 24) that she could hardly have been chafed by the fetters which had been forged with her own consent (§ 73).

91. Out of the house the matron's dress (*stola mātrōnālis*, § 259) secured for its wearer profound respect. Men made way for her in the street; she had a place at the public games, at the theaters, and at the great religious ceremo-nies of state. She could give testimony in the courts, and until late in the Republic might even appear as an advocate. She often managed her own property herself. It is interesting to note that the first book of Varro's work on farming is dedicated to his wife, and intended as a guide for her in the management of her own land. The matron's birthday was sacredly observed and made a joyous occasion by the members of her household, and the people as a whole celebrated the *Mātrōnālia* (the Roman "Mother's Day"), the great festival on the first of March; presents were given to wives and mothers.   Finally, if a woman came of a noble family, she might be honored, after she had passed away, with a public eulogy, delivered from the *rōstra* in the Forum (§ 480).

FIG. 32
PORTRAIT BUST OF A ROMAN LADY
(Third Century A.D.)
Now in the Toronto Museum.

92. It must be admitted that the education of women was not carried far at Rome, and that their accomplishments were few, and useful and homely rather than elegant.   So far as accomplishments were concerned, however, their husbands fared no better.   Even in our own country, restrictions on elementary education for women existed originally and were removed very slowly.   For instance, it is told that in New Haven, in 1684, girls were forbidden to attend the grammar schools.

93. It must be admitted, too, that a great change took place in the last years of the Republic.   With the laxness of the family life, the freedom of divorce, and the inflow of wealth and extravagance, the purity and dignity of the Roman matron declined, as the manhood and the strength of her father and her husband had declined before.   It must be remembered, however, that ancient writers did not dwell upon certain subjects that are favorites with our own. The simple joys of childhood and domestic life, home, the praises of sister, wife, and mother may not have been too sacred for the poet and the essayist of Rome, but the essayist and the poet did not make them their themes; they took such matters for granted, and felt no need to dwell upon them. The mother of Horace may have been a singularly gifted woman, but she is never mentioned by her son. The descriptions of domestic life, therefore, that have come down to us either are from Greek sources, or else they deal with precisely those circles where fashion, profligacy, and impurity made easy the work of the satirist. It is, therefore, safe to say that the pictures painted for us in the verse of Catullus and Juvenal, for example, were not true of Roman women as a class in the times of which they write. The strong, pure woman of the early day must have had many to imitate her virtues in the darkest times of the Empire. There were noble mothers then, as well as in the times of the Gracchi; there were wives as noble as the wife of Marcus Brutus.

Fig. 33
A REPRESENTATION OF A ROMAN WEDDING
From a sarcophagus in the Church of S. Lorenzo Fuori le Mura, Rome.

CHAPTER IV

CHILDREN AND EDUCATION

REFERENCES: Marquardt, 80-134; Blümner, 299-340; Becker-Göll, II, 65-114; Friedländer, I, 156-161, III, Chapter III, 216-281, "Philosophy as a Moral Educator"; Smith, under *lūdus litterārius;* Harper's, under *education,* 571-573; Baumeister, 237, 1588-1591; Schreiber, Plates LXXX, LXXXII, LXXXIX, XC; Sandys, *Companion,* 228-236; Daremberg-Saglio, under *ēducātiō;* Walters, under *education, lūdus;* Pauly-Wissowa, under *Schulen;* Fowler, *Social Life,* 168-203; McDaniel, 60-80; Showerman, 89-111, 194-202; Gwynn; Arthur M. Gates, "Greek and Roman Pets," in *The South Atlantic Quarterly,* 30, 405-419 (October, 1931).

94. Legal Status. The legal position of the children in the *familia* has been already explained (§§ 20-21). It has been

FIG. 34
A ROMAN BABY
A portrait bust now in the Museo Barraco, Rome.

shown that in the eyes of the law they were little better than the chattels of the Head of the House. It rested with him to grant them the right to live; all that they earned was his; they married at his bidding, and either remained under his *potestās* or passed under another no less severe. It has also been suggested that custom and *pietās* had made this condition less rigorous than it seems to us.

95. *Susceptiō.* The power of the *pater familiās* was displayed immediately after the birth of the child. By invariable custom it was laid upon the ground at his feet. If he raised (*tollere, suscipere*) it in his arms, he acknowledged it as his own by the act (*susceptiō*) and admitted it to all the rights and privileges that membership in a Roman family implied. If he should refuse to do so, the child would become an outcast, without family, without the protection of the spirits of the dead (§ 34), utterly friendless and forsaken. The disposal of the child did not call for any act of downright murder, such as was contemplated in the case of Romulus and Remus and was afterwards forbidden by Romulus the King (§ 21). The child was simply "exposed" (*expōnere*), that is, taken by a slave from the house and left on the highway to live or to die. It is improbable, however, that the Roman father was inclined to make actual use of this, his theoretical right. While exposure and "recognition" appear frequently

Fig. 35
GOLDEN BULLA
Now in the Metropolitan Museum of Art,
New York.

in Roman comedies, they are doubtless made use of there as convenient dramatic devices taken over from the Greek originals rather than as a reproduction of actual cases in everyday life. No such actual cases are known during the Republic, at any rate.

96. Birthdays. It was believed that a *Genius*, or guardian spirit, came into the world with the child at birth. In the case of a girl this spirit was called her *Iūnō*. Closely connected with this idea was the celebration of the birthday, as the proper festival of the *Genius*. On that day bloodless offerings, such as flowers, wine, incense, and cakes, were made to the *Genius*. Fresh white garments were worn, friends made visits or sent letters of congratulation, presents were received from friends and members of the household, and there was usually a feast.

97. Diēs Lūstricus. The first eight days of the life of the acknowledged child were called *prīmōrdia*, and were the occasion of various religious ceremonies. During this time the child was called *pūpus* (*pūpa*), although to weak and puny children the *praenōmen* might be given soon after birth. Usually, on the ninth day in the case of a boy, on the eighth in the case of a girl, the *praenōmen* (§ 43) was given with due solemnity. A sacrifice was offered and the ceremony of purification was performed, which gave the day its name, *diēs lūstricus*, although it was also called the *diēs nōminum* and *nōminālia*. These ceremonies seem to have been private, that is, it cannot be shown that there was at this time any

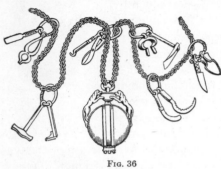

FIG. 36
GIRL'S NECKLACE

taking of the child to a *templum*, as there was among the Jews, or any enrollment of the name upon an official list. Birth registration, which many of our own states have been slow to enforce, was first required under Marcus Aurelius, when it was ordained that the father must register the date of birth and the name of his child within thirty days, at Rome before the *praefectus aerārii*, in the provinces before the *tabulārii pūblicī*. In the case of the boy the registering of the name on the list of citizens may have occurred at the time he put on the *toga virīlis* (§§ 125-127).

98. The *diēs lūstricus* was, however, a time of rejoicing and congratulation among the relatives and friends, and these, together with the household slaves, presented the child with little metal toys or ornaments in the form of flowers, miniature axes and swords, various tools, and especially figures shaped like a half-moon (*lūnulae*), etc. These, called collectively *crepundia*, were strung together and worn around the neck and over the breast. Such strings of these *crepundia* are shown in Figures 36 and 37. They served in the first place as playthings to keep the child amused; hence the name "rattles," from *crepō*. Besides, they were a protection against witchcraft or the evil eye (*fascinātiō*); this was true especially of the *lūnulae*. They could serve also as a means of identification in the case of lost or stolen children, and for this reason Terence calls them *monumenta*. Such

Fig. 37
CREPUNDIA
The original was found in the Crimea.

were the trinkets sometimes left with an "exposed" child (§ 95); their value depended, of course, upon the material of which they were made.

99. The *Bulla*. But of more significance than these was the *bulla*, which the father hung around the child's neck on this day, if he had not done so at the time of the *susceptiō* (§ 95). It consisted frequently of two concave pieces of gold, like a watch case (Fig. 38), fastened together by a wide spring of the same metal, and contained an amulet as a protection against *fascinātiō* (§ 98). It was hung around the neck by a chain or cord and was worn upon the breast. The *bulla* came originally from Etruria.[1] For a

Fig. 38
ROMAN BULLA
Both back (left) and front (right) of this *bulla* are shown.
Now in the Toronto Museum.

<hr />

[1] The influence of Etruria upon Rome faded before that of Greece (§ 6), but from Etruria the Romans got the art of divination, certain forms of architecture, the insignia of royalty, and the games of the circus and the amphitheater.

long time only the children of patricians were allowed to wear *bullae* of gold; the plebeians contented themselves with imitations made of leather, hung on a leather thong. In the course of time the distinction ceased to be observed,

FIG. 39
A ROMAN BOY, WITH TOGA
AND BULLA
A statue in the Louvre, Paris.

as we have seen such distinctions die out in the use of names and in the marriage ceremonies, and by Cicero's time the *bulla aurea* might be worn by the child of any freeborn citizen. The choice of material depended upon the wealth and generosity of the father rather than upon his social position. The girl wore her *bulla* (Figs. 35 and 38) until the eve of her wedding day; then she laid it aside with other childish things, as we have seen (§ 76). The boy wore his until he assumed the *toga virīlis* (§ 127), when it was dedicated to the *Larēs* of the house and carefully preserved. If the boy became a successful general and won the coveted honor of a triumph, he always wore his *bulla* in the triumphal procession as a protection against envy.

100. Nurses. The mother was the child's nurse (§ 90), not only in the days of the Republic but even under the Empire; the Romans heeded the teachings of nature in this respect longer than any other civilized nation of the ancient world. Of course it was not always possible then, as it is not always possible now, for the mother to nurse her children, and then her place was taken by a slave (*nūtrīx*), to whom the name *māter* seems to have been given out of affection. In the ordinary care of the children, too, the mother was assisted, but only assisted, by slaves. Under the eye of the mother, a slave washed and dressed the child, told it stories, sang it lullabies, and rocked it to sleep on her arm or in a cradle (Fig. 40).

The place of the modern baby carriage was taken by a litter (*lectīca*); a terra cotta figure has come down to us (Fig. 41) representing a child carried in such a litter by two men.

FIG. 40
A CRADLE

101. After the Punic Wars (§ 6) it became customary for the well-to-do to select for the child's nurse a Greek

FIG. 41
A CHILD IN A LITTER

slave, that the child might acquire the Greek language as naturally as its own. In Latin literature are many passages that testify to the affection felt for each other by nurse and child, an affection that lasted on into manhood and womanhood. It was a common thing for the young wife to take with her into her new home, as her adviser and confidant, the nurse who had watched over her in her infancy. Faithfulness on the part of such slaves was also frequently repaid by manumission.

102. Playthings. Comparatively little is known of the playthings, pets, and games of Roman children, because, as has been said (§ 93), domestic life was not a theme of Roman writers and no books were then written especially for the young. Still, there are scattered references

FIG. 42
NURSING
BOTTLE

in literature from which we can learn something, and more is known from monumental sources (§ 12). This evidence shows that playthings were numerous and of very many

kinds. The *crepundia* have been mentioned already (§ 98); these miniature tools and implements seem to have been very common. Dolls there were, too, and some of these have come down to us, though we cannot always distinguish between statuettes and genuine playthings. Some dolls were made of clay, others of wax, and even jointed arms and legs were not unknown (Figs. 43 and 44). Quintilian speaks of ivory letters, to be used by children as letter blocks are now. Little wagons and carts were also common. Horace speaks of hitching mice to toys of this sort, of building houses, and riding on "stick-horses." There are numerous pictures and descriptions of children spinning tops, making them revolve by

FIG. 43
JOINTED DOLL
Now in the Toronto Museum.

blows of a whip-lash, as in Europe nowadays. Hoops also were a favorite plaything; they were driven with a stick and had pieces of metal fastened to them to warn people of their approach. Boys walked on stilts. They played with balls, too, but as men enjoyed this sport as well, the account of it may be deferred until we reach the subject of amusements (§ 318).

103. Pets and Games. Pets were even more common then than now (Fig. 45), and then as now the dog was easily first in the affections of children. The house cat began to

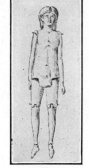

FIG. 44
JOINTED DOLL

be known at Rome in the first century A.D. Birds were very commonly made pets. Thus besides the doves and pigeons which are familiar to us, ducks, crows, and quail, we are told, were pets of children. So also were geese, odd as this seems to us, and there is a statue of a child struggling with a goose as large as himself. Monkeys were known, but could not have been common. Mice have been mentioned already. Games of many kinds were played by children, but we can only guess at the nature of most of them, as we have hardly any formal descriptions. There were games corresponding to our Odd or Even, Blindman's Buff, Hide and Seek, Jackstones (§ 320), and Seesaw. Pebbles and nuts were used in games something like our marbles, and there were board-games also. To these may be added, for boys, riding, swimming, and wrestling, although these were taken too seriously, perhaps, to be called games and belonged rather to the

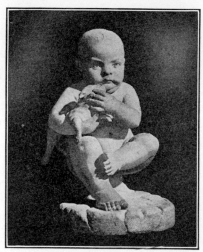

Fig. 45
A LITTLE ROMAN BOY AND HIS PET LAMB
A statue now in the Palazzo dei Conservatori, Rome.

training of boys for the duties of citizenship.

104. Home Training. The training of the children was conducted by the father and mother in person. More stress was laid upon moral than upon intellectual development: reverence for the gods, respect for the law, unquestioning and instant obedience to authority, truthfulness, and self-reliance were the most important lessons for the child to learn. Much of the training came from the constant association of the children with their parents, which was the characteristic feature of the home training of the Romans as compared with that of other peoples of early days. The children sat at table with their elders; in early times they helped to serve the meals. Until the age of seven both boys and girls had their mother for their teacher. From her they learned to speak correctly their native tongue. The mother taught them the elements of reading and writing and as much of the simpler operations of arithmetic as children so young could learn.

FIG. 46

A ROMAN GIRL OF THE FIRST CENTURY, A.D.

A bust now in the Museo Nazionale, Rome.

105. From about the age of seven the boy passed under the care of regular teachers, but the girl remained her mother's constant companion. Her schooling was necessarily cut short, because the Roman girl became a wife so young [§ 68 (2)], and there were things to learn in the meantime that books do not teach. From her mother she learned to spin and weave and sew; even Augustus wore garments woven by his wife. By her mother she was initiated into all the mysteries of household economy and fitted to take her place as the mistress of a household of her own, to be a Roman *mātrōna*, the most dignified position to which a woman could aspire in the ancient world (§§ 90-91).

106. The boy, except during the hours of school, was equally his father's companion. If the father was a farmer, as all Romans were in earlier times, the boy helped in the fields and learned to plow and plant and reap. If the father was a man of high position and lived in the capital, the boy stood by him in his atrium as he received his guests, learned to know their faces, names, and rank, and acquired a practical knowledge of politics and affairs of state. If the father was a senator, the boy (in the earlier days only, it is true) accompanied him to the senate house to hear the debates and listen to the great orators of the time; the son could always go with his father to the Forum when the latter was an advocate or was concerned in a public trial.

107. Then, since every male Roman was bred a soldier, the father trained the son in the use of arms and in the various military exercises, as well as in the manly sports of riding, swimming, wrestling, and boxing. In these exercises strength and agility were kept in view, rather than the grace of movement and symmetrical development of form on which the Greeks laid so much stress. On great occasions, too, when the cabinets in the atrium were opened and the wax busts of the ancestors displayed (§ 200), the boy and girl of noble family were always present and learned the history of the great family of which they were a part, and with it the history of Rome.

Fig. 47

A LITTLE BOY FROM GAUL

A head in the Musée Lapidaire, Arles, France.

108. Schools. The actual instruction given to the children by the father would vary with his own education and would at best be subject to all sorts of interruptions due to his private business or his public duties. We find that this embarrassment was appreciated in very early times, and that it was customary for a *pater familiās* who happened to have among his slaves one competent to give the needed instruction to turn over to him the actual teaching of the children. It must be remembered that slaves taken in war were often much better educated than their Roman masters. Not all households, however, would include a competent teacher, and it would seem only natural for the fortunate owner of such a slave to receive into his house at fixed hours of the day the children of his friends and neighbors to be taught together with his own.

109. For this privilege he might charge a fee for his own benefit, as we are told that Cato actually did, or he might allow the slave to retain as his *peculium* (§§ 22, 162-163) the

FIG. 48
A LITTLE ROMAN BOY
A bust now in the Vatican
Museum, Rome.

little presents given him by his pupils in lieu of direct payment. The next step, one taken in times too early to be accurately fixed, was to select for the school a more convenient place than a private house, one that was central and easily accessible, and to receive as pupils all who could pay the modest fee that was demanded. To these schools girls as well as boys were admitted, but for the reason given in §105 the girls had little time for studying more than their mothers could teach them; those who did carry their studies further came usually of families that preferred to educate their daughters in the privacy of their own homes and could afford to do so. The exceptions to this rule were so few that from this point we may consider the education of boys alone.

110. Subjects Taught in Elementary Schools. In the elementary schools the only subjects taught were reading, writing, and arithmetic. In the first, great stress was laid upon the pronunciation; the sounds were easy enough, but quantity was hard to master. The teacher pronounced first, syllable by syllable, then the separate words, and finally the whole sentence; the pupils pronounced after him at the tops of their voices. In the teaching of writing, wax tablets (Fig. 49) were employed, much as slates were a generation ago. The teacher first traced with a *stilus* (Fig. 49) the letters that served as a copy, then he guided the pupil's hand with his own until the child learned to form the letters independently. When some dexterity had been acquired, the pupil was taught to use the reed pen and write with ink upon papyrus. For practice, the blank sides of sheets that had already been employed for more important purposes were used. If there were any books at all

FIG. 49
WAXED TABLETS AND A STILUS

in these schools, the pupils must have made them for themselves by writing from the teacher's dictation.

111. In arithmetic mental calculation was emphasized, but the pupil was taught to use his fingers in a very

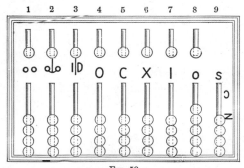

FIG. 50
AN ABACUS

elaborate manner that is not now thoroughly understood. Harder sums were worked out with the help of the reckoning board (*abacus*, Fig. 50). In addition to all this, much attention was paid to train-

ing the memory, and every pupil was made to learn by heart all sorts of wise and pithy sayings, especially the Twelve Tables of the Law. These last became a regular fetich in the schools, and, even when the language in which they were written had become obsolete, pupils continued

to learn and recite them.   Cicero learned them in his boyhood, but within his lifetime they were dropped from the
schools.

112. Grammar Schools.   Among the results of contact
with other peoples that followed the Punic Wars (§6) was
the extension of education at Rome beyond elementary
and strictly utilitarian subjects.   The Greek language came

to be generally learned
(§101), and Greek
ideas of education
were in some degree
adopted. Schools were
established in which
the central task was
the study of the Greek
poets; these schools

Fig. 51
COMPASS AND DIVIDERS
Now in the British Museum, London.

we may call Grammar Schools because the chief study pur-
sued in them was called *grammatica* (a term which included
not merely grammar proper but also literature and literary
criticism, the latter in simple form).   The teacher of such
a school was called *grammaticus*.   Homer was long the
universal textbook, and students were not only taught the
language, but were also instructed in the matters of geography, mythology, antiquities, history, and ethics suggested by
the portions of the text which they read.   The range of
instruction and its value depended largely upon the teacher,
as does such instruction today, but it was at best frag-
mentary and disconnected.   There was no systematic study
of any of these subjects, not even of history, despite its
interest and practical value to a world-ranging people like
the Romans.

113.   The Latin language was soon made the subject of
similar study, at first in separate schools.   The lack of Latin
poetry to work upon (prose writings were not yet used as

textbooks) led to the translation by a Greek slave, Livius Andronicus (third century B.C.), of the *Odyssey* of Homer into Latin Saturnian verses. From this translation, rude as the surviving fragments show it to have been, dates the beginning of Latin literature. It was not until this literature was graced by poets like Terence, Vergil, and Horace that the rough Saturnians of Livius Andronicus disappeared from the schools.

FIG. 52
A ROMAN SCHOOL
From an ancient relief in Trier.

114. In the Grammar Schools, both Greek and Latin, great stress seems to have been laid upon elocution, a fact not surprising when we consider the importance of oratory under the Republic. The teacher had the pupils pronounce after him first the words, then the clauses, and finally the complete sentences. The elements of rhetoric were taught in some of these schools, but technical instruction in the subject was not given until the establishment, early in the first century B.C., of special Schools of Rhetoric. In the Grammar Schools were also taught music and geometry, and these made complete the ordinary education of boyhood.

115. Schools of Rhetoric. The Schools of Rhetoric were formed on Greek lines and conducted by Greek teachers. They were not a part of the regular system of education, but corresponded more nearly to our colleges, since they were frequented by persons beyond the age of boyhood and, usually, of the higher classes only. In these schools the study of prose authors was begun, and philosophy might be studied, but the main work was the practice of composition. This was begun in its simplest form, the narrative (*nārrātiō*), and continued step by step until the end in view was reached, the practice of public speaking (*dēclāmātiō*). One of the intermediate forms was the *suāsōria*, in which a student assumed the character of some famous historical personage at the point of making a decision, and discussed the possible courses of action. A favorite exercise also was the writing of a speech to be put in the mouth of some person famous in legend or history. How effective these could be made is seen in the speeches inserted in their histories by Sallust, Livy, and Tacitus.

116. Travel. In the case of persons of the noblest and most wealthy families, or of those whose talents in early manhood promised a brilliant future, the training of the schools was sure to be supplemented by a period of travel and residence abroad. Greece, Rhodes, and Asia Minor were the places most frequently visited, whether the young Roman cared for the scenes of great historical events and for rich collections of works of literature and art, or merely enjoyed the natural charms and social splendors of the gay and luxurious capitals of the East. For purposes of serious study, Athens offered the greatest attractions and might almost have been called the University for Romans. It must be remembered, however, that the Roman who studied in Athens was thoroughly familiar with Greek, and for this reason was much better prepared to profit by the lectures he heard than is the average American who now studies in Europe.[1]

117. Professional Training. For training in certain matters, a knowledge of which was essential to a successful public life, no provision was made by the Roman system of education. Such matters were jurisprudence, administration and diplomacy, and war. It was customary, therefore, for the young citizen to attach himself for a time to some older man, eminent in these lines or in some one of them, in order to gain an opportunity for observation and practical experience in the performance of duties that would sooner or later devolve upon him. So Cicero learned Roman law under Quintus Mucius Scaevola, the most eminent jurist of the time, and in later years the young Marcus Caelius Rufus in turn served the same

Fig. 53
A YOUNG SOLDIER
A bust of C. Julius Caesar Octavianus, now in the Uffizi Gallery, Florence.

voluntary "apprenticeship" (*tīrōcinium forī*) under Cicero. This arrangement was not only highly advantageous to the young men, but was also considered very honorable for those under whom they studied.

118. In the same way the governors of provinces and generals in the field were attended by a voluntary staff (*cohors*) of young men, whom they had invited to accompany them at state expense for personal or political reasons. These *tīrōnēs* became familiar in this way (*tīrōcinium mīlitiae*) with the practical side of administration and war,

---

[1]See Abbott, *Society and Politics in Ancient Rome*, 191-214, "The Career of a Roman Student."

while at the same time they were relieved of many of the hardships and dangers suffered by those, less fortunate, who had to rise from the ranks. It was this staff of inexperienced young men who hid in their tents or asked for leave of absence when Caesar determined to meet Ariovistus in battle (Caesar, *Dē Bellō Gallicō*, I, 39), although some of them, no doubt, made gallant soldiers and wise commanders afterwards.

119. Remarks on the Schools. Having considered the possibilities in the way of education and training within the reach of the more favored few, we may now go back to the Elementary and Grammar Schools to get an idea of the actual school life of the ordinary Roman boy in Rome and elsewhere (§ 462). Though these were not "public" schools in our sense of the word, that is, though they were not supported or supervised by the State, and, though attendance was not compulsory, it is nevertheless true that the elements at least of education, a knowledge of the three R's, were more generally diffused among the Romans than among any other people of the ancient world. The schools were distinctly democratic in this, that they were open to all classes, that the fees were little more than nominal, that, so far as concerned discipline and the treatment of the pupils, no distinction was made between the children of the humblest and those of the most lordly families.

120. The school was often in a *pergula*, a gallery attached to a public building, or open room like a shop, roofed against the sun and rain, but open at the sides and furnished merely with rough benches without backs. The children were exposed, therefore, to all the distractions of the busy town life around them, and the people living near were in turn annoyed by the noisy recitations (§ 110) and even noisier punishments. A picture of a schoolroom, derived from an ancient relief, is shown in Figure 52.

121. The Teacher. The teacher was originally a slave;

perhaps he was usually a freedman. The position in itself was not honorable, but it might become so through the character of the teacher. Though the pupils feared the master, they seem to have had little respect for him. The pay he received was a mere pittance, varying from three dollars a year from each pupil for the elementary teacher (*litterātor, magister litterārum*) to five or six times that sum for a *grammaticus* (§ 112). In addition to the fee, the pupils were expected to bring the master from time to time little presents, a custom persisting probably from the time when these presents were his only reward (§ 109). The fees varied, however, with the qualifications of the master. Some whose reputations were established and whose schools were "fashionable" charged no fees at all, but left the amount to be paid (*honōrārium*) to the generosity of their patrons. There were no teachers' licenses, and no "Requirements in Education" to be met. Anyone who chose might set up his schoolroom and look for pupils, even as Stephen Douglas walked into Winchester, Illinois, in 1833, and opened a school for three months at three dollars a pupil.

122. Schooldays and Holidays. The schoolday began before sunrise, as did all work at Rome, on account of the heat in the middle of the day (cf. § 302). The pupils brought candles by which to study until it became light, and the roof was soon black with the grime and smoke. The session lasted until time for the noonday luncheon and siesta (§ 302). School was resumed in the afternoon. We do not know definitely that there was any fixed length for the school year. We know that it regularly began on the twenty-fourth of March and that there were numerous holidays, notably the Saturnalia in December and the Quinquatria (from the nineteenth to the twenty-third of March). The great religious festivals, too, especially those celebrated with games, would naturally be observed by the schools, and apparently the market days (*nūndinae*) were also

holidays. It was formerly supposed that there was no
school from the last of June until the first of November,
but this view rested upon an incorrect interpretation of
certain passages of Horace and Martial. It is certain,
however, that the children of wealthy parents would be
absent from Rome during the hot season, and this would
at least cut down the attendance in some of the schools
and might perhaps close them altogether.

123. The *Paedagōgus*. The boy of good family was
always attended by a trustworthy slave (*paedagōgus*), who

FIG. 54
A PAEDAGŌGUS

accompanied him to school, remained
with him during the sessions, and saw
him safely home again when school was
out. If the boy had wealthy parents, he
might have, besides, one or more slaves
(*pedisequī*) to carry his satchel and
tablets. The *paedagōgus* was usually
an elderly man, selected for his good
character; he was expected to keep the
boy out of all harm, moral as well as
physical. He was not a teacher, despite
the meaning of the English word "peda-
gogue," except that, after the learning
of Greek became general, a Greek slave
was usually selected for the position
in order that the boy might not forget what Greek he had
learned from his nurse (§ 101). The scope of the duties of
the *paedagōgus* is clearly shown by the Latin words used
sometimes instead of *paedagōgus: comes, custōs, monitor,*
and *rēctor*. He was addressed by the boy as *dominus,* and
seems to have had the right to compel obedience by mild
punishments (Fig. 54). His duties ceased when the boy
assumed the toga of manhood, but the same warm affection
often continued between the young man and the *paedagōgus* as between a woman and her nurse (§ 101).

124. Discipline.   The discipline was thoroughly Roman
in its severity, if we may judge by the grim references in
Juvenal and Martial to the rod and ferule as used in schools.
Horace has given to his teacher, Orbilius, a deathless fame
by the adjective *plāgōsus.*   From Nepos we learn that

Fig. 55
SCENES IN THE LIFE OF A ROMAN CHILD
From a sarcophagus now in the Louvre, Paris.

then, as now, teachers appealed, at times, to the natural
emulation between well-bred boys, and we know that
prizes, too, were offered.   Perhaps we may think the ferule
well deserved when we read of the schoolboy's trick immor-
talized by Persius.   The passage (III, 44-46) is worth
quoting in full:

> *Saepe oculōs, meminī, tangēbam parvus olīvō,*
> *grandia sī nōllem moritūrī verba Catōnis*
> *discere et īnsānō multum laudanda magistrō . . .* [1]

125. End of Childhood.   There was no special ceremony
to mark the passing of girlhood into womanhood, but for
the boy the attainment of his majority was marked by the
laying aside of the crimson-bordered *toga praetexta* and the
putting on of the pure white *toga virīlis.*   There was no fixed
year, corresponding to the twenty-first with us, in which
the *puer* became *adulēscēns;* something depended upon the

---

[1] "Often, I remember, as a small boy I used to give my eyes a touch with oil,
if I did not want to learn Cato's grand dying speech, sure to be vehemently applauded
by my wrong-headed master . . ."—CONINGTON'S TRANSLATION.

physical and intellectual development of the boy himself, something upon the will or caprice of his *pater familiās*, more perhaps upon the time in which he lived. We may say generally, however, that the *toga virīlis* was assumed between the fourteenth and seventeenth years, the later age belonging to the earlier time when citizenship carried with it more responsibility than under the Empire and consequently demanded a greater maturity.

126. For the classical period we may put the age required at sixteen, and, if we add to this the *tīrōcinium* (§ 117), which followed the donning of the garb of manhood, we shall have the seventeen years after the expiration of which the citizen had been liable in ancient times to military duty. The day was even less precisely fixed. We should expect it to be the birthday at the beginning of the seventeenth year, but it seems to have been the more usual, but by no means invariable, custom to select for the ceremony the feast of Liber which happened to come nearest to the seventeenth birthday. This feast was celebrated on the seventeenth of March and was called the *Līberālia*. No more appropriate time could have been selected to suggest the freer life of manhood upon which the boy was now about to enter.

127. The *Līberālia*. The festivities of the great day began in the early morning, when the boy laid before the *Larēs* of his house the *bulla* (§ 99) and the *toga praetexta*, (§ 125), called together the *īnsignia pueritiae*. A sacrifice was then offered, and the *bulla* was hung up, not to be taken down and worn again except on some occasion when the man who had worn it as a boy should be in danger of the envy of men and gods (§ 99). The boy then dressed himself in the *tunica rēcta* (§ 76), which had one or two crimson stripes if he was the son of a senator or a knight (§ 238); over this was carefully draped the *toga virīlis*. This was also called, in contrast to the gayer garb of boyhood, the *toga pūra*, and, with reference to the freedom of manhood, the *toga lībera*.

128. Then began the procession to the Forum. The father had gathered his slaves and freedmen and clients (§§ 177-180), had notified his relatives and friends, and had used all his personal and political influence to make the escort of his son as numerous and imposing as possible. If the ceremony took place on the *Līberālia*, the Forum was sure to be crowded with similar processions of rejoicing friends. Here were extended the formal congratulations, and the name of one more citizen was added to the official list. An offering was then made in the temple of Liber on the Capitoline Hill, and the day ended with a feast at the father's house.

Fig. 56
MARCUS AURELIUS AS A BOY
A bust in the Capitoline Museum, Rome.

CHAPTER V

DEPENDENTS. SLAVES AND CLIENTS. *HOSPITES*

REFERENCES: Marquardt, 135-212; Becker-Göll, II, 115-212; Friedländer, II, 218-221; Blümner, 277-298; Sandys, *Companion*, 362-365; Pauly-Wissowa, under *clientēs, hospitium;* Daremberg-Saglio, under *servī, lībertus, libertīnus, cliēns, hospitium;* Harper's, Walters, under *servus, lībertus, clientēs;* Fowler, *Social Life*, 204-236; Frank, *An Economic History*, 326-334; McDaniel, 26-40; Showerman, 71-73, and Index, under *slaves;* Duff, throughout.

129. Growth of Slavery. So far as we may learn from history and legend, slavery was always known at Rome. In the early days of the Republic, however, the farm was the only place where slaves were employed. The fact that most of the Romans were farmers and that they and their free laborers were constantly called from the fields to fight the battles of their country led to a gradual increase in the number of slaves, until slaves were far more numerous than the free laborers who worked for hire. We cannot tell when the custom became general of employing slaves in personal service and in industrial pursuits, but it was one of the grossest evils resulting from Rome's foreign conquests. In the last century of the Republic not only most of the manual labor and many trades but also certain of what we now call professions were in the hands of slaves and freedmen. The wages and living conditions of free labor were determined by the necessity of competition with slave labor. Further, every occupation in which slaves engaged was degraded in the eyes of men of free descent until all manual labor was looked upon as dishonorable. The small farms were more and more absorbed in the vast estates of the rich; the sturdy native yeomanry of Rome grew fewer from the constant wars, and were supplanted by foreign stock with the increase of slavery and frequency of manumission (§ 175). By the time of Augustus most of the free-born citizens who were not soldiers were either slaveholders themselves or the idle proletariat of the cities, and the plebeian classes were largely of foreign, not Italian, descent.

130. Ruinous as were the economic results of slavery, the moral effects were no less destructive. To slavery more than to any other one factor is due the change in the character of the Romans in the first century of the Empire. With slaves swarming in their houses, ministering to their love of luxury, pandering to their appetites, directing their amusements, managing their business, and even educating their children, it is no wonder that the old virtues of the Romans, simplicity, frugality, and temperance, declined and perished. And with the passing of Roman manhood into oriental effeminacy began the passing of Roman sway over the civilized world.

131. Numbers of Slaves. We have almost no testimony as to the number of slaves in Italy, none even as to the ratio of the free to the servile population.[1] We have indirect evidence enough, however, to make good the statements in the preceding paragraphs. That slaves were few in early times is shown by their names (§ 59); if it had been usual for a master to have more than one slave, such names as *Mārcipor* and *Ōlipor* would not have sufficed to distinguish them. An idea of the rapid increase in the number of slaves after the Punic Wars may be gained from the number of captives sold into slavery by successful generals. Scipio Aemilianus is said to have disposed in this way of 60,000 Carthaginians, Marius of 140,000 Cimbri, Aemilius Paulus of 150,000 Greeks, Pompeius and Caesar together of more than a million Asiatics and Gauls.

132. The very insurrections of the slaves, unsuccessful

---

[1] We have, indeed, no means of determining the free population of Rome at any period.

though they always were, also testify to their overwhelming numbers. Of the two in Sicily, the first lasted from 134 to 132 B.C., the second from 102 to 98 B.C., in spite of the fact that at the close of the first the consul Rupilius had crucified 20,000, whom he had taken alive, as a warning to others to submit in silence to their servitude. Spartacus defied the armies of Rome for two years, and in the decisive battle with Crassus (71 B.C.) left 60,000 dead upon the field. Cicero's orations against Catiline show clearly that it was the calling out of the hordes of slaves by the conspirators that was most dreaded in the city.

FIG. 57
CAPTIVES ON THEIR WAY TO BE SOLD
AS SLAVES

133. About the number of slaves under the Empire we may get some idea from more direct testimony. Horace implies that ten slaves were as few as a gentleman in even moderate circumstances could afford to own. He himself had two in town and eight on his little Sabine farm, though he was a poor man and his father had been a slave. Tacitus tells us of a city prefect who had four hundred slaves in his mansion. Pliny the Elder says that one Caius Caecilius Claudius Isodorus left at his death over four thousand slaves. Athenaeus (170-230 A.D.) gives us to understand that individuals owned as many as ten thousand and twenty thousand.[1] The fact that house slaves were sometimes

---

[1] The figures are probably exaggerated. However, our own history offers interesting parallels. The famous Virginian, "King" Carter, at his death early in the eighteenth century, is said to have left an estate of 300,000 acres of land and about one thousand slaves; on his plantations the slaves were worked in groups of thirty or fewer with a slave foreman and a white overseer. Nathaniel Heyward of South Carolina died in 1851 possessed of fourteen plantations and 2087 slaves.

divided into "groups of ten" (*decuriae*) indicates how numerous slaves were.

134. Sources of Supply. Under the Republic most slaves brought to Rome and offered there for sale were captives taken in war. An idea of the magnitude of this source of supply has already been given (§ 131). The captives were sold as soon as possible after they were taken, in order that the general might be relieved of the trouble and risk of feeding and guarding such large numbers of men in a hostile country. The sale was conducted by a quaestor; the purchasers were the wholesale slave dealers (§ 135) that always followed an army, along with other traders and peddlers. A spear (*hasta*), which was always the sign of a sale conducted under public authority, was set up in the ground to mark the place of sale, and the captives had garlands on their heads, as did victims offered in sacrifice. Hence the expressions *sub hastā vēnīre* and *sub corōnā vēnīre* came to have practically the same meaning, "to be sold as slaves."

135. The wholesale dealers (*mangōnēs*) assembled their purchases in convenient depots, and, when sufficient numbers had been collected, marched them to Rome, in chains and under guard, to be sold to local dealers or to private individuals. The slaves obtained in this way were usually men, and likely to be physically

Fig. 58
WOUNDED GAUL KILLING HIMSELF
Many prisoners preferred death to slavery.

sound and strong for the simple reason that they had been soldiers. On the other hand they were likely to prove intractable and ungovernable, and many preferred even suicide to servitude. It sometimes happened, of course, that the inhabitants of towns and whole districts were sold into slavery without distinction of age or sex.

136. Under the Empire large numbers of slaves came to Rome as articles of ordinary commerce, and Rome became one of the great slave marts of the world. Slaves were brought from all the provinces of the Empire: blacks came from Egypt, swift runners from Numidia, grammarians from Alexandria; those who made the best house servants came from Cyrene; handsome boys and girls, and well-trained

Fig. 59
A FREEDMAN AND HIS FAMILY
Daughter, father, and mother, from a grave relief now in the
British Museum, London.

scribes, accountants, amanuenses, and even teachers, came from Greece; experienced shepherds came from Epirus and Illyria; Cappadocia sent the most patient and enduring laborers.

137. Some of the slaves were captives taken in the petty wars that Rome was always waging in defense of her boundaries, but they were numerically insignificant. Others had been slaves in the countries from which they came, and merely exchanged old masters for new when they were sent to Rome. Still others were the victims of slave hunters, who preyed on weak and defenseless peoples two thousand years ago much as slave hunters are said to have done in Africa until very recent times. These man-hunts were not prevented, though perhaps not openly countenanced, by the Roman governors.

138. A less important source of supply was the natural increase in the slave population as men and women formed permanent connections with each other, called *contubernia*. This became of general importance only late in the Empire, because in earlier times, especially during the period of conquest, it was found cheaper to buy than to breed slaves. To the individual owner, however, the increase in his slaves in this way was a matter of as much interest as the increase in his flocks and herds. Such slaves would be more valuable at maturity, for they would be acclimated and less liable to disease, and, besides, would be trained from childhood in the performance of the very tasks for which they were destined. They would also have more love for their home and for their master's family, since his children were often their playmates. It was only natural, therefore, for slaves born in the *familia* to have a claim upon their master's confidence and consideration that others lacked, and it is not surprising that they were proverbially pert and forward. They were called *vernae* so long as they remained the property of their first master.

Fig. 60

A YOUNG SLAVE

139. Sales of Slaves. Slave dealers usually offered their wares at public auction sales. These were under the supervision of the aediles, who appointed the placc of the sales and made rules and regulations to govern them. A tax was imposed on imported slaves. They were offered for sale with their feet whitened with chalk; those from the East had their ears bored, a common sign of slavery among oriental peoples. When bids were to be asked for a slave, he was made to mount a stone or platform, corresponding to the "block" familiar to the readers of our own history. From his neck hung a scroll (*titulus*), setting forth his character and serving as a warrant for the purchaser. If the slave had defects not made known in this warrant, the vendor was bound to take him back within six months or make good the loss to the buyer. The chief items in the *titulus* were the age and nationality of the slave, and his freedom from such common defects as chronic ill-health, especially epilepsy, and tendencies to thievery, running away, and suicide. In spite of the guarantee, the purchaser took care to examine the slaves as closely as possible. For this reason they were commonly stripped, made to move around, handled freely by the purchaser, and even examined by physicians. If no warrant

FIG. 61
SALE OF A SLAVE

was given by the dealer, a cap (*pilleus*) was put on the slave's head at the time of the sale, and the purchaser took all risks. The dealer might also offer the slaves at private sale. This was the rule in the case of all slaves of unusual value and especially of those with marked personal beauty. These were not exposed to the gaze of the crowd, but were exhibited only to persons who were likely to purchase. Private sales and exchanges between citizens without the intervention of a regular dealer were as common as the sales of other property, and no stigma was attached to them. The trade of the *mangōnēs* (§ 135), on the other hand, was looked upon as utterly disreputable, but it was very lucrative and great fortunes were often made in it. Vilest of all the dealers were the *lēnōnēs*, who kept and sold women slaves for immoral purposes only.

140. Prices of Slaves. The prices of slaves varied as did the prices of other commodities. Much depended upon the times, the supply and demand, the characteristics and accomplishments of the particular slave, and the requirements of the purchaser. Captives bought upon the battlefield rarely brought more than nominal prices, because the sale was in a measure forced (§ 134), and because the dealer was sure to lose a large part of his purchase on the long march to Rome, through disease, fatigue, and, especially, suicide. There is a famous piece of statuary representing a hopeless Gaul killing his wife and then himself (Fig. 62). We are told that Lucullus once sold slaves in his camp at an average price of eighty cents each. In Rome male slaves varied in value from $100, paid for common laborers in the time of Horace, to $28,000

Fig. 62
THE GAUL AND HIS WIFE
A statue now in the Museo Nazionale, Rome.

paid by Marcus Scaurus for an accomplished *grammaticus* (§ 112). Handsome boys, well trained and educated, sold for as much as $4000. Very high prices were also paid for handsome and accomplished girls. It seems strange to us that slaves were matched in size and color as carefully as horses were once matched, and that a well-matched pair of boys would bring a much larger sum when sold together than when sold separately.

141. Public and Private Slaves. Slaves were called *servī pūblicī* and *servī prīvātī* according as they were owned by the State or by individuals. The condition of the former was considered the more desirable: they were not so likely to be sold, were not worked so hard, and were not exposed to the whims of a capricious master. They were employed to take care of the public buildings and as servants of the magistrates and priests. The quaestors and aediles had great numbers of them in their service. Some *servī pūblicī* were drilled as a corps of firemen to serve at night under the triumvirī nocturnī. Others were employed as lictors, jailers, executioners, etc. The number of public slaves, though considerable in itself, was inconsiderable as compared with that of those in private service.

FIG. 63
A MOSAIC WITH FIGURE
IN RELIEF
Now in the Museo Nazionale,
Naples.

142. Private Slaves. Private slaves were either employed in the personal service of their master and his family or were kept for gain. The former, known together as the *familia urbāna*, will be described later. The latter may be classified according as they were kept for hire or employed in the business enterprises of their master. Of these last the most important as well as the oldest (§ 129) class was that of the farm laborers (*familia rūstica*). Of the others, engaged in all sorts of industries, it may be remarked that it was considered more honorable for a master to employ his slaves in enterprises of his own than to hire them out to others. However, slaves could always be hired for any desired purpose in Rome or in any other city.

143. Industrial Employment. It must be remembered that in ancient times much work was done by hand that is now done by machinery. In work of this sort were

Fig. 64
GLADIATORS
From statuettes now in the British Museum, London.

employed armies of slaves fit only for unskilled labor: porters for the transportation of materials and merchandise, stevedores for the loading and discharging of vessels, men who handled the spade, pickax, and crowbar, men of great physical strength but of little else to make them worth their keep. Above these came artisans, mechanics, and skilled workmen of every kind: smiths, carpenters, bricklayers, masons, seamen, etc. The merchants and shopkeepers required assistants, and so did the millers and bakers, the dealers in wool and leather, the keepers of lodging-houses and restaurants, all who helped to supply the countless wants of a great city. Even the professions, as we should call them, were largely in the hands of slaves.

Books were multiplied by slaves. The artists who carved wood and stone, designed furniture, laid mosaics, painted pictures, and decorated the walls and ceilings of public and private buildings were slaves. . So were the musicians and the acrobats, the actors and the gladiators who amused the people at the public games. So too, as we have seen (§ 121), were some of the teachers in the schools; and physicians were usually slaves.

144. Slaves did not merely perform these various functions under the direction of their master or of the employer to whom he had hired them for the time. Many of them were themselves captains of industry. When a slave showed executive ability as well as technical knowledge, it was common enough for his master to furnish him with the capital necessary to carry on independently the business or profession which he understood. In this way slaves were often the managers of estates, of banks, of commercial enterprises, though these might take them far beyond the reach of their masters' observation, even into foreign countries. Sometimes such a slave was expected to pay the master annually a fixed sum out of the proceeds of the business; sometimes he was allowed to keep for himself a certain share of the profits; sometimes he was merely required to repay the sum advanced, with interest from the time he had received it. In all cases, however, his industry and intelligence were stimulated by the hope of acquiring sufficient means from the venture to purchase his freedom and eventually make the business his own.

Fig. 65
BALANCE AND WEIGHTS
Now in the Museo Nazionale,
Naples.

145. The *Familia Rustica*. Under the name *familia rūstica* are comprised the slaves that were employed upon the vast estates that long before the end of the Republic had begun to supplant the small farms of the earlier day. The very name points to this change, for it implies that the estate was no longer the only home of the master. He had become

FIG. 66
A SEASIDE VILLA
From a Pompeian fresco.

a landlord; he lived in the capital and visited his lands only occasionally for pleasure or for business. The estates may, therefore, be divided into two classes: countryseats for pleasure (§ 448) and farms or ranches for profit (§§ 429-447). The former were selected with great care, the purchaser having regard to their proximity to the city or other resorts of fashion, their healthfulness, and the natural beauty of their scenery. They were maintained upon the most extravagant scale. There were villas and pleasure grounds, parks and game preserves, fish ponds and artificial lakes, everything that ministered to open-air luxury. Great numbers of slaves were required to keep these places in order. Many of them were slaves of the highest class: landscape gardeners, experts in the culture of fruits and flowers, experts even in the breeding and keeping of birds, game, and fish, of which the Romans were inordinately fond. These had under them assistants and laborers of every sort. All the slaves were subject to the authority of a superintendent or steward (*vīlicus*), who had been put in charge of the estate by the master.

146. Farm Slaves. But the name *familia rūstica* is more characteristically used of the drudges upon the farms, because the slaves employed upon the countryseats were more directly in the personal service of the master and can hardly be said to have been kept for profit. The raising of grain for the market had long ceased to be profitable in Italy; various industries had taken its place upon the farms. Wine and oil had become the most important products of the soil, and vineyards and olive orchards were found wherever climate and other conditions were favorable. Cattle and swine were raised in countless numbers, the former more for draft purposes and the products of the dairy than for beef. Pork, in various forms, was the favorite meat dish of the Romans. Sheep were kept for the wool; woolen garments were worn by the rich and by the poor alike. Cheese was made in large quantities, all the larger because butter was unknown. The keeping of bees was an important industry, because honey served, so far as it could, the purposes for which sugar is used in modern times. Besides these things that we are even now accustomed to associate with farming, there were others that are now looked upon as distinct and separate businesses. Of these the most important, perhaps, as it was undoubtedly the most laborious, was the quarrying of stone. Important, too, were the making of brick and tile, the cutting of timber and working it up into rough lumber, and the preparing of sand for the use of the builder. This last was of much greater importance relatively then than now, on account of the extensive use of concrete at Rome.

147. In some of these tasks, intelligence and skill were required as they are today, but in many of them the most necessary qualifications were strength and endurance, as the slaves took the place of much of the machinery of modern times. This was especially true of the men employed in the quarries, who were usually of the rudest and most ungovernable class, and were worked in chains by day and housed in dungeons by night.

148. The *Vīlicus*. The management of such a farm was also intrusted to a *vīlicus* (§145), who was proverbially a hard taskmaster, simply because his hopes of freedom depended upon the amount of profits he could turn into his master's coffers at the end of the year. His task was no easy one. Besides overseeing the gangs of slaves already mentioned and planning their work, he might have under his charge another body of slaves, only less numerous, employed in providing for the wants of the others. On the large estates everything necessary for the farm was produced or manufactured on the place, unless conditions made only highly specialized farming profitable. Enough grain was raised for food, and this grain was ground in the farm mills and baked in the farm ovens by millers and bakers who were slaves on the farm. The mill was usually turned by a horse or a mule, but slaves were often made to do the grinding as a punishment. Wool was carded, spun, and woven Into cloth, and this cloth was made into clothes by the female slaves under the eye of the steward's consort, the *vīlica*. Buildings were erected, and the tools and implements necessary for the work of the farm were made and repaired. These things required a number of carpenters, smiths, and masons, though such workmen were not necessarily of the highest class. It was the touchstone of a good *vīlicus* to keep his men always busy, and it is to be understood that the slaves were alternately plowmen and reapers, vinedressers and treaders of the grapes, perhaps even quarrymen and lumbermen, according to the season of the year and the place of their toiling.

149. The *Familia Urbāna.* The number of slaves kept by the wealthy Roman in his city mansion was measured not by his needs, but by the demands of fashion and his means. In the early days a sort of butler (*ātriēnsis*), or major-domo, had relieved the master of his household cares, had done the buying, had kept the accounts, had seen that the house and furniture were in order, and had looked after the few slaves who did the actual work. Under the late Republic all this was changed. Other slaves, the *prōcūrātor* and *dispēnsātor*, relieved the *ātriēnsis* of the purchasing of the supplies and the keeping of the accounts, and left to him merely the supervision of the house and its furniture. The duties of the slaves under him were, in the same way, distributed among a number many times greater than the slaves of early days. Every part of the house had its special staff of slaves, often so numerous as to be distributed into *decuriae* (§ 133), with a separate superintendent for each *decuria:* one for the kitchen, another for the dining-rooms, another for the bedrooms, etc.

150. The very entrance door had assigned to it its special slave (*ōstiārius* or *iānitor*), who was in early times chained to it like a watchdog, in order to keep him literally at his post. The duties of the several sets were again divided and subdivided; each slave had some one office to perform, and only one. The names of the various functionaries of the kitchen, the dining-rooms, and the bedchambers are too numerous to mention, but an idea of the complexity of the service may be gained from the number of attendants that assisted the master and mistress with their toilets. The former had his *ōrnātor*, *tōnsor*, and *calceātor* (who cared for the feet), the latter her hairdresser (*ciniflō* or *cinerārius*) and *ōrnātrīx;* besides these, each had no fewer than three or four to assist with the bath. The children, too, had each his or her own attendants; these included, for both boy and girl, the *nūtrix*, and, in the case of the boy, the *paedagōgus* and the *pedisequī* (§ 123).

151. When the master or mistress left the house, a numerous retine was deemed necessary. If he or she walked, slaves (*ante-ambulōnēs*) went before to clear the way, and pages and lackeys followed, carrying wraps or the sunshade and fan of the mistress, and ready to perform any little service that might be necessary. The master was often accompanied out of the house by his *nōmen-clātor*, who prompted him in case he had forgotten the name of anyone who greeted

FIG. 67
NURSE, HOLDING A BABY
A terra cotta statuette now in the Metro-
politan Museum of Art, New York.

him. If the master did not walk, he was carried in a litter (*lectīca*, Fig. 41), somewhat like a sedan chair. The bearers were strong men, by preference Syrians or Cappadocians (§ 136), all carefully matched in size (§ 140) and dressed in gorgeous liveries. As each member of the household had his own litter and bearers, this one class of slaves made an important item in the family budget. When master or mistress rode in this way, the same attendants accompanied them as when they walked. At night, as there were no street lights (§ 233), torches had to be carried by some of the attendants to light the way.

152. When the master dined at the house of a friend, his slaves attended him at least as far as the door. Some remained with him to care for his sandals, and others (*adver-sitōrēs*) returned at the appointed hour to see him home. A journey out of the city was a more serious matter and

Fig. 68
A VERY YOUNG SLAVE, WITH A LANTERN
A statue in the Museo Nazionale, Rome.

called for more pomp and display. In addition to the horses and mules that drew the carriages of those who rode, there were mounted outriders and beasts of burden loaded with baggage and supplies. Numerous slaves followed on foot, and an occasional Roman even had a band of gladiators to act as escort and bodyguard. It is not too much to say that the ordinary train of a wealthy traveler included dozens, perhaps scores, of slaves.

153. Among the *familia urbāna* must be numbered also those who furnished amusement and entertainment for the master and his guests, especially during and after meals. There were musicians and readers, and, for persons of less refined tastes, dancers, jesters, dwarfs, and even misshapen freaks. Under the Empire little children were kept for the same purpose.

154. Lastly may be mentioned the slaves of the highest class, the confidential assistants of the master, the amanuenses who wrote his letters, the secretaries who kept his accounts, and the agents through whom he collected his income, audited the reports of his stewards and managers, made his investments, and transacted all sorts of business matters. The greater the luxury and extravagance of the house, the more the master would need these trained and experienced men to relieve him of cares, and by their fidelity and skill to make possible the gratification of his tastes and passions.

155. Such a staff as has been described (§ 154) belonged, of course, only to a wealthy and ostentatiously fashionable man. Persons with really good sense had only such slaves as could be profitably employed. Atticus, the friend of Cicero, a man of sufficient wealth and social position to defy the demands of fashion, kept in his service only *vernae* (§ 138), and had them so carefully trained that the meanest could read and write for him. Cicero, on the other hand, could not think it good form to have a slave do more than one kind of work, and Cicero was not to be considered a rich man.

156. Legal Status of Slaves. The power of the master over the slave, *dominica potestās* (§ 26), was absolute. The master could assign to the slave laborious and degrading tasks, punish him even unto death at his sole discretion, sell him, and kill him (or turn him out in the street to die) when age or illness had made him incapable of labor. Slaves were mere chattels in the eyes of the law, like oxen or horses. They could not legally hold property, they could not make contracts, they could testify in court only on the rack, they could not marry. The free person *in patriā potestāte* was little better off legally (§ 20), but there were two important differences between the son, for example, and the slave. The son was relieved of the *potestās* on the death of the *pater familiās* (§ 29), but the death of the master did not make the slave free. Again, the condition of the son was ameliorated by *pietās* (§ 73) and public opinion (§§ 21-22), but there was no *pietās* for the slave, and public opinion operated in his behalf only to a limited degree. It did enable him to hold as his own his savings (§ 162), and it also gave a sort of sanction to the permanent unions of male and female slaves called *contubernia* (§ 138), but in other respects it did little for his benefit.

157. Under the Empire various laws were passed that seemed to recognize the slave as a person, not a thing: it was forbidden to sell him to become a fighter with wild beasts in the amphitheater; it was provided that the slave should not be put to death by the master simply because he was too old or too ill to work, and that a slave "exposed" (§ 95) should become free by the act; at last the master was forbidden to kill the slave at all without due process of law.   As a matter of fact, these laws were very generally disregarded, much as are our laws for the prevention of cruelty to animals, and it may be said that it was only the influence of Christianity that at last changed the condition of the slave for the better.

158. The Treatment of Slaves.   There was nothing in the stern and selfish character of the Roman that would lead us to expect from him gentleness or mercy in the treatment of his slaves.   At the same time, he was too shrewd and sharp in all matters of business to forget that a slave was a piece of valuable property, and to run the risk of the loss or injury of that property by wanton cruelty.   Much depended, of course, upon the character and temper of the individual owner.   The case of Vedius Pollio, in the time of Augustus, who ordered a slave to be thrown alive into a pond as food for the fish because he had broken a goblet, may be offset by that of Cicero, whose letters to his slave Tiro disclose real affection and tenderness of feeling.   If we consider the age in which the Roman lived, and pass for a moment the matter of punishments, we may say that he was exacting as a taskmaster rather than habitually cruel to his slaves.

159. Of the daily life of the town slave we know little except that his work was light and that he was the envy of the drudge upon the farm.   Of the treatment of the latter we get some knowledge from the writings of the Elder Cato, who may be taken as a fair specimen of the rugged farmer of his time (234-149 B.C.). He held that slaves should always be at work except in the hours, few enough at best, allowed them for sleep, and he took pains to find plenty for his to do even on the public holidays. He advised farmers to sell immediately worn-out draft cattle, diseased sheep, broken implements, aged and feeble slaves, "and other useless things."

160. Food and Dress. Slaves were fed on coarse food, but, when Cato tells us that besides the monthly allowance

Fig. 69
SLAVES AT WORK IN A SMITHY
Fragment of a grave relief in the Museum, Aquileia.

of grain (about a bushel) they were to have merely the fallen olives, or, if these were lacking, a little salt fish and vinegar, we must remember that this allowance corresponded closely to the common food of the poorer Romans. Every student of Caesar knows that grain was the only ration of the sturdy soldiers that won his battles for him. A slave received a tunic every year, and a cloak and a pair of wooden shoes every two years. Worn-out clothes were returned to the *vīlicus* to be made up into patchwork quilts. We are told that the *vīlicus* often cheated the slaves by stinting their allowance for his own benefit, and we cannot doubt that he, a slave himself, was more likely to be brutal and cruel than the master would have been.

161. But, entirely apart from the grinding toil and the harshness and insolence of the overseer, and, perhaps, of the master, the mere restraint from liberty was torture enough in itself. There was little chance of escape by flight. In Greece a slave might hope to cross the boundary of the little state in which he served, to find freedom and refuge under the protection of an adjoining power. But Italy had ceased to be cut up into hostile communities, and, should the slave by a miracle reach the border or the sea, no neighboring state would dare defend him or even hide him from his Roman master. If he attempted flight, he must live the life of an outlaw, with organized bands of slave hunters on his track, with a reward offered for his return, and unspeakable tortures awaiting him as a warning for others. It is no wonder, then, that slaves sometimes sought rest from their labors by a voluntary death (§ 140). It must be remembered that many slaves were men of good birth and high position in the countries from which they came, many of them even soldiers, taken on the field of battle with weapons in their hands.

162. The *Pecūlium*. We have seen that the free man *in patriā potestāte* could not legally hold property, and that all he acquired belonged strictly to his *pater familiās* (§ 20). We have seen, however, that property assigned to him by the *pater familiās* he was allowed to hold, manage, and use just as if it were his own (§ 22). The same thing was true in the case of a slave, and his property was called by the same name (*pecūlium*). His claim to it could not be maintained by law, but was confirmed by public opinion and by inviolable custom. If the master respected these, there were several ways in which an industrious and frugal slave could scrape together bit by bit a little fund of his own; his chance of doing so depended in great measure, of course, upon the generosity of his master and his own position in the *familia*.

163. If the slave belonged to the *familia rūstica*, the opportunities were not so good, but, by stinting himself, he might save something from his monthly allowance of food

(§ 160), and he might do a little work for himself in the hours allowed for sleep and rest, tilling, for example, a few square yards of garden for his own benefit. If he was a city slave, there were, besides these chances, the tips from his master's friends and guests, and perhaps a bribe for some little piece of knavery or a reward for its success. We have already seen that a slave teacher received presents from his pupils (§ 121). It was not at all uncommon, as has been said, for a shrewd master to teach a slave a trade and allow him to keep a portion of the increased earnings which his deftness and skill would bring. Frequently, too, the master would furnish the capital and allow the slave to start in business and retain a portion of the profits (§ 144).

164. For the master such action was undoubtedly profitable in the long run. It stimulated the slave's energy and made him more contented and cheerful. It also furnished a means of control more effective than the severest corporal punishment, and that without physical injury to the chattel. To the ambitious slave the *peculium* gave at least a chance of freedom, for he hoped to save enough in time to buy himself from his master. Many, of course, preferred to use their earnings to purchase little comforts and luxuries nearer than distant liberty. Some upon whom a high price was set by their owners used their *peculium* to buy for themselves cheaper slaves, whom they hired out to the employers of laborers already mentioned (§ 143). In this way they hoped to increase their savings more rapidly. The slave's slave was called *vicārius*, and legally belonged to the owner of his master, but public opinion regarded him as a part of the slave-master's *peculium*. The slave had only a life interest in his savings: a slave could have no heirs, and he could not dispose of his savings by will. If he died in slavery, his property went to his master. Public slaves (§ 141) were allowed as one of their greatest privileges to dispose by will of one-half of their property.

165. At the best the accumulation of a sum large enough to buy his liberty was pitifully slow and painful for the slave, all the more because the more energetic and industrious he was the higher the price that would be set upon him (§ 140). We cannot help feeling a great respect for the man who at so great a price obtained his freedom. We can sympathize, too, with the poor fellows who had to take from their little hoards to make to the members of their masters'

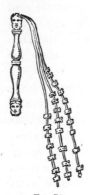

families the presents that were expected on such great occasions as the marriage of one of them, the naming of a child (*diēs lūstricus:* § 98), or the birthday of the mistress (§ 91).

166. Punishments. It is not the purpose of the following sections to catalogue the fiendish tortures sometimes inflicted upon slaves by their masters. They were not very common, for the reason suggested in § 158, and were no more characteristic of the ordinary correction of slaves than lynching is characteristic of the administration of justice in our own states. Certain pun-

Fig. 70
A FLAGELLUM

ishments, however, are so frequently mentioned in Latin literature that a description of them is necessary in order that the passages in which they occur may be understood by the reader.

167. The most common punishment for neglect of duty or petty misconduct was a beating with a stick or a flogging with a lash. The stick or rod was usually of elm wood (*ulmus*); the elm-rod thus used corresponded to the birch of England and the hickory of America, once freely used in flogging. For the lash or rawhide (*scutica* or *lōrum*) was often used a sort of cat-o'-nine-tails, made of cords or thongs of leather. When the offense was more serious, bits of bone, and even metal buttons were attached to this, to tear the flesh, and the instrument was called a *flagrum* or *flagellum* (Fig. 70). It could not have been less severe than the knout of Russia, and we may well believe that slaves died beneath its blows. To render the victim incapable of resistance he was sometimes drawn up to a beam by the arms, and weights were even attached to his feet, so that he could not so much as writhe under the torture.

168. In Roman comedies are references to these punishments, and the slaves make grim jests on the rods and the scourge, taunting each other with the beatings they have had or deserve to have. But such jests are much commoner than the actual infliction of any sort of punishment in the comedies.

169. Another punishment for offenses of a trivial nature resembled the stocks of old New England days. The offender was exposed to the derision of his fellows with his limbs so confined that he could make no motion at all— he could not even brush a fly from his face. A variation of this form of punishment is seen in the *furca*, which was so common that *furcifer* became a mere term of abuse. The culprit was forced to carry upon his shoulders a heavy forked log, and had his arms stretched out before him with his hands fastened to the ends of the fork. This log he had to carry around in order that the other members of the *familia* might see him and take warning. Sometimes to this punishment was added a lashing as he moved painfully along.

170. Less painful and degrading for the moment, but even more dreaded by the slave, was a sentence to harder labor than he had been accustomed to perform. The final penalty for misconduct on the part of a city slave for whom the rod had been spoiled in vain was banishment to the farm, and to this might be added at a stroke the odious task of grinding at the mill (§§ 148, 285), or the crushing toil of labor in the quarries. The last were the punishments of the better class of farm slaves, while the desperate and dangerous class

of slaves who regularly worked in the quarries paid for their
misdeeds by forced labor under the scourge and by having
heavier shackles during the day and fewer hours of rest at
night.   These may be compared to the galley slaves of later
times.   The utterly incorrigible might be sold to be trained
as gladiators.

171. For actual crimes, not mere faults or offenses, the punishments were far more severe.   Slaves were so numerous
(§ 131) and their various employments gave them such free
access to the person of the master that his property and
very life were always at their mercy.   It was indeed a just
and gentle master that did not sometimes dream of a slave
holding a dagger at his throat.   There was nothing within
the confines of Italy so much dreaded as an uprising of the
slaves.   It was simply this haunting fear that led to the
inhuman tortures inflicted upon the slave guilty of an
attempt upon the life of his master or of the destruction of
his property.

172. The runaway slave was a criminal; he had stolen himself. He was also guilty of setting a bad example to his fellow
slaves; and, worst of all, runaway slaves often became ban-
dits (§ 161), and they might find a Spartacus to lead them
(§ 132).   There were, therefore, standing rewards for the
capture of *fugitīvī*, and there were men who made it their
business to track them down and return them to their masters.   The *fugitīvus* was brought back in shackles, and
was sure to be flogged within an inch of his life and sent to
the quarries for the rest of his miserable days.   Besides this,
he was branded on the forehead with the letter F, for *fugitīvus*, and sometimes had a metal collar riveted about his
neck.   One such, which is still preserved at Rome, is shown
in Figure 71.   Another has this inscription:

FUGI. TENE ME. CUM REVOCAVERIS ME D. M.
ZONINO, ACCIPIS SOLIDUM.[1]

---

[1] "I have run away. Catch me. If you take me back to my master Zoninus,
you'll be rewarded."

173. For an attempt upon the life of the master the penalty was death in its most agonizing form, by crucifixion. This was also the penalty for taking part in an insurrection; we may recall the twenty thousand crucified in Sicily (§ 132) and the six thousand crosses that Pompeius erected along the road to Rome, each bearing the body of one of the survivors of the final battle in which Spartacus fell (§ 132).

Fig. 71
SLAVE'S COLLAR

The punishment was inflicted not only upon the slave guilty of taking his master's life, but also upon the family of the slave, if he had a wife (§§ 138, 156) and children. If the guilty man could not be found, his punishment was made certain by the crucifixion of all the slaves of the murdered man. Tacitus tells us that in the reign of Nero four hundred slaves were executed because their master, Pedianus Secundus, had been murdered by one of their number who had not been detected. The cross stood to the slave as the horror of horrors. The very word (*crux*) was used among them as a curse, especially in the expression (*I*) *ad* (*malam*) *crucem*.

174 The minor punishments were inflicted at the order of the master or his representative by some fellow slave called for the time *carnifex* or *lōrārius*, though these words by no means imply that he was regularly or even commonly designated for the disagreeable duty. Still, the administration of punishment to a fellow slave was felt to be degrading, and the word *carnifex* was often applied to the one who administered it and finally came to be a standing term of abuse and taunt. It is applied to each other by quarreling slaves, apparently with no notion of its literal meaning, as many vulgar epithets are applied today. The actual execution of a death sentence was carried out by one of the *servī pūblicī* (§ 141) at a fixed place of execution outside the city walls.

175. Manumission. The slave might purchase freedom from his master by means of his savings, as we have seen (§ 164), or he might be set free as a reward for faithful service or some special act of devotion. In either case it was only necessary for the master to pronounce him free in the presence of witnesses, though a formal act of manumission often took place before a praetor. The new-made freedman

Fig. 72
PILLEUS
On coin of 42 B.C.,
now in the British
Museum, London.

set on his head the cap of liberty (*pilleus*), seen on some Roman coins (Fig. 72). He was called *lībertus* in reference to his master or as an individual, *lībertīnus* as one of a class; his master was now not his *dominus*, but his *patrōnus*. The freedman's relation to the community will be discussed later (§ 423). The relation that existed between the master and the freedman was one of mutual helpfulness. The patron assisted the freedman in business, often supplying the means with which he was to make a start in his new life. If the freedman died first, the patron paid the expenses of a decent funeral and had the body buried near the spot where his own ashes would be laid. He became the guardian of the freedman's children; if no heirs were left, he himself inherited the property. The freedman was bound to show his patron marked deference and respect at all times, to attend him upon public occasions, to assist him in case of reverse of fortune, and in short to stand to him in the same relation as the client had stood to the patron in the brave days of old (§ 176).

176. The Clients. The word *cliēns* is used in Roman history of two very different classes of dependents, who are separated by a considerable interval of time and may be roughly distinguished as Old Clients and New Clients. The former played an important part under the Kings, and especially in the struggles between the patricians and plebeians in the early days of the Republic, but had practically disappeared by the time of Cicero. The latter are first heard of after the Empire was well advanced, and never had any political significance. Between the two classes there is absolutely no connection, and the student must be careful to notice that the later class is not a development of the earlier.

177. The Old Clients. Clientage (*clientēla*) goes back beyond the founding of Rome to the most ancient social institutions of the Italian communities. The *gentēs* that settled on the hills along the Tiber (§ 19) had as a part of their *familiae* (§ 18) numerous free retainers, who farmed their lands, tended their flocks, and did the *gentēs* certain personal services in return for protection against cattle thieves, raiders, and open enemies. These retainers, though regarded as inferior members of the *gēns* to which they had severally attached themselves, had a share in the increase of the flocks and herds (*pecūlium:* § 22), and received the *gēns* name (§ 47), but they had no right of marriage with persons of the higher class and no voice in the government. They were the original *plēbs*, while the *gentīlēs* (§ 19) were the *populus*, or governing body, of Rome.

178. Rome's policy of expansion soon brought within the city a third element, distinct from both *gentīlēs* and *clientēs*. Conquered communities, especially those dangerously near, were made to destroy their own strongholds (*oppida*) and move to Rome. Members of communities that were organized into *gentēs* (§ 19) were allowed to become a part of the *populus*, and these, too, brought their *clientēs* with them. Those who had no such organization either attached themselves to the *gentēs* as clients, or, preferring personal independence, settled here and there, in and about the city, to make a living as best they might. Some were possessed of means as large perhaps as those of the patricians; others were artisans and laborers, hewers of wood and drawers of water;

but all alike were without political rights and occupied the lowest position in the new state. Their numbers increased rapidly with the expansion of Roman territory, and they soon outnumbered the patricians and their retainers, with whom, of course, they, as conquered people, could have no sympathies or social ties. To them also the name of *plēbs* was given, and the old *plēbs*, the *clientēs*, began to occupy an intermediate position in the state, though politically included with the plebeians. Many of the *clientēs*, owing perhaps to the dying out of ancient patrician families, gradually lost their dependent relation and became identified in interests with the newer element.

FIG. 73
ORESTES AND ELECTRA, THE WORK OF
A FREEDMAN
A statue now in the Museo Nazionale, Rome.

179. Mutual Obligations. The relation between patrician patrons and plebeian clients (§ 177) is not now thoroughly understood; the problems connected with it seem beyond solution. We know that it was hereditary and that the great houses boasted of the number of their clients and were eager to increase them from generation to generation. We know that it was regarded as something peculiarly sacred, that the client stood to the patron as little less than a son. Vergil tells us that a special punishment in the underworld awaited the patron who defrauded a client. We read, too, of instances of splendid loyalty to their patrons on the part of clients, a

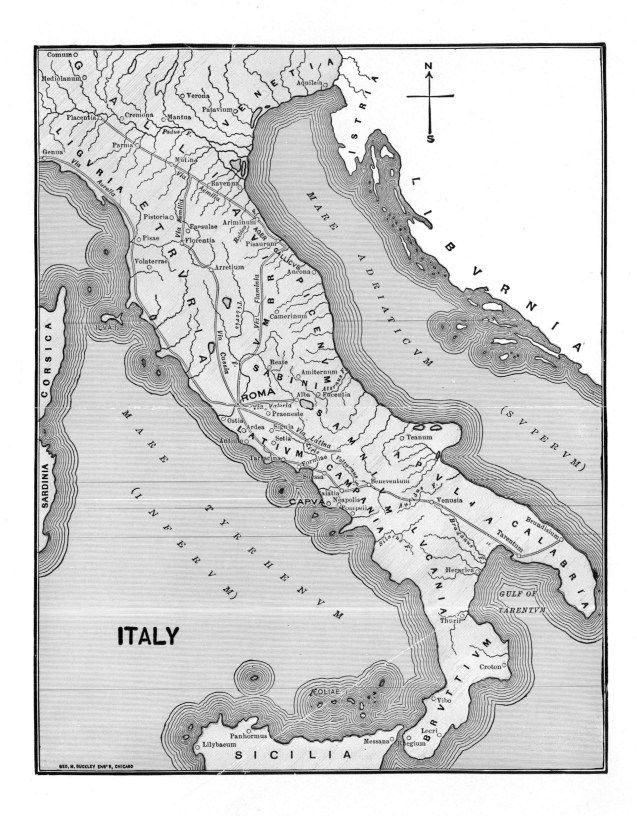

ITALY

loyalty to which we can compare in modern times only that of Highlanders to the chief of their clan. But when we try to get an idea of the reciprocal duties and obligations of clients and patrons, we find little in our authorities that is definite (§ 15). The patron furnished means of support for the client and his family (§ 177), gave him the benefit of his advice and counsel, and assisted him in his transactions with third parties, representing him if necessary in the courts. On the other hand the client was bound to advance the interests of his patron in every way. He tilled his fields, herded his flocks, attended him in war, and assisted him with money in emergencies.

180. It is evident that the value of this relation depended solely upon the predominant position of the patron in the state. So long as the patricians were the only full citizens, so long, that is, as the plebeians had no civil rights, the client might well afford to sacrifice his personal independence for the sake of the countenance and protection of one of the mighty. In the case of disputes over property, for example, the support of his patron would assure him justice even against a patrician, and might secure more than justice were his opponent a plebeian without another such advocate. It is evident that the relation could not long endure after patricians and plebeians became politically equal. For a generation or two patron and client might stand together against their old adversaries, but sooner or later the client would see that he was getting no equivalent for the service he rendered, and his children or his children's children would throw off the yoke. The introduction of slavery, on the other hand, helped to make the patron independent of the client, and, though we can hardly tell whether its rapid growth (§ 129) was the cause or the effect of declining clientage, it is nevertheless significant that the new relation of *patrōnus* and *lībertus* (§ 175) marks the disappearance of that of *patrōnus* and *cliēns* in the old and better sense of the words.

181. The New Clients. The subject of the new clients need not detain us long. They came in with the upstart rich, who counted a long train of dependents as necessary to their state as a string of high-sounding names (§ 50), or a mansion that was crowded with slaves (§§ 149, 155). These dependents were simply needy men and women, usually obscure, who toadied to the rich and great for the sake of the crumbs that fell from their tables. There might be among them men of perverted talents, philosophers or poets like Martial and Statius, but they were, for the most part, a swarm of cringing, fawning, time-serving flatterers and parasites. It is important to understand that there was no personal tie between the new patron and the new client, no bond of hereditary association. A striking difference is in the fact that the new client did not attach himself for life to one patron for better or for worse; he frequently paid his court to several at a time and changed his patrons as often as he could hope for better things. The patron in like manner dismissed a client when he had tired of him.

182. Duties and Rewards. The service rendered by the new clients was easy enough. The chief duty was the *salūtātiō:* the clients, arrayed in the toga, the formal dress for all social functions, assembled early in the morning in the great man's atrium to greet him when he first appeared. This might be all that was required of them for the day, and there might be time to hurry through the streets to another house to pay similar homage to another patron, perhaps to several, for some of the rich slept late. On the other hand, the patron might command their attendance in the house or by his litter (§ 151), if he was going out, and keep them at his side the whole day long. Then there was no chance to wait upon the second patron, but every chance to be forgotten by him. And the rewards were no greater than the services: a few coins for a clever witticism or a fulsome compliment, a cast-off toga occasionally, for a shabby dress disgraced the levee, or an invitation to the dinner table if the patron was particularly gracious. One meal a day was always expected; this was felt to be the due of the client. But sometimes the patron did not receive, and the clients were sent away empty. Sometimes, too, after a day's attendance the hungry and tired *clientēs* were dismissed with a gift of cold food distributed in a little basket (*sportula*), a poor and sorry substitute for the good cheer they had hoped to get. From this basket the "dole" itself, as we should call it now, came to be called *sportula*. In the course of time an equivalent in money, fixed finally at about twenty-five cents a day, took the place of the food. But it was something to be admitted to the familiar presence of the rich and fashionable; there was always the hope of a little legacy, if the flattery was adroit, and even the dole would enable one to live more easily than by work, especially if one could please several patrons and draw the dole from each of them.

183. *Hospitēs*. Finally we come to the *hospitēs*, though these in strictness ought not to be reckoned among the dependents. It is true that they were often dependent on others for protection and help, but it is also true that they were equally ready and able to extend like help and protection to others who had the right to claim assistance from them. It is important to observe that *hospitium* differed from clientship in this respect, that the parties to it were actually on the footing of absolute equality. Although at some particular time one might be dependent upon the other for food or shelter, at another time the relations might be reversed and the protector and the protected change places.

184. *Hospitium*, in its technical sense, goes back to a time when there were no international relations, to a time when there were not two different words for "stranger" and "enemy," but one word (*hostis*) denoted both. In this early stage of society, when distinct communities were numerous, every stranger was looked upon with suspicion, and the traveler in a state not his own found it difficult to get his wants supplied, even if his life was not actually in danger. Hence the custom arose for a man engaged in commerce, or

in any other occupation that might compel him to visit a foreign land, to form previously a connection with a citizen of that country, who would be ready to receive him as a friend, to supply his needs, to vouch for his good intentions, and to act if necessary as his protector. Such a relationship, called *hospitium*, was always strictly reciprocal: if A agreed to entertain and protect B when B visited A's country, then B was bound to entertain and protect A if A visited B's country. The parties to an agreement of this sort were called *hospitēs*, and hence the word *hospes* has a double signification, at one time denoting the entertainer, at another the guest.

185. Obligations of *Hospitium*. The obligations imposed by this covenant were of the most sacred character, and any failure to regard its provisions was sacrilege, bringing upon the offender the

FIG. 74
HOISTING MACHINERY, OPERATED
BY SLAVES
Relief in the Museo Laterano, Rome.

anger of *Iuppiter Hospitālis*. Either of the parties might cancel the bond, but only after a formal and public notice of his intentions. On the other hand the tie was hereditary, descending from father to son, so that persons might be *hospitēs* who had never so much as seen each other, whose immediate ancestors even might have had no personal intercourse. As a means of identification the original parties exchanged tokens (*tessera hospitālis:* see Rich and Harper's, s.v.), by which they or their descendants might recognize each other. These tokens were carefully preserved, and when a stranger claimed *hospitium,* his *tessera* had to be produced and submitted for examination. If it was found to be genuine, he was entitled to all the privileges that the best-known *hospes* could expect. These seem to have been entertainment so long as he remained in his host's city, protection, including legal assistance if necessary, nursing and medical attendance in case of illness, the means necessary for continuing his journey, and honorable burial if he died among strangers. It will be noticed that these are almost precisely the duties devolving upon members of our great benevolent societies at the present time when they are appealed to by a brother in distress.

Fig. 75
TWO PUGILISTS
Ancient relief, now in the Museo Laterano, Rome.

CHAPTER VI

THE HOUSE AND ITS FURNITURE

REFERENCES: Marquardt, 213-250, 607-645; Pauly-Wissowa, under *ātrium, compluvium, impluvium, Römisches Haus;* Blümner, 7-160; Smith, Harper's, Rich, Daremberg-Saglio, Walters, under *domus, mūrus, tegula,* and other Latin words in the text of this book; Baumeister, 631, 927-933, 1364-1384; Friedländer, II, 185-210; Sandys, *Companion,* 217-226; Cagnat-Chapot, I, 1-39, 275-299, II, 1-32, 426-438; Jones, 159-184; Mau-Kelsey, 245-354, 367-382, 456-484; Overbeck, 244-376, 520-540; Gusman, 253-316; McDaniel, 3-22; Fowler, 237-244; Showerman, 76-88. See, also, "The Form of the Early Etruscan and Roman House," by Margaret Waites, in *Classical Philology,* 9, 113-133 (April, 1914).

On Roman building materials and on Roman methods of building construction see Middleton, I, 1-83.

186. *Domus.* The house with which we are first concerned is the residence (*domus*) of the single household in the Italian town, as distinct from lodging houses or apartment houses (*īnsulae*) intended for the accommodation of several families, and the residence, moreover, of the well-to-do citizen, as opposed on the one hand to the mansion of the millionaire and on the other to the hovels of the very poor. Vitruvius (§ 187) says that the house should be suitable to the station of the owner, and that different styles of houses are appropriate in different parts of the world, according to the climate. At the same time it must be understood that the Roman house as we find it does not show as many distinct types as does the American house of the present time. The Roman was naturally conservative—he was particularly reluctant to introduce foreign ideas—and his house preserved in general certain main features essentially unchanged. The proportion of these might vary with the size and shape of the lot at the builder's disposal, and the number of rooms added would depend upon the means and tastes of the owner, but the kernel, so to speak, was always the same.

132

187. Our sources of information are unusually abundant. Vitruvius, an architect and engineer of the time of Caesar and Augustus, has left a work on building, giving in detail his own principles of construction; the works of many of the Roman writers contain either set descriptions of parts of houses or at least numerous hints and allusions that are collectively very helpful; and, finally, the ground plans of many houses have been uncovered in Rome and elsewhere, and in Pompeii we have even the walls of many houses left standing (§ 12). There are still, however, despite the fullness and authority of our sources, many things in regard to the arrangement and construction of the house that are uncertain and disputed (§ 15).

Fig. 76

A CINERARY URN IN THE SHAPE OF AN OVAL HUT

188. The Development of the House. The primitive Roman house goes back to the simple farm life of early times, when all members of the household, father, mother, children, and dependents, lived in one large room together. In this room (*ātrium*) the meals were cooked, the table spread, all indoor work done, and the sacrifices offered to the *Larēs* (§ 490); at night a space was cleared in which to spread the hard beds or pallets. The primitive house had no chimney; the smoke escaped through a hole in the roof. There were no windows; all natural light came through the hole in the roof. There was but one door; the space opposite it seems to have been reserved as much as possible for the father and mother. Here was the hearth, where the mother prepared the meals, and near it stood the implements she used in spinning and weaving; here was the strong box (*arca*) in which the master kept his valuables, and here the bed was spread.

189. The earliest house was a round or oval hut with thatched roof such as was reproduced in the traditional hut of Romulus (§ 214) on the Palatine.[1] The round shape was retained in the form assigned to the Temple of Vesta, whose worship began at the hearth in such huts. The later huts were oval. Later still came a rectangular form. The outward appearance of such a hut is shown in the Etruscan cinerary urns, found in various places in Italy. The ground plan was a simple rectangle without partitions. This may be regarded as historically and architecturally the kernel of the Roman house. Its very name (*ātrium*), which originally denoted the whole house, was also preserved; it appears in the names of certain very ancient buildings in Rome used for religious purposes, the

Fig. 77

A BRONZE CINERARY URN

This urn, in the shape of an early rectangular house, is now in the Museo di Villa Giulia, Rome.

Ātrium Vestae, the *Ātrium Lībertātis*, etc. In later times, however, *ātrium* was applied to a single characteristic room of the house. The origin of the name *ātrium* is still a mystery. The funerary urn from Chiusi, often illustrated (Schreiber, LIII, Fig. 5; Baumeister, Fig. 146, etc.), has a square opening in the top. This has been taken to show that the early house of the rectangular type had such an opening in the middle of the roof for the escape of smoke. It has been shown, however, that this particular urn has lost the toppiece that completed its roof. Urns of this type have regularly one door, and occasionally windows.

190. A feature of the later house, so commonly found in connection with the *ātrium* that one is tempted to suppose it an early addition, is the *tablīnum*, the wide recess opposite the entrance door. The origin of the *tablīnum*, and the uses to

[1] The hut of Romulus, now standing on the Palatine, is a modern reconstruction, based on the round hut-shaped urns found in Latin graves (Fig. 76).

which it was put, alike in earlier and in later times, are still matters of dispute. It may have been intended at first for merely temporary purposes, being built of boards (*tabulae*), and having an outside door and no connection with the *ātrium*. It could not have been long, however, until the wall between was broken through. When this was once done and its convenience demonstrated, the partition wall was removed. Varro explained the *tablīnum* as having been a sort of balcony or porch, used as a dining-room in hot weather.

191. Later, the *ātrium* received its light from a central opening in the roof, the *compluvium*,[1] which derived its name from the fact that rain, as well as air and light, could enter here. Just beneath this a basin, the *impluvium*, was hollowed out in the floor to catch the water for domestic purposes. As more space and privacy were demanded, the house was enlarged by small rooms opening out of the *ātrium* at the sides. The *ātrium* at the end next the *tablīnum* had the full width between the outside walls, and the additional spaces, or alcoves, one on each side, were called *ālae*. The appearance of such a house as seen from the entrance door must have been much like that of an Anglican or Roman Catholic church. The *ātrium* corresponded to the nave, the two *ālae* to the transepts,

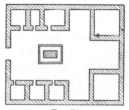

Fig. 78

PLAN OF A TYPICAL
EARLY ROMAN HOUSE

while the bay-like *tablīnum* resembled the chancel. So far as we know, the outside rooms received light only from the *ātrium*. From this ancient house we find preserved in its successors all that was opposite the entrance door, the *ātrium* with its *ālae* and *tablīnum*, the *impluvium* and *compluvium*. These are the characteristic features of the Roman house, and must be so regarded in the description which follows of later developments under foreign influence.

---

[1] The opening in the roof is called the *impluvium* in Plautus, and by later writers when they refer to a certain ancient religious usage (e. g., Aulus Gellius 10.15.8). Hence it is probable that the terms were interchanged later.

192. The Greeks seem to have furnished the idea next adopted by the Romans, a court at the rear of the *tablīnum*, open to the sky, surrounded by rooms, and set with flowers, trees, and shrubs. The open space had columns around it and often a fountain in the middle (Fig. 79). This court was called the *peristȳlium* or *peristȳlum*. According to Vitruvius (§ 187) its breadth should exceed its depth by one-third, but we do not find these or any other pro-portions strictly observed in the houses that are known to us. Access to the *peristȳlium* from the *ātrium* could be had through

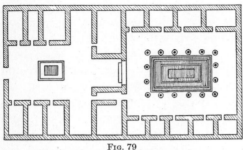

Fig. 79
PLAN OF A GRECO-ROMAN HOUSE
The original house is combined with the *peristȳlium.*

the *tablīnum*, though this might be cut off from it by fold-ing doors, and by a narrow passage (*andrōn:* Fig. 88) at one side. The latter would naturally be used by slaves and by others when they were not privileged to pass through the *tablīnum* (§201). Both passage and *tablīnum* might be closed on the side of the *ātrium* by portières. The arrangement of the various rooms around the *peristȳlium* seems to have va-ried with the notions of builder or owner; no one plan for them can be laid down. According to the means of the owner there were bedrooms, dining-rooms, libraries, drawing-rooms, kitchen, scullery, closets, private baths, together with the simple accommodations necessary for a varying number of slaves. But, whether these rooms were many or few, they all faced the court, receiving from it light and air, as did the rooms along the sides of the *ātrium*. There was often a gar-den behind the *peristȳlium*.

193. The next change took place in the city and town house only, because it was due to conditions of town life that did not obtain in the country. In ancient as well as in modern times business was likely to spread from the center of the town into residence districts, and it often became desirable for the owner of a dwelling house to adapt it to the new conditions. This was easily done in the case of the Roman house on account of the arrangement of the rooms. Attention has already been called to the fact that the rooms all opened to the interior of the house, that few windows were placed in the outer walls, and that there was frequently only one door, and that in front. If the house faced a business street, it is evident that the owner could, without interfering with the privacy of his house or decreasing its light, build rooms in front of the *ātrium* for commercial purposes. He reserved, of course, a passageway to his own door, narrower or wider according to the circumstances. If the house occupied a corner, such rooms might be added on the side as well as in the front (Fig. 95), and, as they had no necessary connection with the interior, they might be rented as living-rooms, as separate rooms often are in our own cities. It is probable that rooms were first added in this way for business purposes by an owner who expected to carry on some enterprise of his own in them, but even men of good position and considerable means did not hesitate to add to their incomes by renting to others these disconnected parts of their houses. All the larger houses uncovered in Pompeii are arranged in this manner. One occupying a whole block and having rented rooms on three sides is described in § 208 (Fig. 95). Such a detached house was called an *insula*.

194. The *Vēstibulum*. Having traced the development of the house as a whole and described briefly its permanent and characteristic parts, we may now examine these more closely and at the same time call attention to other parts introduced at a later period. It will be convenient to begin with the front of the house. The city house was built on the street line. In the poorer houses the door opening into the *ātrium* was in the front wall, and was separated from the street only by the width of the threshold. In the better sort of houses, those described in the last section, the separation of the *ātrium* from the street by the row of shops gave opportunity for arranging a more imposing entrance. Sometimes a part, at least, of this space was left as an open court, with a costly

FIG. 80
MOSAIC DOG FROM POMPEII
Now in the Museo Nazionale, Naples.

pavement running from the street to the door; the court was adorned with shrubs, flowers, statuary even, and trophies of war, if the owner was rich and a successful general. This courtyard was called the *vēstibulum*. The important point to notice is that it does not correspond at all to the part of a modern house called, after it, the vestibule. In this *vēstibulum* the clients gathered, before daybreak perhaps (§ 182), to wait for admission to the *ātrium*, and here the *sportula* (§ 182) was doled out to them. Here, too, was arranged the wedding procession (§ 86), and here was marshaled the train that escorted the boy to the Forum the day that he put away childish things (§§127-128). Even in the poorer houses the same name was given to the little space between the door and the inner edge of the sidewalk.

195. The Ōstium. The entrance to the house was called the *ōstium*. This includes the doorway and the door itself, and the word is applied to either, though *forēs* and *iānua* are the more precise words for the door. In the poorer houses (§ 194) the *ōstium* was directly on the street, and there can be no doubt that it originally opened directly into the *ātrium;* in other words, the ancient *ātrium* was separated from the street only by its own wall. The refinement of later times led to the introduction of a hall or passageway between the *vēstibulum* and the *ātrium,* and the *ōstium* opened into this hall and gradually gave its name to it. The door was placed well back, leaving a broad threshold (*līmen*), which often had the word *Salvē* worked on it in mosaic. Sometimes over the door were words of good omen, *Nihil intret malī,* for example, or a charm against fire. In the houses where an *ōstiārius* or *iānitor* (§ 150) was kept on duty, his place was behind the door; sometimes he had here a small room. A dog was often kept chained inside the *ōstium,* or in default of one a picture of a dog was painted on the wall or worked in mosaic on the floor (Fig. 80) with the warning beneath it: *Cavē canem!* The hallway was closed on the side of the *ātrium* with a curtain (*vēlum*). Through this hallway persons in the *ātrium* could see passers-by in the street.

196. The Ātrium. The *ātrium* (§§ 188-189) was the kernel of the Roman house. The most conspicuous features of the *ātrium* were the *compluvium* and the *impluvium* (§ 191). The water collected in the latter was carried into cisterns; across the former a curtain could be drawn when the light was too intense, as across a photographer's skylight nowadays. We find that the two words were carelessly used for each other by Roman writers

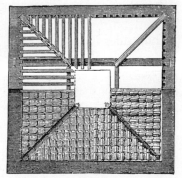

FIG. 81
COMPLUVIUM IN A TUSCAN ĀTRIUM

(§ 191, note). So important was the *compluvium* to the *ātrium* that the *ātrium* was named from the manner in which the *compluvium* was constructed. Vitruvius tells us that there were four styles. The first was called the *ātrium Tus-canicum.* In this the roof was formed by two pairs of beams crossing each other at right angles; the inclosed

FIG. 82
SECTION OF A TUSCAN ĀTRIUM

space was left uncovered and thus formed the *com-pluvium* (Figs. 81, 82). It is evident that this mode of construction could not be used for rooms of large dimensions. The second was called *ātrium tetrastȳ-lon.* The beams were supported at their intersections by pillars or columns. The third, *ātrium Corin-thium,* differed from the second only in having more than four supporting pillars. The fourth was called the *ātrium displuviātum.* In this the roof sloped toward the outer walls, and the water was carried off by gutters on the outside; the *impluvium* collected only so much water as actually fell into it from the heavens. We are told that there was another style of *ātrium,* the *testūdi-nātum,* which was covered all over and had neither *impluvium* nor *compluvium.* We do not know how this was lighted.

197. The Change in the Ātrium. The *ātrium* as it was in the early days of

FIG. 83
AN ĀTRIUM TETRASTȳLON IN A HOUSE AT POMPEII

the Republic has been described in §§ 188-189. The simplicity and purity of the family life of that period lent a dignity to the one-room house that the vast palaces of the late Republic and Empire failed utterly to inherit. By Cicero's time the *ātrium* had ceased to be the center of domestic life; it had become a state apartment used only for

display. We do not know the successive steps in the process of change. Probably the rooms along the sides of the *ātrium* (§ 191) were first used as bedrooms, for the sake of greater privacy. The necessity of a detached room for the cooking, and then of a dining-room, must have been felt as

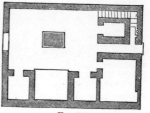

FIG. 84

A SMALL HOUSE AT POMPEII

soon as the *peristȳlium* was adopted (it may well be that this court was originally a kitchen garden). Then other rooms were added about the *peristȳlium*, and these were made sleeping apartments for the sake of still greater privacy. Finally these rooms were needed for other purposes (§ 192) and the sleeping rooms were moved again, this time to an

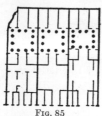

FIG. 85

PLANS OF THREE HOUSES AT ROME

From the Marble Plan, now in the courtyard of the Palazzo dei Conservatori, Rome.

upper story. When this second story was added we do not know, but it presupposes the small and costly lots of a city. Even unpretentious houses in Pompeii have in them the remains of staircases (Fig. 84).

198. The *ātrium* was now fitted up with all the splendor and magnificence that the owner's means would permit. The opening in the roof was enlarged to admit more light, and the supporting pillars (§ 196) were made of marble or costly woods. Between these pillars and along the walls, statues and other works of art were placed. The *impluvium* became a marble basin, with a fountain in the center, and was often richly carved or adorned with figures in relief. The floors were mosaic, the walls painted in brilliant colors or paneled with marbles of many hues, and the ceilings were covered with ivory and gold. In such an *ātrium* (Fig. 86) the host greeted his guests (§ 106), the patron, in the days of the Empire, received his clients

FIG. 86
ĀTRIUM OF THE HOUSE OF SALLUST, IN POMPEII
(A restoration.)

(§ 182), the husband welcomed his wife (§ 89), and here the master's body lay in state when the pride of life was over.

199. Still, some memorials of the older day were left in even the most imposing *ātrium*. The altar to the *Larēs* and *Penātes* sometimes remained near the place where the hearth had been, though the regular sacrifices were made in a special chapel in the *peristȳlium*. In even the grandest houses the implements for spinning (§§ 86, 105) were kept in the place where the matron had once sat among her slave women, as Livy tells us in the story of Lucretia. The cabinets retained the masks of simpler and, perhaps, stronger men (§ 107), and the marriage couch stood opposite the *ōstium* (hence its other name, *lectus adversus*), where it had been placed on the wedding night (§ 89), though no one slept in the *ātrium*. In the country much of the old-time use of the *ātrium* survived even in the days of Augustus, and the poor, of course, had never changed their style of living. What use

Fig. 87
VIEW FROM THE ĀTRIUM ACROSS THE TABLĪNUM
IN A POMPEIAN HOUSE

was made of the small rooms along the sides of the *ātrium*, after they had ceased to be bedchambers, we do not know; they served, perhaps, as conversation rooms, private parlors, and drawing-rooms.

200. The Ālae. The manner in which the *ālae*, or wings, were formed has been explained (§ 191); they were simply the rectangular recesses left on the right and left of the *ātrium* when the smaller rooms on those sides were walled off. It must be remembered that they were entirely open to the *ātrium* and formed a part of it. In them were kept the *imāginēs* (the wax busts of those ancestors who had held curule offices), arranged in cabinets in such a way that, by the help of cords running from one to another and of inscriptions under each of them, the relations of the men to one another could be made clear and their great deeds kept in mind.   Even when Roman writers or those of modern times speak of the *imāginēs* as in the *ātrium*, it is the *ālae* that are intended.

Fig. 88
INTERIOR OF A POMPEIAN HOUSE
This shows the *ātrium* with the *impluvium*, the *tablīnum* with the *andrōn* to the
right of it, and a small *peristȳlium* in the rear.

201. The *Tablīnum*.   The possible origin of the *tablīnum* has already been explained (§ 190).   Its name has been derived from the material (*tabulae*, "planks") of the "lean-to," from which, perhaps, it developed.   Others think that the room received its name from the fact that in it the master kept his account books (*tabulae*) as well as all his business and private papers.   This is unlikely, for the name was probably fixed before the time when the room was used for this purpose. He kept here also the money chest or strong box (*arca*),

which in the olden time had been chained to the floor of
the *ātrium*, and made the room in fact his office or study.
By its position it commanded the whole house, as the rooms
could be entered only from the *ātrium* or *peristȳlium*, and
the *tablīnum* was right between them. The master could
secure entire privacy by closing the folding doors which cut

Fig. 89
PERISTȲLIUM OF A HOUSE IN POMPEII
(A restoration.)
The fence is modern to protect the little garden, which has been replanted.

off the *peristȳlium*, the private court, or by pulling the cur-
tains across the opening into the *ātrium*, the great hall.
On the other hand, if the *tablīnum* was left open, the guest
entering the *ōstium* must have had a charming vista, commanding at a glance all the public and semi-public parts of
the house (Fig. 86). Even when the *tablīnum* was closed,
there was free passage from the front of the house to the
rear through the short corridor (§ 192) by the side of the
tablīnum.

202. The *Peristȳlium*. The *peristȳlium*, or *peristȳlum*, was adopted, as we have seen (§ 192), from the Greeks, but despite the way in which the Roman clung to the customs of his fathers it was not long in becoming the more important of the two main sections of the house. We must think of a spacious court (Fig. 89) open to the sky, but surrounded by rooms, all facing it and having doors and latticed windows opening upon it. All these rooms had covered porches on the side next the court (Fig. 89). These porches, forming an unbroken colonnade on the four sides, were strictly the peristyle, though the name came to be used of this whole section of the house, in-

Fig. 90
THE ROOF OF A PERISTȲLIUM

cluding court, colonnade, and surrounding rooms. The court was much more open to the sun than the *ātrium* was; all sorts of rare and beautiful plants and flowers flourished in this spacious court, protected by the walls from cold winds. The *peristȳlium* was often laid out as a small formal garden, having neat geometrical beds edged with bricks. Careful excavation at Pompeii has even given an idea of the planting of the shrubs and flowers. Fountains and statuary adorned these little gardens; the colonnade furnished cool or sunny promenades, no matter what the time of day or the season of the year. Since the Romans loved the open air and the charms of nature, it is no wonder that they soon made the peristyle the center of their domestic life in all the houses of the better class, and reserved the *ātrium* for the more formal functions which their political and public position demanded (§ 199). It must be remembered that there was often a garden behind the peristyle, and there was also very commonly a direct connection between the peristyle and the street.

203. Private Rooms. The rooms surrounding the *peristȳlium* varied so much with the means and tastes of the owners of the houses that we can hardly do more than give a list of those most frequently mentioned in literature. It is important to remember that in the town house all these

FIG. 91
CORNER OF A KITCHEN IN POMPEII

rooms received their light by day from the *peristȳlium* (§ 192). First in importance comes the kitchen (*culīna*), placed on the side of the *peristȳlium* opposite the *tablīnum*. It was supplied with an open fireplace for roasting and boiling, and with a

FIG. 92
ROMAN KITCHEN UTENSILS
Now in the British Museum, London.

stove (Fig. 91) not unlike the charcoal stoves still used in Europe. This was regularly of masonry, built against the wall, with a place for fuel beneath it, but there were occasional portable stoves. Kitchen utensils have been found at Pompeii. The spoons, pots and pans, kettles and pails, are graceful in form and often of beautiful workmanship (Fig. 92). There are interesting pastry molds. Trivets held the pots and pans above the glowing charcoal on the top of the stove. Some pots stood on legs. The shrine of the household gods sometimes followed the hearth into the kitchen from its old place in the *ātrium*. Near the kitchen was the bakery, if the mansion required one, supplied with an oven. Near it, too, was the bathhouse with the necessary closet (*lātrīna*), in order that kitchen and bathhouse might use the same sewer connection. If the house had a stable, it was also put near the kitchen, as nowadays in Latin countries.

204. The dining-room (*trīclīnium*) may be mentioned next. It was not necessarily closely connected with the kitchen, because, as in the Old South, the numbers of slaves made its position of little importance so far as convenience was concerned. It was customary to have several *trīclīnia* for use at different seasons of the year, in order that one room might be warmed by the sun in winter, and another might in summer escape its rays. Vitruvius thought the length of the *trīclīnium* should be twice its breadth, but the ruins show no fixed proportions. The Romans were so fond of air and sky that the *peristȳlium*, or part of it, must often have served as a dining-room. An outdoor dining-room is found in the so-called House of Sallust at Pompeii. Horace has a charming picture of a master, attended by a single slave, dining under an arbor.

FIG. 93
A BEDROOM
Drawing from the Vatican Manuscript of Vergil.

205. The sleeping rooms (*cubicula*) were not considered so important by the Romans as by us, for the reason, probably, that they were used merely to sleep in and not for living-rooms as well. They were very small, and their furniture was scant (Fig. 93), even in the best houses. Some of these seem to have had anterooms in connection with the *cubicula*, which were probably occupied by attendants

(§ 150). Even in the ordinary houses there was often a recess for the bed. Some of the bedrooms seem to have been used merely for the midday siesta (§ 122); these were naturally situated in the coolest part of the *peristȳlium;* they were called *cubicula diurna.* The others were called by way of distinction *cubicula nocturna* or *dormītōria,* and were placed so far as possible on the west side of the court in order that they might receive the morning sun. It should be remembered that, finally, in the best houses bedrooms were preferably in the second story of the peristyle (§ 197).

FIG. 94
A SACRĀRIUM IN POMPEII

206. A library (*bibliothēca*) had its place in the house of every Roman of education. Collections of books were large as well as numerous, and were made then, as now, even by persons who cared nothing about their contents. The books, or rolls, which will be described later, were kept in cases or cabinets around the walls. In one library discovered in Herculaneum an additional rectangular case occupied the middle of the room. It was customary to decorate the room with statues of Minerva and the Muses, and also with the busts and portraits of distinguished men of letters. Vitruvius recommends an eastern aspect for the *bibliothēca*, probably to guard against dampness.

207. Besides these rooms, which must have been found in all good houses, there were others of less importance, some of which were so rare that we scarcely know their uses.

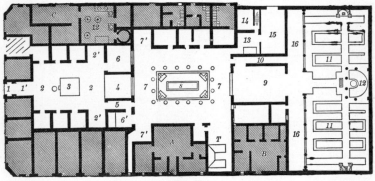

Fig. 95
PLAN OF THE HOUSE OF PANSA, IN POMPEII

The *sacrārium* was a private chapel (Fig. 94) in which the images of the gods were kept, acts of worship performed, and sacrifices offered. The *oecī* were halls or saloons, corresponding perhaps to our parlors and drawing-rooms, and probably used occasionally as banquet halls. The *exedrae* were rooms supplied with permanent seats; they seem to have been used for lectures and various entertainments. The *sōlārium* was a place in which to bask in the sun, sometimes a terrace, often the flat part of the roof, which was then covered with earth and laid out like a garden and made beautiful with flowers and shrubs. Besides these there were, of course, sculleries, pantries, and storerooms. The slaves had to have their quarters (*cellae servōrum*), in which they were packed as closely as possible. Cellars under the houses seem to have been rare, though some have been found at Pompeii.

208. The House of Pansa. Finally, we may describe a house that actually existed, taking as an illustration one that must have belonged to a wealthy and influential man, the so-called House of Pansa at Pompeii (Figs. 95, 96). The house occupied an entire block; it faced a little east of south. Most of the rooms on the front and sides were rented out for shops or stores or apartments; in the rear was a garden. The rooms that did not belong to the house proper are shaded in the plan given. The *vēstibulum*, marked *1* in the plan, is the open space between two of the shops (§§ 193-194). Be-

Fig. 96
SECTION OF THE HOUSE OF PANSA

hind it are the *ōstium* (*1′*), with a figure of a dog (§ 195) in mosaic, opening into the *ātrium* (*2, 2*). The *ātrium* had three rooms on each side, the *ālae* (*2′, 2′*) in the regular place, the *impluvium* (*3*) in the middle, the *tablīnum* (*4*) opposite the *ōstium*, and the passage on the eastern side (*5*). The *ātrium* is of the *Tuscanicum* style (§ 196), and is paved with concrete; the *tablīnum* and the passage have mosaic floors. From these, steps lead down into the *peristȳlium*, which is lower than the *ātrium*, measures 65 by 50 feet, and is surrounded by a colonnade with sixteen pillars in all. There are two rooms on the side next the *ātrium*. One of these (*6*) has been called the *bibliothēca* (§ 206), because a manuscript was found in it, but its purpose is uncertain; the other (*6′*) was possibly a dining-room. The *peristȳlium* has two projections (*7′, 7′*), much like the *ālae*, which have been called *exedrae* (§ 207); it will be noticed that one of these has the convenience of an exit (§ 202) to the street. The rooms on the west and the small room on the east cannot be definitely named. The large room on the east (*T*) is the main dining-room (§ 204); the remains of the dining couches are marked on the plan. The kitchen is at the northwest corner (*13*), with the stable (*14*) next to it (§ 203, at the end); off the kitchen is a paved yard (*15*) with a gateway from the street by which a cart could enter. East of the kitchen and yard

FIG. 97
MODEL OF A ROMAN HOUSE, BASED ON THE HOUSE OF PANSA
In the Metropolitan Museum of Art, New York.

is a narrow passage connecting the *peristȳlium* with the garden (§ 202). East of this are two rooms, the larger of which (*9*) is one of the most imposing rooms of the house, 33 by 24 feet in size, with a large window guarded by a low balustrade, and opening into the garden. This was probably an *oecus* (§ 207). In the center of the *peristȳlium* is a basin about two feet deep, the rim of which was once decorated with figures of water plants and fish. Along the whole north end of the house ran a long veranda (*16, 16*), overlooking the garden (*11, 11*) in which was a sort of summer house (*12*). The house had an upper story, but the stairs leading to it are in the rented rooms, suggesting that the upper floor was not occupied by Pansa's family.

209. Of the rooms facing the street it will be noticed that one, lightly shaded in the plan, is connected with the *ātrium;* it was probably used for some business conducted by Pansa himself (§ 193, at the end), possibly with a slave (§ 144) or a freedman (§ 175) in immediate charge of it. Of the others the suites on the east side (*A, B*) seem to have been rented out as

Fig. 98
MODEL OF A ROMAN HOUSE, WITH ROOF REMOVED
In the Metropolitan Museum of Art, New York.

living apartments. The others were shops and stores. The four connected rooms on the west, near the front, seem to have been a large bakery; the room marked *C* was the sales-room, with a large room opening off it containing three stone mills (§ 418),[1] troughs for kneading the dough, a water tap with sink, and an oven in a recess. The uses of the others are uncertain. The section plan (Fig. 96) represents the appearance of the house if all were cut away on one side of a line drawn from front to rear through the middle of the house. It is, of course, largely conjectural, but it gives a clear idea of the general way in which the dividing walls and roof must have been arranged.

---

[1] The Romans had no public mills distinct from bakeries; each baker was also a miller. (See § 283 and Figure 166.)

210. The Walls.   The materials of which the walls
(*parietēs*) were composed varied with the time, the place, and
the cost of transportation.   Stone and unburned bricks
(*laterēs crūdī*) were the earliest materials used in Italy, as almost everywhere else, timber being employed for merely
temporary structures, as in the addition (§ 190) from which
the *tablīnum*, perhaps, developed.   For private houses in early
times and for public buildings in all times, walls of dressed

Fig. 99
OPUS QUADRĀTUM
This is a section of the Servian Wall.

stone (*opus quadrā-
tum*) were laid in
regular courses, pre-
cisely as in modern
times (Fig. 99).   As
the *tufa*, the volcanic
stone first easily
available in Latium,
was dull and unat-
tractive in color, over
the wall was spread,
for decorative pur-
poses, a coating of fine
marble stucco which
gave it a finish of daz-
zling white.   For less
pretentious houses,
not for public build-
ings, sun-dried bricks (the adobe of our southwestern states)
were largely used until the beginning of the first century
B.C.   These, too, were covered with stucco, for protection
against the weather as well as for decoration, but even
the hard stucco has not preserved walls of this perishable
material to our times.   In classical times a new material had
come into use, better than either brick or stone, cheaper, more
durable, more easily worked and transported, which was employed almost exclusively for private houses, and very gen-

erally for public buildings. Walls constructed in the new way (*opus caementīcium*) are variously called "rubble-work" or "concrete" in our books of reference, but neither term is quite accurate; the *opus caementīcium* was not laid in courses, as is our rubble-work, while on the other hand larger stones were used in it than in the concrete of which walls for buildings are now constructed.

FIG. 100
OPUS RĒTICULĀTUM AT OSTIA

211. Pariēs Caementīcius. The materials of the *pariēs caementīcius* varied with the place. At Rome lime and volcanic ashes (*lapis Puteolānus*) were used with pieces of stone as large as or larger than the fist.

FIG. 101
METHOD OF CASTING CONCRETE WALLS

Brickbats sometimes took the place of stone, and sand (§ 146) that of the volcanic ashes; potsherds crushed fine were better than the sand. The harder the stones the better the concrete; the best concrete was made with pieces of lava, the material with which the roads were generally paved. The method of forming the concrete walls was the same as that of modern times. The method employed by the Romans will be easily understood by examining Figure 101. First, upright posts, about 5 by 6 inches thick, and from

10 to 15 feet in height, were fixed about 3 feet apart along the line of both faces of the projected wall. Outside these

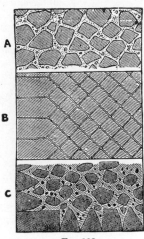

FIG. 102
WALL FACINGS

were nailed, horizontally, boards 10 or 12 inches wide. Into the intermediate space the semi-fluid concrete was poured, receiving the imprint of posts and boards. When the concrete had hardened, the framework was removed and raised; thus the work was continued until the wall had reached the required height. Walls made in this way varied in thickness from a seven-inch partition wall in an ordinary house to the eighteen-foot walls of the Pantheon of Agrippa. They were far more durable than stone walls, which might be removed stone by stone with little more labor than was required to put them together; the concrete wall was a single slab of stone throughout its whole extent, and large parts of it might be cut away without in the slightest degree diminishing the strength of the rest.

212. Wall Facings. Impervious to the weather though these walls were, they were usually faced with stone or kiln-burned bricks (*laterēs coctī*). The stone employed was com-

FIG. 103
BRICKS FOR FACING WALL

monly the soft tufa, not nearly so well adapted to stand the weather as the concrete itself. The earliest fashion

was to take bits of stone having one smooth face but of no
regular size or shape and arrange them, with the smooth faces
against the framework, as fast as the concrete was poured in;
when the framework was removed, the wall presented the appearance shown at *A* (Fig. 102). Such a wall was called *opus
incertum*. In later times the tufa was used in small blocks having the smooth face square and of a uniform size. A wall so
faced looked as if covered with a net (*B* in Fig. 102) and was
therefore called *opus rēticulātum* (Fig. 100). A corner section
is shown at *C* (Fig. 102). In either case the exterior face of
the wall was usually covered with a fine limestone or marble
stucco, which gave a hard finish, smooth and white. The
burned bricks were triangular in shape, but their arrangement and appearance can be more easily understood from
the illustration (Fig. 103). It must be noticed that there
were no walls made of *laterēs coctī* alone; even the thin
partition walls had a core of concrete.

213. Floors and Ceilings. In the poorer houses the floor
(*solum*) of the first story was made by smoothing the ground
between the walls, covering it
thickly with small pieces of stone,
bricks, tile, and potsherds, and
pounding all down solidly and
smoothly with a heavy rammer
(*fistūca*). Such a floor was called
pavīmentum, but the name came
gradually to be used of floors of
all kinds. In houses of a better
sort the floor was made of stone
slabs fitted smoothly together.
The more pretentious houses
had concrete floors, made as
has been described. Floors of upper stories were sometimes
made of wood, but concrete was used here, too, poured over
a temporary flooring of wood. Such a floor was very heavy,

Fig. 104
ROMAN-BRITISH FLOOR
MOSAIC
Now in the Toronto Museum.

and required strong walls to support it; examples are preserved of floors with a thickness of eighteen inches and a span
of twenty feet. A floor of this kind made a perfect ceiling for
the room below, requiring only a finish of stucco. Other
ceilings were made much as they are now: laths were nailed
on the stringers or rafters and covered with mortar and
stucco.

214. Roofs. The construction of the roofs (*tēcta*) differed
very little from the modern method, as may readily be seen
in Figures 81 and 82. Roofs varied as much as ours do in

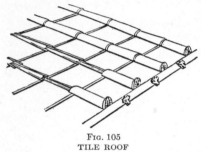

FIG. 105
TILE ROOF

shape; some were flat,
others sloped in two di-
rections, others in four.
In the most ancient times
the covering was a thatch
of straw, as in the so-
called hut of Romulus
(*casa Rōmulī*) on the Palatine Hill, preserved even
under the Empire as a
relic of the past (see note, page 134). Shingles followed
the straw, only to give place, in turn, to tiles. These
were at first flat, like our shingles, but were later made
with a flange on each side in such a way that the lower
part of one would slip into the upper part of the one
below it on the roof. The tiles (*tēgulae*) were laid side by
side and the flanges covered by other tiles, called *imbricēs*
(Fig. 105), inverted over them. Gutters also of tile ran
along the eaves to conduct the water into cisterns, if it
was needed for domestic use. The appearance of the completed roof is shown in Figure 90.

215. The Doors. The Roman doorway, like our own, had
four parts: the threshold (*līmen*), the two jambs (*postēs*),
and the lintel (*līmen superum*). The lintel was always of a
single piece of stone and peculiarly massive. The doors
were exactly like those of modern times, except in the matter

of hinges, for, though the Romans had hinges like ours, they did not use them on their doors. The door-support was really a cylinder of hard wood, a little longer than the door and of a diameter a little greater than the thickness of the door, terminating above and below in pivots. These pivots turned in sockets made to receive them in the threshold and the lintel. To this cylinder the door was mortised, so that the combined weight of cylinder and door came upon the lower pivot. Figure 106 makes this clear, and reminds one of an old-fashioned homemade gate. The Roman comedies are full of references to the creaking of the front doors of houses.

FIG. 106
DOOR OF A ROMAN HOUSE

216. The outer door of the house was properly called *iānua*, an inner door *ōstium*, but the two words came to be used indiscriminately, and the latter was even applied to the whole entrance (§ 195). Double doors were called *forēs;* the back door, opening into a garden (§ 208) or into a *peristȳlium* from the rear or from a side street, was called *postīcum.* The doors opened inward; those in the outer wall were supplied with slide-bolts (*pessulī*) and bars (*serae*). Locks and keys by which the doors could be fastened from without were not unknown, but were very heavy and clumsy. In the interiors of private houses doors were less common than now, as the Romans preferred portières (*vēla, aulaea.*)

FIG. 107
WINDOW OF A ROMAN HOUSE

217. The Windows. In the principal rooms of a private house the windows (*fenestrae*) opened on the *peristȳlium*, as has been seen, and it may be set down as a rule that in private houses rooms situated on the first floor and used for domestic purposes did not often have windows opening on the street. In the upper floors there were outside windows in such apartments as had no outlook on the *peristȳlium*, as in those above the rented rooms in the House of Pansa (§ 208) and in *īnsulae*

(§ 232) in general.   Country houses might have outside windows in the first story.   Some windows were provided with shutters, which were made to slide from side to side in a framework on the outside of the wall.   These shutters (*foriculae, valvae*) were sometimes in two parts moving in opposite directions; when closed they were said to be *iūnctae*.

Other windows were latticed; others, again, were covered with a fine network to keep out mice and other objectionable animals.   Glass was known to the Romans of the Empire, but was too expensive for general use in windows.   Talc and other translucent materials were also employed in window frames as a protection against cold, but only in very rare instances.

218. Heating. Even in the mild climate of Italy the houses must often have been too cold for comfort. On merely chilly days the occupants probably contented themselves with moving into rooms warmed by the direct rays of the sun (§ 204), or with wearing wraps or heavier clothing. In the more severe weather of actual winter they used *foculī*,

Fig. 108
STOVE FOR HEATING

charcoal stoves or braziers of the sort still used in the countries of southern Europe.   These were merely metal boxes (Fig. 108) in which hot coals could be put, with legs to keep the floors from injury and handles by which they could be carried from room to room. The wealthy sometimes had furnaces resembling ours under their houses; in such cases, the heat was carried to the rooms by tile pipes.   The partitions and floors then were generally hollow, and the hot air circulated through them, warming the rooms without being admitted directly to them (§ 368). These furnaces had chimneys, but furnaces were seldom used in private houses in Italy. Remains of such heating arrangements are found more commonly in the northern provinces, particularly in Britain, where the furnace-heated house seems to have been common in the Roman period.

219. Water Supply.[1] All the important towns of Italy and many cities throughout the Roman world had abundant supplies of water brought by aqueducts from hills, sometimes at a considerable distance. The aqueducts of the Romans were among their most stupendous and most successful works of engineering. The first great aqueduct (*aqua*) at Rome (see Fig. 2) was built in 312 B.C. by the famous censor Appius Claudius. Three more were built during the Republic and at least seven under the Empire, so that ancient Rome was at last supplied by eleven or more aqueducts. Modern Rome is well supplied by four, which are the sources and occasionally the channels of as many of the ancient ones. Mains were laid down the middle of the streets, and from these the water was piped into the houses. There was often a tank in the upper part of the house from which the water was distributed as needed. It was not usually carried into many of the rooms, but there was always a fountain in the *peristȳlium* and its garden (§ 202), and a jet in the bathhouse and in the closet. The bathhouse had a separate heating apparatus of its own, which kept the room or rooms at the desired temperature and furnished hot water as required. The poor must have carried the water for household use from the public fountains in the streets.

The necessity for drains and sewers was recognized in very early times, the oldest at Rome dating traditionally from the time of the kings. Some of the ancient drains, among them the famous Cloaca Maxima, were in use until recent years.

[1] For a fuller discussion see Chapter XVI.

220. Decoration. Houses were small and simple with little decoration until the last century of the Republic. The outside of the house was usually left severely plain; the walls were merely covered with stucco, as we have seen (§ 212). The interior was decorated to suit the tastes and means of the owner; not even the poorer houses lacked charming effects. At first the stucco-finished walls were merely

Fig. 109

A CUBICULUM IN A VILLA AT BOSCOREALE, NEAR POMPEII

These frescoes are now in the Metropolitan Museum of Art, New York, set up as they were in the villa.

marked off into rectangular panels (*abacī*), which were painted in deep, rich colors; reds and yellows predominated. Then in the middle of these panels simple centerpieces were painted, and the whole was surrounded with the most brilliant arabesques. Then came elaborate pictures, figures, interiors, landscapes, etc., of large size and most skillfully executed, all painted directly upon the wall, as in some of our public buildings today. A little later the walls began to be covered with panels of thin slabs of marble with a baseboard and cornice. Beautiful effects were produced by combining marbles of different tints, since the Romans ransacked the world for striking colors. Later still came raised figures of stucco work, enriched with gold and colors, and mosaic work, chiefly of minute pieces of colored glass, which had a jewel-like effect.

221. The doors and doorways gave opportunities for treatment equally artistic. The doors were richly paneled and carved, or were plated with bronze, or made of solid bronze. The threshold was often of mosaic (see the example from Pompeii in Figure 126). The *postēs* were sheathed

FIG. 110
PART OF A CARVED DOORWAY FROM POMPEII

with marble usually carved in elaborate designs, as in the one shown in part here in Figure 110. The floors were covered with marble tiles arranged in geometrical figures with contrasting colors, much as they are now in public buildings, or with mosaic pictures only less beautiful than those upon the walls. The most famous of these, "Darius at the Battle of Issus,"[1] measures sixteen feet by eight, but despite its size has no less than one hundred fifty separate pieces to each square inch. The ceilings were often barrel-vaulted and painted in brilliant colors, or were divided into panels (*lacūs, lacūnae*), deeply sunk, by heavy intersecting beams of wood or marble, and then decorated in

[1] See Baumeister, "*Mosaik*," Fig. 1000; Overbeck, between pages 612 and 613; Mau-Kelsey, Fig. 137.

the most elaborate manner with raised stucco work, or gold or ivory, or with bronze plates heavily gilded.[1]

222. Furniture. Our knowledge of Roman furniture is largely indirect, because only such articles have come down to us as were made of stone or metal. Fortunately the secondary sources are abundant and good. Many articles are incidentally described in works of literature, many are shown in the wall paintings mentioned above (§ 220), and some have been restored from casts taken in the hardened ashes of Pompeii and Herculaneum. In general we may say that the Romans had very few articles of furniture in their houses, and that they cared less for comfort, not to say luxurious ease, than they did for costly materials, fine workmanship, and artistic forms. The mansions on the Palatine were enriched with all the spoils of Greece and Asia, but it may be doubted whether there were many comfortable beds within the walls of Rome.

Fig. 111
WALL DECORATION FROM A HOUSE IN POMPEII
Now in the Museo Nazionale, Naples.

223. Principal Articles. Many of the most common and useful articles of modern furniture were entirely unknown to the Romans. No mirrors hung on their walls. They had no

[1] The magnificence of some of the great houses at Rome, even in Republican times, may be inferred from the prices paid for them. Cicero paid about $140,000, the consul Messala the same price, Clodius $600,000, the highest price known to us. All these were on the Palatine Hill, where ground, too, was expensive.

desks or writing tables, no dressers or chiffoniers, no glass-doored cabinets for the display of bric-a-brac, tableware, or books, no mantels, no hat-racks even. The principal articles found in even the best houses were couches or beds, chairs, tables, and lamps. If to these we add chests or wooden cabinets with doors, an occasional brazier (§ 218), and still rarer, a water-clock, we shall have everything that can be called furniture, except tableware and kitchen utensils. Still it must not be thought that their rooms presented a desolate or dreary appearance. When one considers the decorations (§§ 220, 221), the stately pomp of the *ātrium* (§ 198), and the rare beauty of the *peristȳlium* (§ 202), it is evident that a very few articles of real artistic excellence were more in keeping with the Roman house than would have been the litter and jumble that we sometimes have in our rooms.

224. The Couches. The couch (*lectus, lectulus*) was found everywhere in the Roman house, as a sofa by day, a bed by night. In its simplest form it consisted of a frame of wood with straps across the top on which was laid a mattress. At one end there was an arm, as in the case of our sofas; sometimes there was an arm at each end, and a back besides.

The back seems to have been a Roman addition to the ordinary form of the ancient couch. The couch was always provided with pillows and rugs or coverlets. The mattress was originally stuffed with straw, but this gave place to wool and even feathers. In some of the bedrooms of Pom-

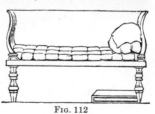

Fig. 112
A LECTUS
From a relief in the British
Museum, London.

peii the frame seems to have been lacking; in such cases the mattress was laid on a support built up from the floor. The couches used for beds seem to have been larger than those used as sofas, and they were so high that stools (Fig. 112)

or even steps were necessary accompaniments. As a sofa
the *lectus* was used in the library for reading and writing;
the student supported himself on his left arm and held the
book or writing with the right hand. In the dining-room it
had a permanent place, as will be described later. Its
honorary position in the great hall has already been mentioned (§ 199). It will be seen that the *lectus* could be made
highly ornamental. The legs and arms were carved or made

Fig. 113
A ROMAN EMPEROR SEATED ON THE CURULE CHAIR
From the Arch of Constantine, Rome.

of costly woods, or inlaid or plated with tortoise-shell, ivory,
or the precious metals. We read even of frames of solid silver.
The coverings were often made of the finest fabrics, dyed in
the most brilliant colors, and worked with figures of gold.

225. The Chairs. The primitive form of seat (*sedīle*)
among the Romans, as elsewhere, was the stool or bench
with four perpendicular legs and no back. The remarkable
fact is that it did not give place to something better as

soon as means permitted. The stool (*sella*) was the ordinary seat for one person (Fig. 114), used by men and women resting or working, and by children and slaves at their meals as well. The bench (*subsellium*)

differed from the stool only in accommodating more than one person. It was used by senators in the *cūria*, by jurors in the courts, and by boys in the school (§ 120), as well as in private houses. A special form of the *sella* was the famous curule chair (*sella cu-rūlis*), having curved legs of ivory (Fig. 113). The curule

FIG. 115
THE SOLIUM
Drawing from the
Vatican Manu-
script of Vergil.

FIG. 114
THE SELLA
From a Pompeian
fresco.

chair folded up like our camp-stools for convenience of carriage and had straps across the top to support the cushion which formed the seat.

226. The first improvement upon the *sella* was the *soli-um*, a stiff, straight, high-backed chair with solid arms; it looked as if cut from a single block of wood (Fig. 115), and was so high that a footstool was as necessary with it as with a bed (§ 224). Poets represented gods and kings as seated in such a chair, and it was kept in the *ātrium* for the use of the patron when he received his clients (§§ 182, 198). Lastly, we find the *cathedra* (Fig. 116), a chair without arms, but with a

FIG. 116
THE CATHEDRA

curved back sometimes fixed at an easy angle (*cathedra supīna*), the only approximation to a comfortable seat that the Romans knew. It was at first used by women only, as it was regarded too luxurious for men, but finally came into general use. Its employment by teachers in the Schools of Rhetoric (§ 115) gave rise to the expression *ex cathedrā*, applied to authoritative utterances of every kind, and its use by bishops explains our word "cathedral." Neither the *solium* nor the *cathedra* was upholstered, but cushions and coverings were used with them both as with the *lectī*, and they afforded like opportunities for skillful workmanship and lavish decoration.

227. Tables. The table (*mēnsa*) was the most important article of furniture in the Roman house, whether we consider

FIG. 117
A MARBLE TABLE WITH BRONZE FITTINGS
Now in the Metropolitan Museum of Art,
New York.

its manifold uses, or the prices often paid for certain kinds. Tables varied in form and construction as much as our own, many of which are copied directly from Roman models. All sorts of materials were used for their supports and tops: stone, wood, solid or veneered, the precious metals, probably in thin plates only. The most costly, so far as we know, were the round tables made from cross sections of the citrus tree. The wood was beautifully marked and single pieces could be had from three to four feet in diameter. Cicero paid $20,000 for such a table, Asinius Pollio $44,000 for another, King Juba $52,000 for a third; the family of the Cethegi possessed one valued at $60,000. Special names were given to tables of certain forms. The *monopodium* was a table or stand with but one support, used especially to hold a lamp (§ 228) or toilet articles.   The *abacus* was a table with a rectangular top having a raised rim; it was used for plates and dishes, in the place of the modern sideboard.   The *delphica* (sc. *mēnsa*) had three legs.   Tables were frequently made with adjustable legs, so that the height might be altered.   On the other hand the permanent tables in the *trĭclīnia* (§ 204) were often of solid masonry or concrete built up from the floor; they had tops of polished stone or mosaic.   The table gave a better opportunity than even the couch or chair for artistic workmanship, especially in the matter of carving and inlaying the legs and top.

Fig. 118
ROMAN LAMPS FROM POMPEII

228. The Lamps.   The Roman lamp (*lucerna*) was essentially simple enough, merely a vessel that would hold olive oil or melted grease with threads twisted loosely together for a wick or wicks, drawn out through one or more holes in the cover or top (Fig. 118).   Usually there was a special hole through which the lamp was filled.   The light thus furnished must have been very uncertain and dim.   There was no glass to keep the flame steady; there was never a chimney or central draft.   As works of art, however, lamps were often exceedingly beautiful.   Even those of the cheapest material were frequently of graceful form and proportions, while to those of costly material the skill of the artist in many cases must have given a value far above that of the rare stones or precious metals of which they were made.

Some of these lamps (Fig. 118) were intended to be carried in the hand, as shown by the handles, others to be suspended from the ceiling by chains. Others were kept on tables expressly made for them, as the *monopodia* (§ 227) commonly used in the bedrooms, or the tripod shown in Figure 119. For lighting the public rooms there were, besides these, tall stands, like those of our "floor lamps," an example of which may be seen in Figure 120. On some of these, several lamps were placed or hung at a time. Some stands were adjustable in height. The name of the lamp-stands (*candēlābra*) shows that they were originally intended to hold wax or tallow candles (*candēlae*), and the fact that these candles were supplanted in the houses of the rich by the smoking and ill-smelling lamp is good proof that the Romans were not skilled in the art of candle-making. Finally, it may be noticed that a supply of torches (*facēs*) of dry, inflammable wood, often soaked in oil or smeared with pitch, was kept near the outer door for use upon the streets, because the streets were not lighted at night (§§ 151, 233).

FIG. 119
BASE FOR A LAMP

FIG. 120
A CANDĒLĀ-
BRUM

229. Chests and Cabinets. Every house was supplied with chests (*arcae*) of various sizes for the purpose of storing clothes and other articles not always in use, and for the safe keeping of papers, money, and jewelry. The material was usually wood; the *arcae* were often bound with iron and ornamented with hinges and locks of bronze. The smaller *arcae*, used for jewel cases, were often made of silver or even of gold. Of most importance, perhaps, was the strong box, kept in the

tablīnum (§ 201), in which the *pater familiās* stored his ready
money. It was made as strong as possible so that it could not

FIG. 121
AN ARCA

easily be opened by force,
and was so large and
heavy that it could not
be carried away entire.
As an additional precau-
tion it was sometimes
chained to the floor. Of-
ten, too, it was richly
carved and mounted, as
is seen in the illustration
in Figure 121.

230. The cabinets (*armāria*) were designed for similar purposes and made of similar materials. They were often
divided into compartments and were always supplied with
hinges and locks. Two of the most important uses of these
cabinets have been mentioned already: in the library (§ 206)
they preserved books against mice and
men, and in the *ālae* (§ 200) they held
the *imāginēs,* or death masks of wax.
It must be noticed that the *armāria*
lacked the convenient glass doors of
the cabinets or cases that we use for
books and similar things, but they
were as well adapted to decorative
purposes as the other articles of furniture that have been mentioned.

FIG. 122
A ROMAN SUNDIAL

231. Other Articles. The heating
stove, or brazier, has already been
described (§ 218). It was at best a
poor substitute for the poorest modern
stove. The place of our clock was
taken in the *peristȳlium* or garden by the sundial (*sōlārium*), such as is often seen nowadays in our parks and

gardens; this measured the hours of the day by the shadow of a stick or pin.   It was introduced into Rome from Greece in 268 B.C.   About a century later the water-clock (*clepsydra*) was also borrowed from the Greeks.   This was more useful, because it marked the hours of the night as well as of the day and could be used in the house.   It consisted essentially of a vessel filled at a regular time with water, which was allowed to escape from it at a fixed rate, the changing level marking the hours on a scale.   As the length of the Roman hours varied with the season of the year and the flow of the water with the temperature, the apparatus was far from accurate. Shakespeare's reference in *Julius Caesar* (II, i, 192) to the striking of the clock is an anachronism.

232. Ī́nsulae.   Before the end of the Republic, in Rome and other cities only the wealthy could afford to live in pri-

FIG. 123
RUINS OF AN INSULA AT OSTIA

vate houses.   By far the greater part of the city population lived in apartment buildings and tenement houses.   These were called *īnsulae*, a name originally applied to city blocks.   They were sometimes six or seven stories high.   Augustus limited their height to seventy feet; Nero, after the great fire of his reign, set a limit of sixty feet.   They were frequently built poorly and cheaply for speculative purposes; and Juvenal speaks of the great danger of fire and collapse.   Except for the lack of glass in the windows they must have looked rather like modern buildings of the sort.   Outside

Fig. 124
A STREET IN POMPEII SHOWING STEPPING-STONES
This picture shows stepping-stones such as are mentioned on page 175.

rooms were lighted by windows (§ 217). There were sometimes balconies (§ 233) overhanging the street. These, like the windows, could be closed by wooden shutters. The inner rooms were lighted by courts if, indeed, they were lighted at all.

The *insulae* were sometimes divided into apartments of several rooms, but were frequently let by single rooms. At Ostia remains of *insulae* have been found in which each of the upper apartments has its own stairway. The ground floors were regularly occupied by shops. The superintendent of the building, who looked after it and collected the rents, was a slave of the owner and was called the *insulārius*.

233. The Street. It is evident from what has been said that a street in a residence quarter of an ordinary Roman

town must have been plain and monotonous in appearance.
The houses were all of practically one style, they were finished
alike in stucco (§ 210), the windows were few and mainly
in the upper stories, there were no lawns or gardens facing
the streets; there was, in short, nothing to lend variety or
to please the eye, except, perhaps, the decorations of the
vēstibula (§ 194), or the occasional balcony (*maeniānum*,
see § 232), or a public fountain.

In the shopping streets the open fronts of the small shops,
as well as the balconies and windows above them, gave color

FIG. 125
A STREET SCENE
From a fresco in a villa at Boscoreale,
now in the Metropolitan Museum of Art,
New York.

and variety during the day;
the shops, however, were closed
and blank at night. In Pompeii some streets show colonnades extending along the
fronts of the buildings. These
offered shade and shelter to
the shopper and the passer-
by; walls thus protected were
sometimes adorned with paintings. Such advertisements as
notices of elections and announcements of gladiatorial
fights (§ 361) were very often
painted on the walls. In the
city streets the rows of tall
apartment buildings would
seem much like such buildings

in the same cities today. The galleries and balconies were
full of life in warm weather. There were often flowerpots
or window boxes in upper windows.

In Rome most of the streets were narrow and crooked
(§ 382). Juvenal, in his third satire, gives a vivid description of the discomfort and even danger involved in threading
one's way through the crowd. Conditions were worse at

night because of the lack of any system of street lighting (§ 151). The street itself was paved (§ 385), and was supplied with a footway on either side raised from twelve to eighteen inches above the carriageway. The inconvenience of crossing from the one to the other was relieved at Pompeii by stepping-stones (§ 386), of the same height, firmly fixed at suitable distances from one another across the carriageway. These stepping-stones were placed at convenient intervals on each street, not merely at the intersections. They were usually oval in shape, had flat tops, and measured about three feet by eighteen inches; the longer axis was parallel with the walk. The spaces between them were often cut into deep ruts by the wheels of the vehicles, the distance between the ruts showing that the wheels were about three feet apart. The arrangement of the stepping-stones is shown clearly in Figure 124.

FIG. 126
A MOSAIC THRESHOLD OF POMPEII
A border mosaic with tragic masks, fruits, flowers, and garlands.
From the Museo Nazionale, Naples.

CHAPTER VII

DRESS AND PERSONAL ORNAMENTS

REFERENCES: Marquardt, 475-606; Blümner, 205-277; Becker-Göll, III, 189-310; Smith, Harper's, Daremberg-Saglio, Walters, under *toga, tunica, stola, palla* or *pallium,* and other Latin words in the text of this book; Baumeister, 574-576, 1822-1846; Pauly-Wissowa, under *calceus, clāvus, lacerna, Schuh;* Sandys, *Companion,* 190-200; Cagnat-Chapot, II, 364-408; Friedländer, II, 173-185; McDaniel, 81-100; Showerman, 56-64; Wilson.

234. From the earliest to the latest times the clothing of the Romans was very simple, consisting ordinarily of two or three articles only, besides the covering of the feet. These articles varied in material, style, and name from age to age, it is true, but their forms were practically unchanged during the Republic and the early Empire. The mild climate of Italy (§ 218) and the hardening effect of physical exercise on the young (§ 107) made unnecessary the closely fitting garments to which we are accustomed, while contact with the Greeks on the south and perhaps the Etruscans on the north gave the Romans a taste for the beautiful that found expression in the graceful arrangement of their loosely flowing robes. The clothing of men and women differed much less than in modern times, but it will be convenient to describe their garments separately. Each article was assigned by Latin writers to one of two classes and called, from the way it was worn, *indūtus* ("put on") or *amictus* ("wrapped around"). To the first class we may give the name of undergarments, to the second outer garments, though these terms very inadequately represent the Latin words.

235. The *Subligāculum.* Next the person was worn the *subligāculum,* the loin cloth familiar to us in pictures of ancient athletes and gladiators (Figs. 64 and 196), or per-

haps the short drawers (trunks) worn nowadays by bathers
or athletes. We are told that in the earliest times this was
the only undergarment worn by the Romans, and that the
family of the Cethegi adhered to this ancient practice
throughout the Republic, wearing the toga immediately
over it. This was done, too, by individuals who wished
to pose as the champions of old-fashioned simplicity, as,
for example, the Younger Cato, and by candidates for
public office. In the best times, however, the *subligāculum*
was worn under the tunic or was replaced by it.

236. The Tunic. The tunic was also adopted in very
early times and came to be the chief article of the kind
covered by the word *indūtus*. It was a plain woolen shirt,
made of two pieces, back and front,
which were sewed together at the
sides. It usually had very short
sleeves, covering hardly half of the
upper arm, as shown in Figure 128.
It was long enough to reach from the
neck to the calf, but if the wearer desired greater freedom for his limbs he
could shorten it by merely pulling it
through a girdle or belt worn around
the waist. Tunics with sleeves reaching to the wrists (*tunicae manicātae*),
and tunics falling to the ankles (*tunicae tālārēs*) were not unknown in the
late Republic, but were considered
unmanly and effeminate.

Fig. 127
A TUNIC WITH LONG
SLEEVES
A bronze statue of a *camillus*,
in the Palazzo dei Conserva-
tori, Rome.

237. The tunic was worn in the house without any outer
garment and probably without a girdle; in fact it came to be
the distinctive house-dress as opposed to the toga, the dress
for formal occasions only. The tunic was also worn with
nothing over it by the citizen while at work (§§ 240, 268),
but no citizen of any pretension to social or political im-

portance ever appeared at social functions or in public places at Rome without the toga over it; and even then, though it was hidden by the toga, good form required the wearing of the girdle with it. Two tunics were often worn (*tunica interior*, or *subūcula*, and *tunica exterior*), and persons who suffered from the cold, as did Augustus for example, might

wear an even larger number when the cold was very severe. The tunics intended for use in the winter were probably thicker and warmer than those worn in the summer, though both kinds were of wool.

238. The tunic of the ordinary citizen was the natural color of the white wool of which it was made, without trimmings or ornaments of any kind. Knights and senators, on the other hand, had stripes of crimson (§ 270), narrow and wide, respectively, running from the shoulders to the bottom of the tunic both behind and in

FIG. 128
BOY DRESSED IN A TUNIC
A bronze figure of a *camillus*, now in the Metropolitan Museum of Art, New York.

front. These stripes were either woven in the garment or sewed upon it. From them the tunic of the knight was called *tunica angustī clāvī* (or *angusticlāvia*), and that of the senator *lātī clāvī* (or *lāticlāvia*). Some authorities think that the badge of the senatorial tunic was a single broad stripe running down the middle of the garment in front and behind, but unfortunately no picture has come down to us that absolutely decides the question. It seems probable that the knight's tunic had two stripes, one running from each shoulder. Under this official tunic the knight or senator wore usually a plain *tunica interior*. When in the house he left the outer tunic unbelted in order to display the stripes as conspicuously as possible.

239. Besides the *subligāculum* and the *tunica* the Romans had no regular underwear. Those who were feeble through age or ill health sometimes wound strips of woolen cloth (*fasciae*), like the modern spiral puttees, around the legs for the sake of additional warmth. These were called *feminālia* or *tībiālia* according as they covered the upper or lower part of the leg. Feeble persons might also use similar wrappings for the body (*ventrālia*) and even for the throat (*fōcālia*), but all these were looked upon as badges of senility or decrepitude and formed no part of the regular costume of sound men. It must be especially noticed that the Romans had nothing corresponding to our trousers or even long drawers. *Brācae*, "trousers," were a Gallic article that was not used at Rome until the time of the latest emperors.[1] *Nātiōnēs brācātae* in classical times was a contemptuous expression for Gauls in particular and for barbarians in general.

240. The Toga. Of the outer garments or wraps the most ancient and the most important was the *toga* (cf. *tegere*). It goes back to the very earliest time of which tradition tells, and was the characteristic garment of the Romans for more than a thousand years. It was a heavy, white, woolen robe, enveloping the whole figure, falling to the feet, cumbrous but graceful and dignified in appearance. All its associations suggested formality. When the Roman of old tilled his fields, he was clad only in the *subligāculum;* in the privacy of his home or at his work the Roman of every age wore the comfortable, blouse-like *tunica;* but in the Forum, in the *comitia*, in the courts, at the public games, and wherever social forms were observed, he appeared and had to appear in the toga. In the toga he assumed the responsibilities of

---

[1] The Roman armies sometimes adopted the *brācae* when they were campaigning in the northern provinces. Tacitus tells a story of the offense given by Caecina on his return from his campaign in Gaul because he continued to wear the *brācae* while he was addressing the toga-clad citizens of the Italian towns through which he passed. (*Hist.* 2.20)

citizenship (§ 127); in the toga he took his wife from her father's house to his own (§ 78); in the toga he received his clients, also toga-clad (§ 182); in the toga he discharged his duties as a magistrate, governed his province, celebrated his triumph; and in the toga he was wrapped when he lay for the last time in his *ātrium* (§ 198).   No foreign nation had a robe of the same material, color, and arrange-

FIG. 129
THE EARLY TOGA
A bronze statue of an orator in the Museo Archeologico, Florence.

ment; no foreigner was allowed to wear it, though he lived in Italy or even in Rome itself; even the banished citizen left the toga, with his civil rights, behind him.   Vergil merely gave expression to the national feeling when he wrote the proud verse (*Aeneid* I, 282):

> *Rōmānōs, rērum dominōs,*
> *gentemque togātam.*[1]

241. Form and Arrangement. The general appearance of the toga is well known; of few ancient garments are pictures so common and in general so good.   They are derived from numerous statues of men clad in it, which have come down to us from ancient times, and we have, besides, full and careful descriptions of its shape and of the manner of wearing it, left to us by writers who had worn it themselves.   The cut and draping of the toga varied from generation to generation.   In its earlier form it was simpler, less cumbrous, and more closely fitted to the figure than in later times.   Even as early as the classical period its arrangement was so complicated that the man of fashion could not array himself in it

---

[1] "The Romans, lords of the world, the race that wears the toga."

without assistance. A few forms of the toga will be discussed here, but it is best studied in Miss Wilson's treatise.

242. In its original form the toga was probably a rectangular blanket much like that of our own Indians, or the plaid of the Highlanders, except for the lack of color, as that of the private citizen seems to have been always of undyed wool. Its development into its characteristically Roman form began when one

FIG. 130
AN EARLY SHAPE OF THE TOGA

edge of the garment came to be curved instead of straight. The statue in Florence known as the "Arringatore" (Fig. 129), supposed to date from the third century B.C., shows a

FIG. 131
BACK OF A TOGA

toga of this sort, so cut or woven that the two lower corners are rounded off. Such a toga for a man who was five feet six inches in height would be about four yards long, and one yard and three-quarters in width.[1] The toga was thrown over the left shoulder from the front (Fig. 129), so that the curved edge fell over the left arm, and the end hung in front so as to fall about halfway between the knee and the ankle. On the left shoulder a few inches of the straight or upper edge were gathered into folds. The long portion remaining was now drawn across the back, the folds were passed under the right arm, and again thrown over the left shoulder, the end falling down the back to a point a trifle higher than the corresponding end in front. The right shoulder and arm were free, the left covered by the folds.

[1]Wilson, 120-121.

243. Statues of the third and second centuries B.C. show a larger and longer toga, more loosely draped, drawn around over the right arm and shoulder instead of under the arm as before (Fig. 133). By the end of the Republic and the beginning of the Empire the toga was of the same size as that just described, but with some difference in shape and draping. For a man who was five feet six inches in height it would have been about four yards and a half in length and two and two-thirds yards across at the widest part. The lower corners were rounded much as before (Fig. 132). From each of the upper corners a triangular section was cut. This toga was then folded lengthwise so that the lower section was deeper than the other. The end *A* hung in front, between the feet, not quite to the ground. The section *AFEB* was

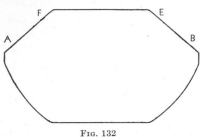

FIG. 132
SHAPE OF THE LARGER TOGA

folded over. The folded edge lay on the left shoulder against the neck. The rest of the folded length was then brought around under the right arm and over the left shoulder again, as in the case of the earlier toga. The upper section fell in a curve over the right hip, and then crossed the breast diagonally, forming the *sinus* or bosom. This was deep enough to serve as a pocket for the reception of small articles. The part running from the left shoulder to the ground in front was pulled up over the *sinus* to fall in a loop a trifle to the front, as in Figure 134. This seems to have been the toga as worn by Caesar and Cicero. This might also be drawn over the right shoulder, as was the earlier form of the large toga, and as is shown in Figures 133 and 157. The early toga may well have been woven in one piece, but the larger forms must have been woven or cut in two sections, which were then sewed together. It will be clearly found in practice that much of the grace of the toga must have been due to the trained *vestiplicus*, who kept it properly creased when it was not in use and carefully arranged each fold after his master had put it on. We are not told of any pins or tapes to hold the toga in place,[1] but are told that the part falling

Fig. 133
ROMANS IN A RELIGIOUS PROCESSION
Note three styles of wearing the toga.
A fragment from the Ara Pacis relief, now in the Uffizi Gallery, Florence.

from the left shoulder toward the ground behind kept all in position by its own weight, and that this weight was sometimes increased by lead sewed in the hem of this part.

244. It is evident that in this fashionable toga the limbs were completely fettered, and that all rapid, not to say violent, motion was absolutely impossible. In other words the toga of the ultrafashionable in the time of Cicero was fit only for the formal, stately, ceremonial life of the city. It is easy to see, therefore, how it had come to be the emblem of peace, being too cumbrous for use in war, and how Cicero could sneer at the young dandies of his time for wearing

[1] See, however, Wilson, 48–49.

"sails, not togas." We can understand also the eagerness
with which the Roman welcomed a respite from civic and
social duties. Juvenal sighed for the freedom of the
country, where only the dead had to wear
the toga. For the same reason Martial
praised the unconventionality of the provinces. Pliny the Younger counted it one
of the attractions of his villa that no
guest need wear the toga there. Its cost,
too, made it all the more burdensome for
the poor, and the working classes could
scarcely have afforded to wear it at all.

FIG. 134
AUGUSTUS WITH HIS
TOGA DRAWN OVER
HIS HEAD
A statue found near
Rome, now in the
Museo Nazionale,
Rome.

245. For certain ceremonial observances the toga, or rather the *sinus*, was
drawn over the head from the rear, as
shown in Figure 134. The *cīnctus Gabīnus*
was another manner of arranging the toga
for certain sacrifices and official rites; it
is supposed to be shown in Figure 135.
For this the *sinus* was drawn over the head
and then the long end which usually hung
down the back from the left shoulder was
drawn under the left arm and around the
waist behind to the front and tucked in there.[1]

246. Kinds of Togas. The toga of the ordinary citizen
was, like the tunic (§ 238), of the natural color of the white
wool of which it was made, and varied in texture, of course,
with the quality of the wool. It was called *toga pūra* (or
virīlis, lībera: § 127). A dazzling brilliancy could be given
to the toga by a preparation of fuller's chalk, and one
so treated was called *toga splendēns* or *candida*. In such
a toga all persons running for office arrayed themselves,
and from it they were called *candidātī*. The curule magistrates, censors, and dictators wore the *toga praetexta*, differ-

---

[1] Wilson, 86-88.

ing from the ordinary toga only in having a "purple" (garnet: § 270) border. It was worn also by boys (§ 127) and by the chief officers of the free towns and colonies. In the early toga (§ 242) this border seems to have been woven or sewed on the curved edge. It was probably on the edge of the *sinus* in the later forms. The *toga picta* was wholly of crimson covered with embroidery of gold, and was worn by the victorious general in his triumphal procession, and later by the emperors. The *toga pulla* was simply a dingy toga worn by persons in mourning or threatened with some calamity, usually a reverse of political fortune. Persons assuming it were called *sordidātī* and were said *mūtāre vestem*. This *vestis mūtātiō* was a common form of public demonstration of sympathy with a fallen leader. In this case curule magistrates contented themselves with merely laying aside the *toga praetexta* for the *toga pūra;* only the lower orders wore the *toga pulla*.

Fig. 135
CĪNCTUS
GABĪNUS

247. The *Lacerna*. In Cicero's time there was just coming into fashionable use a mantle called a *lacerna*, which seems to have been used first by soldiers and the lower classes and then adopted by their betters on account of its convenience. The better citizens wore it at first over the toga as a protection against dust and sudden showers. It was a woolen mantle, short, light, open at the side, without sleeves, but fastened with a brooch or buckle on the right shoulder. It was so easy and comfortable that it began to be worn not over the toga but instead of it, and so generally that Augustus issued an edict forbidding it to be used in public assemblages of citizens. Under the later emperors, however, it came into fashion again, and was the common outer garment at the theaters. It was made of various colors, dark, naturally, for the lower classes, white for formal occasions, but also of brighter hues. It was sometimes supplied with a

hood (*cucullus*), which the wearer could pull over his head
as a protection or a disguise. No representation in art of
the *lacerna* that can be positively identified has come down

FIG. 136
HOODED CLOAK, PER-
HAPS THE PAENULA

to us. The military cloak, called at first
trabea, then *palūdāmentum* and *sagum*,
was much like the *lacerna*, but made of
heavier material.

248. The *Paenula*. Older than the
lacerna and used by all sorts and conditions of men was the *paenula* (Fig.
136), a heavy coarse wrap of wool,
leather, or fur, used merely for protection against rain or cold, and therefore never a substitute for the toga or
made of fine materials or bright colors.
It seems to have varied in length and
fullness, but to have been a sleeveless
wrap, made chiefly of one piece with a
hole in the middle, through which the wearer thrust his
head. It was, therefore, classed with the *vestīmenta clausa*,
or closed garments, and must have been much like the modern poncho. It was drawn on over the head, like
a tunic or sweater, and covered the arms, leaving them much less freedom than the *lacerna* did.
In the *paenula* of some length there was a slit in
front running from the waist down, and this
enabled the wearer to hitch the cloak up over
one shoulder, leaving one arm comparatively
free, but at the same time exposing it to the
weather. The *paenula* was worn over either
tunic or toga according to circumstances, and
was the ordinary traveling habit of citizens
of the better class. It was also commonly worn by slaves,
and seems to have been furnished regularly to soldiers
stationed in places where the climate was severe. Like the
lacerna it was sometimes supplied with a hood.

FIG. 137
A SOLDIER
WEARING
THE ABOLLA

249. Other Wraps. Of other articles included under the general term *amictus* (§ 234) we know little more than the names. The *synthesis* was a dinner dress worn at table over the tunic by the ultrafashionable, and sometimes dignified by the special name of *vestis cēnātōria*, or *cēnātōrium* alone. It was not worn out of the house except during the Saturnalia, and was usually of some bright color. Its shape is unknown. The *laena* and *abolla* were very heavy woolen cloaks; the latter (Fig. 137) was a favorite with poor people who had to make one garment do duty for two or three. It was used especially by professional philosophers, who were proverbially careless about their dress. Cloaks of several shapes are shown in the hunting group in Figure 138. The *endromis* was something like the modern bath robe, used by the men after violent gymnastic exercise to keep from taking cold, and hardly belongs under the head of dress.

FIG. 138

THE LION HUNT
These Romans are dressed in tunics and cloaks.
A relief from the Arch of Constantine, Rome.

250. Footwear: the *Soleae*. It may be set down as a rule that freemen did not appear in public at Rome with bare feet, except under the compulsion of the direst poverty. Two styles of footwear were in use, slippers or sandals (*soleae*) and shoes (*calceī*). The slipper consisted essentially of a sole of leather or matting attached to the foot in various ways (note the style in Fig. 139). Custom limited its use to the house, and it went characteristically with the tunic (§ 237), when that was not covered by an outer garment. Oddly enough, it seems to us, the slippers were not worn at meals. Host and guests wore them into the dining-room, but, as soon as they had taken their places on the couches (§ 224), slaves removed the slippers

from their feet and cared for them until the meal was over (§ 152). Hence the phrase *soleās poscere* came to mean "to prepare to take leave." When a guest went out to dinner in a *lectīca* (§ 151), he wore the *soleae*, but if he walked, he wore the regular outdoor shoes (*calceī*) and had his slippers carried by a slave.

251. The *Calceī*. Out of doors, when a man walked, the *calceus* was always worn, although it was much heavier and less comfortable than the *solea*. Good form forbade the toga to be worn without the *calceī*. The *calceī* were worn also with all the other garments included under the word *amictus* (§ 234). The *calceus* was essentially our shoe, of leather, made on a last, covering the upper part of the foot as well as protecting the sole, and fastened with laces or straps. The higher classes had shoes peculiar to their rank. The shoe for senators (*calceus senātōrius*) is best known to us; but we know only its shape, not its color. It had a thick sole, was open on the inside at the ankle, and was fastened by wide straps which ran from the juncture of the sole and the upper, were wrapped around the leg and tied above the instep. The *mulleus*, or *calceus patricius*, was worn originally by patricians only, but later by all curule magistrates. It was shaped like the senator's shoe, was red in color like the fish from which it was named, and had an ivory or silver ornament of crescent shape (*lūnula*) fastened on the outside of the ankle. We know nothing of the shoe worn by the knights. Ordinary citizens wore shoes that opened in front and were fastened by a strap of leather running from one side of the shoe near the top. They did not come up so high on the leg as those of the senators and were probably of uncolored leather. The poorer classes naturally wore shoes (*pērōnēs*) of coarser material, often of untanned leather, and laborers and soldiers had half-boots (*caligae*)

Fig. 140
THE PETASUS

of the stoutest possible make, or wore wooden shoes. No stockings were worn by the Romans, but persons with tender feet might wrap them with *fasciae* (§ 239) to keep the shoes and boots from chafing them. A well-fitting shoe was of great importance for appearance as well as for comfort, and the satirists speak of the embarrassment of the poor client who had to appear in patched or broken shoes. Vanity seems to have led to the wearing of tight shoes.

252. Coverings for the Head. Men of the upper classes in Rome had ordinarily no covering for the head. When they went out in bad weather, they protected themselves, of course, with the *lacerna* or the *paenula;* these, as we have seen (§§ 247, 248), were sometimes provided with hoods (*cuculli*). If the men were caught without wraps in a sudden shower, they made shift as best they could by pulling

Fig. 141
THE CAUSIA

the toga up over the head. Persons of lower standing, especially workmen who were out of doors all day, wore a conical felt cap which was called the *pilleus* (see Fig. 72). It is probable that the *pilleus* was a survival of what had been in prehistoric times an essential part of the Roman dress, for it was preserved among the insignia of the oldest priesthoods, the Pontifices, Flamines, and Salii, and figured in the ceremony of manumission. Out of the city, that is, while he was traveling or was in the country, a man of the upper classes, too, protected his head, especially against the sun, with a broad-brimmed felt hat of foreign origin, the *causia* or *petasus*. Such hats are shown in Figures 140 and 141. They were worn in the city also by the old and feeble, and in later times by all classes in the theaters. In the house, of course, the head was left uncovered.

Fig. 142

M. VIPSANIUS AGRIPPA

A bust in the Uffizi Gallery, Florence.

253. The Hair and Beard. The Romans in early times wore long hair and full beards, as did uncivilized peoples. Varro tells us that professional barbers first came to Rome in the year 300 B.C., but we know that the razor and shears were used by the Romans long before history begins. Pliny the Elder says that the Younger Scipio (died 129 B.C.) was the first Roman to shave every day, and the story may be true. People of wealth and position had the hair and beard kept in order by their own slaves (§ 150); these slaves, if they were skillful barbers, brought high prices in the market. People of the middle class went to public barber shops, and gradually made them places of general resort for the idle and the gossiping. But in all periods the hair and beard were allowed

Fig. 143

ANTONINUS PIUS, EMPEROR
FROM 136-161 A.D.

A bust in the Vatican Museum, Rome.

to grow as a sign of sorrow, and were the regular accompaniments of the mourning garb already mentioned (§ 246). The very poor went usually unshaven and unshorn; this was the cheap and easy fashion.

254. Styles of wearing hair and beard varied with the years of the persons concerned and with the period. The hair of children, boys and girls alike, was allowed to grow long and hang around the neck and shoulders. When the boy assumed the toga of manhood, the long locks were cut off, sometimes with a good deal of formality, and under the Empire they were often made an offering to some deity. In the classical period young men seem to have worn close-clipped beards; at least Cicero jeers at those who

Fig. 144
THE EMPEROR HADRIAN
Hadrian was the first Roman emperor to wear a full beard. A bust in the Capitoline Museum, Rome.

followed Catiline for wearing full beards, and on the other hand declares that their companions who could show no signs of beard on their faces were worse than effeminate. Mature men wore the hair cut short and the face shaved clean. Most of the portraits that have come down to us show beardless men until well into the second century of our era, but after the time of Hadrian the full beard became fashionable.

255. Jewelry. The ring was the only article of jewelry worn by a Roman citizen after he reached the age of manhood (§§ 125-127), and good taste limited him to a single ring. It was originally of iron, and, though it was often set with a precious stone and made still more valuable by the artistic cutting of the stone, it was always worn more for use than for ornament. The ring was in fact in almost all cases a seal ring, having some device upon it (Fig. 145) which the

wearer imprinted in melted wax when he wished to acknowledge some document as his own, or to secure cabinets and coffers against prying curiosity. The iron ring was worn generally
until late in the Empire,
even after the gold ring
had ceased to be the
special privilege of the
knights and had be-
come merely the badge
of freedom. Even the
engagement ring (§ 71)

Fig. 145
SEAL RINGS

was usually of iron; the jewel gave it its material value,
although, we are told, this particular ring was often the
first article of gold that a young girl possessed.

256. Of course there were not wanting men as ready to
violate the canons of taste in the matter of rings as in the
choice of their garments or the style of wearing the hair
and beard. We need not be surprised, then, to read of one
having sixteen rings, or of another having six for each finger.
One of Martial's acquaintances had a ring so large that the
poet advised him to wear it on his leg. It is a more surprising fact that the ring was often worn on the joint of
the finger, perhaps for convenience in using the seal.

257. Dress of Women. It has been remarked already

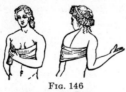

Fig. 146
MAMILLĀRE

(§ 234) that the dress of men and
women differed less in ancient than
in modern times, and we shall find
that in the classical period at least
the principal articles worn were practically the same, however much they
differed in name and, probably, in the
fineness of their materials. At this period the dress of the
matron consisted in general of three articles: the *tunica interior*, the *tunica exterior* or *stola*, and the *palla*. Beneath
the *tunica interior* there was nothing like the modern brassiere

or corset, intended to modify the figure, but a band of soft leather (*mamillāre*) was sometimes passed around the body under the breasts for a support (Fig. 146), and the *subligāculum* (§ 235) was also worn by women.

258. The *Tunica Interior*. The *tunica interior* did not differ much in material or shape from the tunic for men already described (§ 236). It fitted the figure more closely perhaps than the man's, was sometimes supplied with sleeves, and as it reached only to the knee did not require a belt to keep it from interfering with the free use of the limbs. A soft sash-like band of leather (*strophium*), however, was sometimes worn over it, close under the breasts, but merely to support them; in this case, we may suppose, the *mamillāre* was discarded. For this sash (Fig. 147), the more general terms *zōna* and *cingulum* are sometimes used. This tunic was not usually worn alone, even in the house, except by young girls.

Fig. 147
THE
STROPHIUM

Fig. 148

A ROMAN MATRON WEARING THE STOLA
She has a *palla* across her lap.
A statue in the Capitoline Museum, Rome.

259. The *Stola*. Over the *tunica interior* was worn the *tunica exterior*, or *stola*, the distinctive dress of the Roman matron (§ 91). It differed in several respects from the tunic worn as a house-dress by men. It was open at both sides above the waist and fastened on the shoulders by brooches. It was much longer, reaching to the feet when ungirded and having in addition a wide border (*īnstita*) on its lower edge. There was also a border around the neck, which seems to have been of some color, perhaps often crimson. The *stola* was sleeveless if the *tunica interior* had sleeves, but, if the tunic itself was sleeveless, the *stola* had sleeves, so that the arm was always protected. These sleeves, however, whether in tunic or in *stola*, were open on the front of the upper arm and were only loosely clasped with brooches or buttons, often of great beauty and value.

Fig. 149
MEMBERS OF A ROMAN FAMILY
The women wear the *palla* and *stola;* a young girl and two small boys wear the
toga; one man wears cloak and tunic, the other the *toga.*
A relief from the Ara Pacis, now in the Uffizi Gallery, Florence.

260. Owing to its great length the *stola* was always worn with a girdle (*zōna*) above the hips; through this girdle the *stola* itself was pulled until the lower edge of the *īnstita* barely cleared the floor. This gave the fullness about the waist seen in Figures 24, 116, and 148, in which the cut of the sleeves can also be seen. The *zōna* was usually entirely hidden by the overhanging folds. The *stola* was the distinctive dress of the matron, as has been said, and it is probable that the *īnstita* was its special feature.

261. The *Palla*. The *palla* was a shawl-like wrap for use out of doors. It was a rectangular piece of woolen goods, as simple as possible in its form, but worn in the most diverse fashions in different times. In the classical period it seems to have been wrapped around the figure, much as the toga

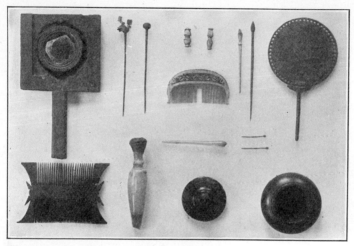

FIG. 150
TOILET ARTICLES
In the Toronto Museum.

was. One-third was thrown over the left shoulder from behind and allowed to fall to the feet. The rest was carried around the back and brought forward either over or under the right arm at the pleasure of the wearer. The end was then thrown back over the left shoulder after the style of the toga, as is shown in the relief from the Ara Pacis in Figure 149, or was allowed to hang loosely over the left arm, as in Figure 7. It was possible also to pull the *palla* up over the head (Figs. 7, 149).

262. Shoes and Slippers. What has been said of the footgear of men (§§ 250-251) applies also to that of women. Slippers (*soleae*) were worn in the house, differing from those of men only in being embellished as much as possible, sometimes even with pearls. An idea of their appearance may be had from the statues in Figures 24, 116, and 148. Shoes (*calceī*) were insisted upon for outdoor use, and differed from those of men, as they differ from them now, chiefly in being

FIG. 151
STYLES IN HAIRDRESSING, AS SHOWN IN PORTRAITS
Busts in the Museo Nazionale, Rome.

made of finer and softer leather. They were often white, or gilded, or of bright colors; those intended for winter wear sometimes had cork soles.

263. Dressing of the Hair. The Roman woman regularly wore no hat, but covered her head when necessary with the *palla* or with a veil. Much attention was given to the arrangement of the hair, the fashions being as numerous and as inconstant as they are today. For young girls the favorite arrangement, perhaps, was to comb the hair back and gather it into a knot (*nōdus*) on the back of the neck. For matrons it will be sufficient to call attention to the Figures (e.g., Figs. 1, 13, 14, 23, 30, 32) already given, and to show from

busts five styles (Fig. 151) worn at different times under the
Empire, all by ladies of the court.

264. For keeping the hair in place pins were used, of ivory,
silver, and gold, often mounted with jewels (Fig. 152). Nets
(*rēticula*) and ribbons (*vittae, taeniae, fasciolae*) were also
worn, but combs were not made a part of the headdress.

The Roman woman of
fashion did not scruple,
if she chose, to color
her hair (the golden-red
color of the Greek hair
was especially admired)
or to use false hair, which
had become an article
of commercial impor-
tance early in the Empire.
Mention should also be
made of the garlands (*corōnae*) of flowers, or of flowers and

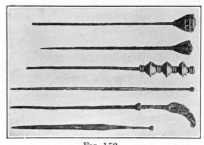

Fig. 152
HAIRPINS

foliage, and of the coronets of pearls and other precious
stones that were used to supplement the natural or artificial beauty of the hair.

265. The woman's hairdresser was a female slave (§ 150).
This *ōrnātrīx* was an adept in all the tricks of the toilet
already mentioned, and, besides, used all sorts of unguents,
oils, and tonics to make the hair soft and lustrous and to
cause it to grow abundantly. In Figure 150 are shown a
number of common toilet articles: hairpins, hand mirrors
made of highly polished metal, combs, and boxes for un-
guent or powder.

266. Accessories. The parasol (*umbrāculum, umbella*) was
commonly used by women at Rome at least as early as the
close of the Republic, and was all the more necessary because
they wore no hats or bonnets. The parasols were usually
carried for them by attendants (§ 151). From vase paint-

ings we learn that they were much like our own in shape (Fig. 153), and could be closed when not in use. The use of umbrellas by men was considered effeminate. The fan

FIG. 153
THE PARASOL
Drawing from a vase.

(*flābellum*) was used from the earliest times and was made in various ways (Fig. 154), sometimes of wings of birds, sometimes of thin sheets of wood attached to a handle, sometimes of peacock's feathers artistically arranged, and sometimes of linen stretched over a frame. These fans were not used by the woman herself; they were always handled by an attendant, who was charged with the task of keeping her cool and untroubled by flies. Handkerchiefs (*sūdāria*), the finest made of linen, were used by both sexes, but only for wiping the perspiration from the face or hands. For keep-

FIG. 154
FANS

ing the palms cool and dry, ladies seem also to have used glass balls or balls of amber, the latter, perhaps, for the fragrance also.

FIG. 155
A NECKLACE OF THE
IMPERIAL PERIOD
In the Metropolitan
Museum of Art,
New York.

267. Jewelry. The Roman woman was passionately fond of jewelry, and incalculable sums were spent upon it for the adornment of her person. Rings, brooches, pins, jeweled buttons, and coronets have been mentioned; and, besides these, bracelets, necklaces, and earrings or pendants were worn from the earliest times by all who could afford them. Not only were they made of costly materials, but their value was also enhanced by the artistic workmanship that was lavished upon them. Almost all the precious stones

that are known to us were familiar to the Romans and
were to be found in the jewel-casket (§ 29) of the wealthy
lady. The pearl, however, seems to have been in all times
the favorite. No adequate description of these articles can
be given here; no illustrations
can do them justice. It will
have to suffice that Suetonius
says that Caesar paid six million sesterces (nearly $300,000)
for a single pearl, which he

gave to Servilia, the mother of Marcus Brutus, and that
Lollia Paulina, the wife of the Emperor Caligula, possessed
a single set of pearls and emeralds which is said by Pliny
the Elder to have been valued at forty million sesterces
(nearly $2,000,000).

268. Dress of Children and Slaves. Boys wore the *subligāculum*, and, as is shown in Figures 7, 52, and 157, the
tunica; it is very probable that no other articles of clothing were worn by either boys or girls of the poorer classes.
Besides these garments, children of well-to-do parents
wore the *toga praetexta* (§ 246, and Figs. 39, 55, 149), which the
girl laid aside on the eve of her marriage (§ 76) and the boy
when he reached the age of manhood (§ 127). Slaves were
supplied with a tunic, wooden shoes, and in stormy weather
a cloak, probably the *paenula* (§ 248). This must have been
the ordinary garb of the poorer citizens of the working
classes, for they would have had little use for the toga, at
least in later times, and could hardly have afforded so
expensive a garment.

269. Materials. Fabrics of wool, linen, cotton, and silk
were used by the Romans. For clothes woolen goods were the
first to be used, and naturally so, since the early inhabitants
of Latium were shepherds, and woolen garments best suited
the climate. Under the Republic, wool was almost exclusively used for the garments of both men and women, as we

have seen, though the *subligāculum* was frequently, and the woman's tunic sometimes, made of linen. The best native wools came from Calabria and Apulia; wool from the neighborhood of Tarentum was the finest. Native wools did not suffice, however, to meet the great demand, and large quantities were imported. Linen goods were early manu-

Fig. 157
A GROUP OF ROMANS IN A RELIGIOUS PROCESSION
The men wear the toga, the child a tunic.
A fragment from the Ara Pacis relief, now in the Uffizi Gallery, Florence.

factured in Italy, but were used chiefly for other purposes than clothing until the days of the Empire; only in the third century of our era did men begin to make general use of them. The finest linen came from Egypt, and was as soft and transparent as silk. Little is positively known about the use of cotton, because the word *carbasus*, the genuine Indian name for it, was used by the Romans for linen goods also; hence when we meet the word we cannot always be sure of the material meant. Silk, imported from China directly or indirectly, was first used for garments under Tiberius, and then only in a mixture of linen and silk (*vestēs sēricae*). These were forbidden for the use of men in his reign, but the law was powerless against the love of luxury. Garments of pure silk were first used in the third century.

270. Colors. White was the prevailing color of all articles of dress throughout the Republic, in most cases the natural color of the wool, as we have seen (§ 246). The lower classes, however, selected for their garments shades that required cleansing less frequently, and found them, too, in the undyed wool. From Canusium came a brown wool with a tinge of red, from Baetica in Spain a light yellow, from Mutina a gray or a gray mixed with white, from Pollentia in Liguria the dark gray (*pulla*), used, as has been said (§ 246), in public mourning. Other shades from red to deep black were furnished by foreign wools. Almost the only artificial color used for garments under the Republic was *purpura*, which seems to have varied from what we call garnet, made from the native trumpet shell (*būcinum* or *mūrex*), to the true Tyrian purple. The former was brilliant and cheap, but likely to fade. Mixed with the dark *purpura* in different proportions, it furnished a variety of permanent tints. One of the most popular of these tints, violet, made the wool cost twenty dollars a pound, while the genuine Tyrian cost at least ten times as much. Probably the stripes worn by the knights and senators on the tunics and togas were much nearer our crimson than purple. Under the Empire the garments worn by women were dyed in various colors, and so, too, perhaps, the fancier articles worn by men, such as the *lacerna* (§ 247) and the *synthesis* (§ 249). The *trabea* of the augur seems to have been striped with scarlet and "purple," the *palūdāmentum* of the general to have been at different times white, scarlet, and "purple," and the robe of the *triumphātor* "purple."

271. Manufacture. In the old days the wool was spun at home by the women slaves, working under the eye of the mistress (§ 199), and woven into cloth on the family loom. This custom was kept up throughout the Republic by some of the proudest families. Augustus wore such homemade garments. By the end of the Republic, however, this was no longer general, and, though much of the native wool was worked up on the farms by the slaves, directed by the *vīlica* (§ 148), cloth of any desired quality could be bought in the open market. It was formerly supposed that the garments came from the loom ready to wear, but this view is now known to be incorrect. We have seen that the tunic was made of two separate pieces sewed together (§ 236), and that the toga had to be measured, cut, and sewed to fit the wearer (§ 243), and that even the coarse *paenula* (§ 248) could not have been woven in one piece. But ready-made garments, though perhaps of the cheaper qualities only, were on sale in the towns as early as the time of Cato; under the Empire the trade reached large proportions. It is remarkable that, though there were many slaves in the *familia urbāna* (§§ 149-155), it never became usual to have soiled garments cleansed at home. All garments showing traces of use were sent by the well-to-do to the fullers (*fullōnēs*) to be washed (Fig. 158), whitened (or redyed), and pressed. The fact that almost all were of woolen materials made skill and care the more necessary.

FIG. 158
CUPIDS WORKING AS FULLERS
From a fresco in the House of the Vettii, Pompeii.

CHAPTER VIII

FOOD AND MEALS

REFERENCES: Marquardt, 264-268, 300-340, 414-465; Becker-Göll, III, 311-454; Blümner, 160-209, 385-419; Sandys, *Companion*, 71-82, 205-207; Friedländer, II, 146-173; Pauly-Wissowa, under *cēna, cōmissātiō;* Smith, Harper's, Walters, under *cēna, cōmissātiō, olea,* or *oleum,* or *olīva, vīnum;* Rich, under *coena, cōmissātiō;* Daremberg-Saglio, under *cibāria;* Baumeister, 845-846, 2086-2088; Mau-Kelsey, 262-268, 273-276; Fowler, *Social Life,* 270-284; Cagnat-Chapot, II, 229-251, 426-438; McDaniel, 120-135; Showerman, 124-136.

272. Natural Conditions. Italy is blessed above all the other countries of central Europe with the natural conditions that go to yield an abundant and varied supply of food. The soil is rich and composed of different elements in different parts of the country. The rainfall is abundant, and rivers and smaller streams are numerous. The line of greatest length runs northwest to southeast, but the climate depends little upon latitude, as it is modified by surrounding bodies of water, by mountain ranges, and by prevailing winds. These agencies in connection with the varying elevations of the land itself produce such widely different conditions that somewhere within the confines of Italy almost all the grains and fruits of the temperate and subtropic zones find the soil and climate most favorable to their growth.

273. The earliest inhabitants of the peninsula, the Italian peoples, seem to have left for the Romans the task of developing and improving these means of subsistence. Wild fruits, nuts, and flesh have always been the support of uncivilized peoples, and must have been so for the shepherds who laid the foundations of Rome. The very word *pecūnia* (from *pecū;* cf. *pecūlium,* §§22, 162-163) shows that herds of domestic animals were the first source of Roman wealth. But other words show just as clearly that the cultivation of the soil was understood by the Romans in very early times: the names Fabius, Cicero, Piso, and Caepio are no less ancient than Porcius, Asinius, Vitellius, and Ovidius.[1] Cicero puts into the mouth of the Elder Cato the statement that to the farmer the garden was a second meat supply, but

FIG. 159
CAST OF BRONZE
PITCHER FROM
POMPEII
In the Field Museum
of Natural History,
Chicago.

long before Cato's time meat had ceased to be the chief article of food. Grain and grapes and olives furnished subsistence for all who did not live to eat. These gave "the wine that maketh glad the heart of man, and oil to make his face to shine, and bread that strengtheneth man's heart." On these three abundant products of the soil the mass of the people of Italy lived of old as they live today. Something will be said of each, after less important products have been considered.

274. Fruits. The apple, pear, plum, and quince were either native to Italy or, like the olive and the grape, were introduced into Italy long before history begins. Careful attention had long been given to their cultivation, and by Cicero's time Italy was covered with orchards. All these fruits were abundant and cheap in their seasons, and were used by all sorts and conditions of men. By Cicero's time, too, had begun the introduction of new fruits from foreign lands and the improvement of native varieties. Great statesmen and generals gave their names to new and better sorts of apples and pears, and vied with one another in producing fruits out of season by hothouse culture (§ 145). Every fresh extension of Roman territory brought new fruits and nuts into Italy. Among the nuts were the walnut, hazelnut, filbert, almond (after Cato's time), and the pistachio (not

---

[1]The names are connected respectively with *faba*, a bean, *cicer*, a chick-pea, *pistor*, a miller, *caepe*, an onion, *porcus*, a pig, *asinus*, an ass, *vitellus*, a calf, and *ovis*, a sheep.

introduced until the time of Tiberius). Among the fruits were the peach (*mālum Persicum*), the apricot (*mālum Armeniacum*), the pomegranate (*mālum Pūnicum* or *grānātum*), the cherry (*cerasus*, brought by Lucullus from the town Cerasus in Pontus), and the lemon (*citrus*, not grown in Italy until the third century of our era). Similarly, the fruits, grains, and vegetables known at home were carried out through the provinces wherever the Romans established themselves. Cherries, for instance, are said to have been grown in Britain in 47 A.D., four years after its conquest. Besides the introduction of fruits for culture, large quantities, either dried or otherwise preserved, were imported for food. The orange, however, strange as this seems to us, was not grown by the Romans.

275. Garden Produce. The garden did not yield to the orchard in the abundance and variety of its contributions to the supply of food. We read of artichokes, asparagus, beans, beets, cabbage, carrots, chicory, cucumbers, garlic, lentils, melons, onions, peas, the poppy, pumpkins, radishes, and turnips, to mention only those whose names are familiar to us all. It will be noticed, however, that the vegetables perhaps most prized by us, the potato and the tomato, were not known to the Romans. Of those mentioned the oldest seem to have been the bean and the onion, as shown by the names Fabius and Caepio already mentioned (§ 273), but the latter came gradually to be looked upon as unrefined and the former to be considered too heavy a food except for persons engaged in the hardest toil. Cato pronounced the cabbage the finest vegetable known, and the turnip figures in the well-known anecdote of Manius Curius (§ 299).

276. The Roman gardener gave great attention, too, to the raising of green stuffs that could be used for salads. Among these the sorts most often mentioned are cress and lettuce, with which we are familiar, and the mallow, no longer used for food. Plants in great variety were cultivated for seasoning. Poppy seed was eaten with honey

as a dessert, or was sprinkled over bread before baking.
Anise, cumin, fennel, mint, and mustard were raised everywhere. Besides these seasonings that were found in every

kitchen garden, spices were
brought in large quantities
from the East, and rich men
imported vegetables of larger
sizes or finer quality than
could be raised at home.
Fresh vegetables, like fresh
fruits, could not be brought
from great distances.

277. Meats. Besides the
pork, beef, and mutton that
we still use, the Roman farmer
had goat's flesh at his dis-

Fig. 160
A POMPEIAN STOVE
The original is now in the Museo
Nazionale, Naples.

posal; all of these meats were sold in the towns. Goat's
flesh was considered the poorest of all and was used by
the lower classes only. Beef had been eaten by the Romans
from the earliest times, but its use was a mark of luxury
until very late in the Empire. Under the Republic the ordinary citizen ate beef only on great occasions when he had
offered a steer or a cow to the gods in sacrifice. The flesh
then furnished a banquet for his family and friends; the
heart, liver, and lungs (called collectively the *exta*) were the
share of the priest, while certain portions were consumed
on the altar. Probably the great size of the carcass had
something to do with the rarity of its use at a time when
meat could be kept fresh only in the coldest weather; at
any rate we must think of the Romans as using cattle for
draft and dairy purposes (§ 281), rather than for food.

278. Pork was widely used by rich and poor alike, and was
considered the choicest of all domestic meats. The very
language testifies to the important place the pig occupied in
the economy of the larder, for no other animal has so many

words to describe it in its different functions. Besides the general term *sūs* we find *porcus, porca, verrēs, aper, scrōfa, maiālis*, and *nefrēns*. In the religious ceremony of the *suovetaurīlia (sūs+ovis+taurus)*, the swine, it will be noticed, has the first place, coming before the sheep and the bull. The vocabulary describing the parts of the pig used for food is

Fig. 161
POMPEIAN MOSAIC SHOWING DUCKS AND FISH
Now in the Museo Nazionale, Naples.

equally rich; there are words for no less than half a dozen kinds of sausages, for example, with pork as their basis. We read, too, of fifty different ways of cooking pork.

279. Fowl and Game. The common domestic fowls— chickens, ducks, geese, as well as pigeons —were eaten by the Romans, and, besides these, the wealthy raised various sorts of wild fowl for the table, in the game preserves that have been mentioned (§ 145). Among these were cranes, grouse, partridges, snipe, thrushes, and woodcock. In Cicero's time the peacock was most highly esteemed, having at the feast much the same place of honor as the turkey has with us; the birds cost as much as ten dollars each. Wild animals also were bred for food in similar preserves; the hare and the wild boar were the favorite. The latter was served whole upon the table, as in feudal times.

As a contrast in size the dormouse (*glīs*) may be mentioned; it was thought a great delicacy.

280. Fish. The rivers of Italy and the surrounding seas must have furnished always a great variety of fish, but in early times fish were not much used as food by the Romans. By the end of the Republic, however, matters had changed, and no article of food brought higher prices than the rarer sorts of fresh fish. Salt fish was exceedingly cheap and was imported in many forms from almost all the Mediterranean harbors. One dish especially, *tȳrotarīchus*, made of salt fish, eggs, and cheese, and there-

FIG. 162
MOSAIC FROM POMPEII SHOWING SEA FISH
Now in the Museo Nazionale, Naples.

fore something like our codfish balls, is mentioned by Cicero in about the same way as we speak of hash. Fresh fish were all the more expensive because they could be transported only while alive. Hence the rich constructed fish ponds on their estates—Lucius Licinius Crassus setting the example in 92 B.C.—and both fresh-water and salt-water fish were raised for the table. The names of the favorite sorts mean little to us, but we find the mullet (*mullus*) and a kind of turbot (*rhombus*) bringing high prices, while oysters (*ostreae*) were as popular as they are now.

281. Before passing to the more important matters of bread, wine, and oil, it may be well to mention a few articles that are still in general use. The Romans used freely the products of the dairy—milk, cream, curds, whey, and cheese. They drank the milk of sheep and goats as well as that of cows, and made cheese of the three kinds of milk. The cheese from ewes' milk was thought more digestible, though less palatable, than that made from cows' milk, while cheese from goats' milk was more palatable but less digestible. It is remarkable that they had no knowledge of butter except as a plaster for wounds. Honey took the place of sugar on the table and in cooking, for the Romans had only a botanical knowledge of the sugar cane. Salt was at first obtained by the evaporation of sea water, but was afterwards mined. Its manufacture was a monopoly of the government, and care was taken always to keep the price low. It was used not only for seasoning, but also as a preservative agent. Vinegar was made from grapes (§ 297). Among the articles of food unknown to the Romans were tea and coffee, along with the orange, tomato, potato, butter, and sugar.

282. Cereals. The word *frūmentum*[1] was a general term applied to any of the many sorts of grain that were grown for food. Of those now in use barley, oats, rye, and wheat were known to the Romans, though rye was not cultivated, and oats served only as feed for cattle. Barley was not much used, for it was thought to lack nutriment, and therefore to be unfit for laborers. In very ancient times another grain, spelt (*far*), a very hardy kind of wheat, had been grown extensively, but it had gradually gone out of use except for the sacrificial cake that had given its name to the confarreate ceremony of marriage (§ 82). In classical times wheat was the staple grain grown for food, not differing much from that which we have today. It was usually planted in the

---

[1] The word *frūmentum* occurs fifty-five times in Caesar's *Gallic War*, meaning any kind of grain that happened to be grown for food in the country in which Caesar was campaigning at the time. The word "corn" used to translate it in many of our books of reference is the worst possible for the young American student, because to him the word "corn" means a particular kind of grain, a kind which was unknown to the Romans. The general word "grain" is much better for translation purposes.

fall, though on some soils it would mature as a spring wheat. After grain ceased to be much grown in Central Italy and the land was diverted to other purposes (§§ 146, 442), wheat had to be imported from the provinces, first from Sicily, then from Africa and Egypt, as the home supply became inadequate to the needs of the teeming population.

283. Preparation of the Grain. In the earliest times the grain (*far*) had not been ground, but had been merely

FIG. 163
A POMPEIAN MILL WITHOUT ITS
FRAMEWORK

pounded in a mortar. The meal was then mixed with water and made into a sort of porridge (*puls*, whence our word "poultice"), which long remained the national dish, something like the oatmeal of Scotland. Plautus (died 184 B.C.) jestingly refers to his countrymen as "pulse-eaters." The persons who crushed the grain were called *pīnsitōrēs*, or *pīstōrēs*, whence the cognomen *Pīsō*, as was said above (§ 273), was derived; in later times the bakers were also called *pīstōrēs*, because they ground the grain as well as baked the bread. In the ruins of bakeries we find mills as regularly as ovens. Figure 166 shows a bakery with mills.

284. In such mills the grain was ground into regular flour. The mill (*mola*) consisted of three parts, the lower millstone (*mēta*), the upper stone (*catīllus*), and the framework that surrounded and supported the latter and furnished the means to turn it upon the *mēta*. All these parts are shown distinctly in Figure 164, and hence require little explanation. The *mēta* was, as the name suggests, a cone-shaped stone (*A*) resting on a bed of masonry (*B*) with a raised rim, between which and the lower edge of the *mēta* the flour was collected. In the upper part of the *mēta* a beam (*C*) was mortised, ending above in an iron pin or pivot (*D*), on which hung and turned the framework that supported the *catīllus*. The *catīllus* (*E*) itself was shaped something like an hourglass, or two funnels joined at their necks. The upper funnel served as a hopper into which the grain was poured; the lower funnel fitted closely over the *mēta*. The distance between the lower funnel and the *mēta* was

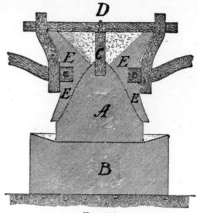

FIG. 164
SECTION OF A MILL

regulated by the length of the pin, mentioned above, according to the fineness of the flour desired. A mill without framework is shown in Figure 163.

285. The framework was very strong and massive on account of the heavy weight that was suspended from it. The beams used for turning the mill were fitted into holes in the narrow part of the *catīllus*, as shown in Figure 164. The power required to do the grinding was furnished by horses or mules pulling the beams (Fig. 165), or by slaves pushing against them. This last method was often used as a punishment, as we have seen (§§ 148, 170). Of

FIG. 165
HORSES TURNING A MILL
From a relief in the Vatican Museum, Rome.

the same form but much smaller were the hand mills used by soldiers for grinding the *frūmentum* furnished them as rations. Under the Empire, water mills were introduced, but they are rarely mentioned in literature.

286. The transition from the ancient porridge (§ 283) to bread baked in the modern fashion must have been through the medium of thin cakes baked in or over the fire. We do not

Fig. 166
A POMPEIAN BAKERY WITH MILLS

know when bread baked in ovens came into use. Bakers (§ 283) as representatives of a trade do not go back beyond 171 B.C., but long before this time, of course, the family bread had been made by the *māter familiās*, or by a slave under her supervision. After public bakeries were once established, it became less and less usual for bread to be made in private houses in the towns. Only the most pretentious of the city mansions had ovens attached, as shown by the ruins. In the country, on the other hand, the older custom was always retained (§ 148). Under Trajan (98-118 A.D.) it became the custom to distribute bread to the people daily, instead of grain once a month, and the bakers were organized into a guild (*corpus, collēgium*), and as a corporation enjoyed certain privileges and immunities. In Figure 166 are shown the ruins of a Pompeian bakery with several mills which were, of course, turned by hand.

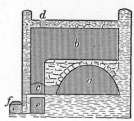

287. Breadmaking. After the flour collected about the edge of the *mēta* (§ 284) had been sifted, water and salt were added and the dough was kneaded in a trough by hand or by a simple machine shown in the illustration in Schreiber, Plate LXVII.

FIG. 167
AN OVEN FOR BAKING BREAD

Yeast was added as nowadays, and the bread was baked in an oven much like those still found in parts of Europe. One preserved in the ruins of Pompeii is well shown in Figure 167: at the point marked *a* is the oven proper, in which a fire was built; the draft was furnished by the opening at *d*. The surrounding chamber (*b*) is intended to retain the heat after the fire (usually of charcoal) had been raked out into the ashpit (*e*) and the vent closed. The letter *f* marks a receptacle for water, which seems to have been used for moistening the bread while it was baking. After the oven had been heated to the proper temperature and the fire raked out, the loaves were put in, the vents closed, and the bread left to bake. The principle is the same as that of the modern fireless cooker, which uses heated soapstone disks.

288. There were several qualities of bread, varying with the sort of grain, the setting of the millstones (§ 284), and the fineness of the sieves (§ 287). The very best, made of pure wheat flour, was called *pānis silīgineus;* that made of coarse flour, of flour and bran, or of bran alone was called *pānis* *plēbēius, castrēnsis, sordidus, rūsticus,* etc. In the first century A.D. people preferred the fine white bread, even

though as now the whole wheat bread was thought to be more nutritious. The loaves were circular and rather flat—some have been found in the ruins of Pompeii—and had their surfaces marked off, by lines drawn from the center, into four or more parts (Fig. 168). The wall painting (Fig. 169) of a salesroom of a bakery, also found in Pompeii, gives a good idea of the appearance of the bread. Various kinds of cakes and confections also were sold at these shops.

289. The Olive. Next in importance to the wheat came the olive. It was introduced into Italy from Greece, and from Italy has spread through all the Mediterranean countries; but in ancient times the best olives were those of Italy, even as today the best olives come from Italy. The olive was an important article of food merely as a fruit. It was eaten both fresh and preserved in various ways, but it found its significant place in the domestic economy of the Romans in the form of the olive oil with which we are familiar.

FIG. 169
THE SALESROOM OF A BAKERY
From a fresco in the Museo Nazionale, Naples.

It is the value of the oil that has caused the cultivation of the olive to become so general in southern Europe. Many varieties of the olive were known to the Romans; they required different climates and soils and were adapted to different uses. In general it may be said that the larger fruit were better suited for eating than for oil.

290. The olive was eaten fresh as it ripened and was also preserved in various ways. The ripe olives were sprinkled with salt and left untouched for five days; the salt was then shaken off, and the olives dried in the sun. They were also preserved sweet without salt in boiled must (§ 296). Half-ripe olives were picked (Fig. 170) with their stems and covered over in jars with the best quality of oil; in this way they are said to have retained for more than a year the flavor of the fresh fruit. Green olives were preserved whole in strong

FIG. 170
PICKING OLIVES

brine, the form in which we know them now, or were beaten into a mass and preserved with spices and vinegar. The preparation called *epitȳrum* was made by taking the fruit in any of the three stages, removing the stones, chopping up the pulp, seasoning it with vinegar, coriander seeds, cumin, fennel, and mint, and covering the mixture in jars with oil enough to exclude the air. The result was a salad that was eaten with cheese.

291. Olive Oil. Olive oil was used for several purposes. It was employed at first to anoint the body after bathing, especially by athletes; it was used as a vehicle for perfumes (the Romans knew nothing of distillation by means of alcohol); it was burned in lamps (§ 228); it was an indispensable article of food. As a food it was employed in its natural state as butter is now in cooking, or in relishes, or dressings. The olive when subjected to pressure yields two fluids. The first to flow (*amurca*) is dark and bitter, having the consistency of water. It was largely used as a fertilizer, but not as a food. The second, which flows after greater pressure, is the oil (*oleum, oleum olīvum*). The best oil was made from olives not fully ripe, but the largest quantity was yielded by the ripened fruit.

292. The olives were picked from the tree; those that fell of their own accord were thought inferior (§ 160), and

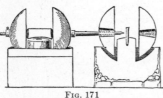

FIG. 171
AN OLIVE CRUSHER FOUND AT POMPEII

were spread upon sloping platforms in order that a part of the *amurca* might flow away by itself. Here the fruit remained until a slight fermentation took place. It was then subjected to the action of a machine (Fig. 171) that bruised and pressed it to separate the pulp from the stones. The pulp was then crushed in a press. The oil that flowed out was caught in a jar and from it ladled into a receptacle (*lābrum fictile*), where it was allowed to settle; the *amurca* and other impurities went to the bottom. The oil was then skimmed off into another like receptacle and again allowed to settle; the process was repeated (as often as thirty times if necessary) until all impurities had been left behind. The best oil was made by subjecting the olives at first to a gentle pressure only. The bruised pulp was then taken out, separated from the stones or pits, and pressed a second or even a third time, the quality becoming poorer each time. The oil was kept in jars which were glazed on the inside with wax or gum to prevent absorption; the covers were carefully secured and the jars stored away in vaults (Fig. 172).

293. Grapes. Grapes were eaten fresh from the vines and were also dried in the sun and kept as raisins, but they owed their real importance in Italy as elsewhere to the wine made from them. It is believed that the grapevine was not native to Italy, but was introduced, probably from Greece, in very

early times. The first name for Italy known to the Greeks
was *Oenōtria*, a name which may mean "the land of the
vine"; very ancient legends ascribe to Numa restrictions
upon the use of wine. It is probable that up to the time
of the Gracchi wine was rare and expensive. The quantity produced gradually increased as the cultivation of
cereals declined (§ 146), but the quality long remained

FIG. 172
A VAULT AT OSTIA FOR STORING OIL IN DŌLIA
The man's figure will give an idea of the size of the jars.

inferior; all the choice wines were imported from Greece
and the East. By Cicero's time, however, attention
was being given to viticulture and to the scientific making of wines, and by the time of Augustus vintages were
produced that vied with the best brought from abroad.
Pliny the Elder says that of the eighty really choice wines
then known to the Romans two-thirds were produced in
Italy; and Arrian, about the same time, says that Italian
wines were famous as far away as India.

294. Viticulture. Grapes could be grown almost anywhere in Italy, but the best wines were made south of Rome, within the confines of Latium and Campania. The cities of Praeneste, Velitrae, and Formiae were famous for the wines grown on the sunny slopes of the Alban hills. A little farther south, near Terracina, was the *ager Caecubus*, where was produced the Caecuban wine, pronounced by Augustus the noblest of all. Then came Mt. Massicus with the *ager Falernus* on its southern side, producing the Falernian wines, even more famous than the Caecuban. Upon and around Vesuvius, too, fine wines were grown, especially near Naples, Pompeii, Cumae, and Surrentum. Good wines, but less noted than these, were produced in the extreme south, near Beneventum, Aulon, and Tarentum. Of like quality were those grown east and north of Rome, near Spoletium, Caesena, Ravenna, Hadria, and Ancona. Those of the north and west, in Etruria and Gaul, were not so good.

295. Vineyards. The sunny side of a hill was the best place for a vineyard. The vines were supported by poles or trellises in the modern fashion, or were planted at the foot of trees up which they were allowed to climb. For this purpose the elm (*ulmus*) was preferred, because it flourished everywhere, could be closely trimmed without endangering its life, and had leaves that made good food for cattle when they were plucked off to admit the sunshine to the vines. Vergil speaks of "marrying the vine to the elm," and Horace calls the plane tree a bachelor (*platanus caelebs*), because its dense foliage made it unfit for the vineyard. Before the gathering of the grapes the chief work lay in keeping the ground clear; it was spaded over once each month in the year. One man could properly care for about four acres.

296. Wine Making. The making of the wine took place usually in September; the season varied with the soil and the climate. It was anticipated by a festival, the *vīnālia rūstica*, celebrated on the nineteenth of August. Precisely what the festival meant the Romans themselves did not fully understand, perhaps, but it was probably intended to secure a favorable season for the gathering of the grapes. The general process of making the wine differed little from that familiar to us in Bible stories and still practiced in modern times. After the grapes were gathered, they were first trodden with the bare feet (Fig. 173) and then pressed in the *prē-lum* or *torcular*. The juice as it came from the press was

FIG. 173
MAKING WINE

called *mustum* (*vīnum*), "new (wine)," and was often drunk unfermented, as sweet cider is now. It could be kept sweet from vintage to vintage by being sealed in a jar smeared within and without with pitch and immersed for several weeks in cold water or buried in moist sand. It was also preserved by evaporation over a fire; when it was reduced one-half in this way, it became a grape jelly (*dēfrutum*) and was used as a basis for various beverages and for other purposes (§ 290).

297. Fermented wine (*vīnum*) was made by collecting the *mustum* in huge vat-like jars (*dōlia:* Fig. 172). One of these was large enough to hide a man and held a hundred gallons or more. These were covered with pitch within and without and partially buried in the ground in cellars or vaults (*vīnāriae cellae*), in which they remained permanently. After they were nearly filled with the *mustum*, they were left uncovered during the process of fermentation, which lasted under ordinary circumstances about nine days. They were then tightly sealed, and opened only when the wine required attention[1] or was to be removed. The cheaper wines were

---

[1]Spoiled wine was used as vinegar (*acētum*), and vinegar that became insipid and tasteless was called *vappa*. This latter word was used also as a term of reproach for shiftless and worthless men.

used directly from the *dōlia;* but the choicer kinds were drawn off after a year into smaller jars (*amphorae*), clarified and even "doctored" in various ways, and finally stored in depositories often entirely distinct from the cellars (Fig. 174). A favorite place was a room in the upper story of the house, where the wine was aged by the heat rising from a furnace

FIG. 174
A WINE CELLAR

or even by the smoke from the hearth.   The *amphorae* were often marked with the name of the wine, and the names of the consuls for the year in which they were filled.

298. Beverages. After water and milk, wine was the ordinary drink of the Romans of all classes. It must be distinctly understood, however, that they always mixed it with water and used more water than wine. Pliny the Elder mentions one wine that would stand being mixed with eight times its own bulk of water. To drink wine unmixed was thought typical of barbarism; wine was so drunk only by the dissipated at their wildest revels. Under the Empire the ordinary qualities of wine were cheap enough to be sold at three or four cents a quart (§ 388); the choicer kinds were very costly, entirely beyond the reach, Horace gives us to understand, of a man in his circumstances. More rarely used than wine were other beverages that are mentioned in literature. A favorite drink was *mulsum,* made of four measures of wine and one of honey. A mixture of water and honey allowed to ferment together was called *mulsa.* Cider was made by the Romans, and wines from mulberries and dates. They also made various cordials from aromatic plants, but they had no knowledge of tea or coffee.

299. Style of Living. The table supplies of a given people vary from age to age with the development of civilization and refinement, and in the same age with the means and tastes of classes and individuals. Of the Romans it may be said that during the early Republic, perhaps almost through the second century B.C., they cared little for the pleasures of the table. They lived frugally and ate sparingly. They were almost strictly vegetarians (§ 273), much of their food was eaten cold, and the utmost simplicity characterized the cooking and the service of their meals. Everything was prepared by the *māter familiās* or by the women slaves under her supervision (§ 90). The table was set in the *ātrium* (§ 188); the father, mother, and the children sat around it on stools or benches (§ 225), waiting on one another and on their guests

FIG. 175
ROMAN SILVER SPOONS
From the Metropolitan Museum of Art,
New York.

FIG. 176
ROMAN-BRITISH POTTERY
From the Toronto Museum.

(§ 104). Dependents ate of the same food, but apart from the family. The dishes were of the plainest sort, of earthenware or even of wood, though a silver saltcellar was often the cherished ornament of the humblest board. Table knives and forks were unknown; the food was cut into convenient portions before it was served, and spoons were used to convey to the mouth what the fingers could not manage. During this period there was little to choose between the fare of the proudest patrician and the humblest client. The Samnite envoys found Manius Curius, the conqueror of Pyrrhus (275 B.C.), eating his dinner of vegetables (§ 275) from an earthen bowl. A century later the poet Plautus calls his countrymen a race of porridge-eaters (*pultiphagōnidae:* § 283), and gives us to understand that in

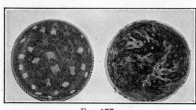

FIG. 177
ROMAN MILLEFIORI GLASS BOWLS
In the Metropolitan Museum of Art,
New York.

his time even the wealthiest Romans had in their households no specially trained cooks. When a dinner out of the ordinary was given, a professional cook was hired, who brought with him to the house of the host his own utensils and his own helpers, just as a caterer does nowadays.

300. The last two centuries of the Republic saw all this changed. The conquest of Greece and the wars in Asia Minor gave the Romans a taste of Eastern luxury and altered their simple table customs, as other customs had been altered by like contact with the outside world (§§ 6, 101, 112, 192). From this time the poor and the rich no longer fared alike. The former, constrained by poverty, lived frugally as of old; students of Caesar know that the soldiers who won Caesar's battles for him lived on grain (§ 282, and note), which they ground in their handmills and baked at their campfires. Some of the very rich, on the other hand, aping the luxury of the Greeks but lacking their refinement, became gluttons instead of gourmets. They ransacked the world for articles of food,[1] preferring the rare and the costly to

[1]Gellius (6.16.5) gives a list from a satirical poem of Cicero's contemporary, Varro: peacock from Samos, heath-cock from Phrygia, crane from Media, kid from Ambracia, young tunny-fish from Chalcedon, *mūrēna* from Tartessus, cod (?) from Pessinus, oysters from Tarentum, scallops (?) from Chios, sturgeon (?) from Rhodes, *scarus* from Cilicia, nuts from Thasos, dates from Egypt, chestnuts (?) from Spain.

what was really palatable and delicate. The separate dining-room (*triclīnium*) was introduced, the great houses having two or more (§ 204), and the *oecī* (§ 207) were, perhaps, pressed into service for banquet halls. The dining couch (§§ 224, 304) took the place of the bench or stool, slaves served the food to the reclining guests, a dinner dress (§ 249) was devised, and every *familia urbāna* (§ 149) included a high-priced chef with a staff of trained assistants. Of course, there were always wealthy men (Atticus, the friend of Cicero [§ 155], for example) who clung to the simpler customs of the earlier days, but these could make little headway against the current of senseless dissipation and extravagance. Over against these must be set the fawning poor, who preferred the fleshpots of the rich patron (§§ 181-182) to the bread of honest independence. Between the two extremes was a numerous middle class of the well-to-do, with whose ordinary meals we are most concerned. These meals were the *ientāculum*, the *prandium*, and the *cēna*.

301. Hours for Meals. Three meals a day were the regular number with the Romans as with us, though hygienists were found then, as they may be found nowadays, who believed two meals more healthful than three, and then as now high livers often indulged in an extra meal taken late at night. Custom fixed more or less rigorously the hours for meals, though these varied with the period, and to a less extent with the occupations and even with the inclinations of indi-viduals. In early times in the city and in all periods in the country the chief meal (*cēna*) was eaten in the middle of the day, preceded by a breakfast (*ientāculum*) in the early morning and followed in the evening by a supper (*vesperna*). In classical times the hours for meals in Rome were about as they are now in our large cities, that is, the *cēna* was post-poned until the work of the day was finished, thus crowding out the *vesperna*, and a luncheon (*prandium*) took the place of the old-fashioned "noon dinner." The late dinner came

to be more or less of a social function, as guests were present
and the food and service were the best the house could afford.
The *ientāculum* and *prandium* were in comparison very simple
and informal meals.

302. Breakfast and Luncheon. The breakfast (*ientāculum*
or *iantāculum*) was eaten immediately after rising, the hour
varying, of course, with the occupation and social position of
the individual. Usually it consisted merely of bread, eaten
dry or dipped in wine or sprinkled over with salt, though
raisins, olives, and cheese were sometimes added. Workmen
pressed for time seem to have taken their breakfast in their
hands to eat as they went to the place of their labor, and
schoolboys often stopped on their way to school (§ 122) at a
public bakery (§ 286) to buy a sort of shortcake or pancake,
on which they made a hurried breakfast. More rarely the
breakfast became a regular meal: eggs were served in addition to the things just mentioned, and *mulsum* (§ 298) and
milk were drunk with them. It is likely that such a breakfast was taken at a later hour and by persons who dispensed
with the noon meal. The luncheon (*prandium*) came about
eleven o'clock. It, too, consisted usually of cold food:
bread, salads (§ 276), olives, cheese, fruits, nuts, and cold
meats from the dinner of the day before. Occasionally,
however, warm meat and vegetables were added, but the
meal was never an elaborate one. It is sometimes spoken of
as a morning meal, but in this case it must have followed
at about the regular interval an extremely early breakfast,
or it must itself have formed the breakfast, taken later than
usual, when the *ientāculum* for some reason had been
omitted. After the *prandium* came the midday rest or
siesta (*merīdiātiō*), when all work was laid aside until the
eighth hour, except in the law courts and in the senate. In
the summer, at least, everybody went to sleep, and even in
the capital the streets were almost as deserted as at midnight. The *vesperna*, entirely unknown in city life, closed

the day on the farm. It was an early supper which consisted largely of the leavings of the noonday dinner with the addition of such uncooked food as a farm would naturally supply. The word *merenda* seems to have been applied in early times to this evening meal, and then to refreshments taken at any time (cf. English "lunch").

303. The Formal Meal. The busy life of the city had early crowded the dinner out of its original place in the middle

Fig. 178
ROMAN GLASSWARE
Now in the Museo Nazionale, Naples.

of the day and fixed it in mid-afternoon. The fashion soon spread to the towns and was carried by city people to their country estates (§ 145), so that in classical times the late dinner (*cēna*) was the regular practice for all persons of any social standing throughout the length and breadth of Italy. It was even more of a function than it is with us, because the Romans knew no other form of purely social intercourse. They had no receptions, balls, musicales, or theater parties, no other opportunities to entertain their friends or be entertained by them. It is safe to say, therefore, that, when the

Roman was in town he was, every evening, host or guest at a dinner as elaborate as his means or those of his friends permitted, unless, of course, urgent business claimed his atten-

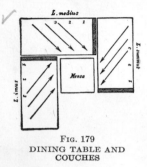

Fig. 179

DINING TABLE AND
COUCHES

tion or some unusual circumstances had withdrawn him temporarily from society. On the country estates the same custom prevailed: the guests came from neighboring estates or were friends who stopped unexpectedly, perhaps, to claim entertainment for a night as they passed on a journey to or from the city (§ 388). These dinners, formal as they were, are to be distinguished carefully from the extravagant banquets of the ostentatious rich. They were in themselves thoroughly wholesome, the expression of genuine hospitality. The guests were friends, their number was limited, the wife and children of the host were present, and social enjoyment was the end in view.

304. The Dining Couch. The position of the dining-room (*trīclīnium*) in the Roman house has been described already (§ 204), and it has been re-marked (§ 300) that in classical times the stool or bench had given place to the couch. This couch (*lectus trīclīniāris*) was constructed much as the common *lectī* were (§ 224), except that it was made broader and lower, had an arm at one end only, was without a back, and sloped from the front to the rear.

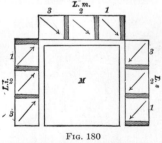

Fig. 180

DINING TABLE AND COUCHES

At the end where the arm was, a cushion or bolster was placed, and parallel with it two others were arranged in such a way as to divide the couch into three parts. Each part was for one person, and a single couch would, therefore, accommodate three persons. The dining-room received its name (*trīclīnium*) from the fact that it was planned to hold three of these couches (κλίναι in Greek), set on three sides of a table, the fourth side of which was open. The arrangement varied a little with the size of the room. In a large room the couches were set as in Figure 180, but if economy of space was necessary they were placed as in Figure 179; the latter was, probably, the more common arrangement of the two. Nine may be taken, therefore, as the normal upper limit of the number at an ordinary table. On unusual occasions, a larger

Fig. 181
WOMAN SITTING ON A DINING COUCH

room would be used where two or more tables could be arranged in the same way, each accommodating nine guests. In the case of members of the same family, especially if one was a child, or when the guests were very intimate friends, a fourth person might find room on a couch, but this was certainly unusual; probably when a guest unexpectedly presented himself, some member of the family would surrender his place to him. Often the host reserved a place or places for friends that his guests might bring without notice. Such uninvited persons were called *umbrae*. When guests were present, the wife sat on the edge of the couch (Fig. 181) instead of reclining, and children were usually accommodated on seats.

305. Places of Honor. The guest approached the couch from the rear and took his place upon it, lying on his left side, with his face to the table, and supported by his left elbow, which rested on the cushion or bolster mentioned above. The position of his body is indicated by the arrows in Figures 179 and 180. Each couch and each place on the couch had its own name according to its position with reference to the others. The couches were called respectively *lectus summus, lectus medius,* and *lectus īmus;* it will be noticed that persons reclining on the *lectus medius* had the *lectus summus* on the left and the *lectus īmus* on the right. Etiquette assigned the *lectus summus* and the *lectus medius* to guests, while the *lectus īmus* was reserved for the host,

FIG. 182
CAST OF BRONZE TABLE FROM BOSCOREALE
In the Field Museum of Natural History, Chicago.

his wife, and one other family member. If the host alone represented the family, the two places beside him on the *lectus īmus* were given to the humblest of the guests.

306. The places on each couch were named in the same way, (*locus*) *summus, medius,* and *īmus,* denoted respectively by the figures *1, 2,* and *3* in Figure 179. The person who occupied the place numbered *1*

was said to be above (*super, suprā*) the person to his right, while the person occupying the middle place (*2*) was above the person on his right and below (*īnfrā*) the one on his left. The place of honor on the *lectus summus* was that numbered *1,* and the corresponding place (*1*) on the *lectus īmus* was taken by the host. To the most distinguished guest, however, was given the place on the *lectus medius* marked *3;* this place was called by the special name *locus cōnsulāris,* because if a consul was present, it was always assigned to him. It was next to the place of the host, and, besides, was especially convenient for a public official; if he found it necessary to receive or send a message during the dinner, he could communicate with the messenger without so much as turning on his elbow.

In the early years of the Empire a new type of couch was

made to be used with the round table. From its semicircular shape it was called *sigma*, from one form of the Greek letter. The cushion curved around the inner side of the couch, which apparently served for all. The number accommodated seems to have varied. The places of honor were at the ends; the place at the right[1] end of the couch was called the *locus cōnsulāris*.

FIG. 183
ROMAN SIDEBOARD

307. Other Furniture. In comparison with the *lectī* the rest of the furniture of the dining-room played an insignificant part. In fact, the only other absolutely necessary article was the table (*mēnsa*), placed, as shown in Figures 179 and 180, between the three couches in such a way that all were equally distant from it and free access to it was left on the fourth side. The space between the table and the couches was so little that the guests could help themselves. The guests had no individual plates to be kept upon the table; it

FIG. 184
ROMAN SIDEBOARD

was used merely to receive the large dishes in which the food was served, and certain formal articles, such as the saltcellar (§ 299) and the things necessary for the offering to the gods. The table, therefore, was never very large, but it was often exceedingly beautiful and costly (§ 227). At first its beauties were not hidden by any cloth or covering; the tablecloth did not come into use until about the end of the first century of our era. The usual tableware in the time of Augustus was the Arretine ware, a red glazed pottery with

---

[1]"Right" here means right as one stood behind the couch and faced the table.

designs in relief; the cost and the beauty of the dishes were limited only by the means and taste of the owner.   Besides the couches and the table, sideboards (*abacī*) were the only articles of furniture usually found in the *trīclīnium*.   These varied from a simple shelf to tables of different forms and

sizes such as are shown in Figures 183 and 184, and open cabinets. They were set out of the way against the walls and served as do ours to display plate and porcelain when such articles were not in use on the table.

308. Courses. In classical times even the simplest dinner was divided into three parts, the *gustus* ("appetizer"), the

cēna ("dinner proper"), and the *secunda mēnsa*[1] ("dessert"); the dinner was made elaborate by having each part served in several courses. The *gustus* consisted only of things that were believed to excite the appetite or aid the digestion: oysters and other shell-fish fresh, sea-fish salted or pickled, certain vegetables that could be eaten uncooked, especially onions, and almost invariably lettuce and eggs, all with piquant sauces.   With these appetizers *mulsum* (§ 298) was drunk, as wine was thought too heavy for an empty stomach. From this drink the *gustus* was also called the *prōmulsis;* another and more significant name for it was *antecēna.* Then followed the real dinner, the *cēna*, which consisted of the more substantial viands, fish, flesh, fowl, and vegetables. With this part of the meal wine was drunk, but in modera-

---

[1] This is the most common form of the term for "dessert," but the plural also occurs, and the adjective may follow the noun.

tion, for it was thought to dull the sense of taste; the real drinking began only when the *cēna* was over. The *cēna* almost always consisted of several courses (*mēnsa prīma, altera, tertia,* etc.). Three were thought neither niggardly nor extravagant; we are told that Augustus often dined on three courses and never went beyond six. The *secunda mēnsa* closed the meal with all sorts of pastry, sweets, nuts, and fruits, fresh and preserved, with which wine was freely drunk. From the fact that eggs were eaten at the beginning of the meal and apples at the close came the proverbial expression, *ab ōvō ad māla* (compare our expression "from soup to nuts").

309. Bills of Fare. We have preserved to us in literature the bills of fare of a few meals, probably actually served, which may be taken as typical at least of the homely, the generous, and the sumptuous dinner. The simplest is given by Juvenal (60-140 A.D.): for the *gustus*, asparagus and eggs; for the *cēna*, young kid and chicken; for the *secunda mēnsa*, fruits. Two other menus are given by Martial (43-101 A.D.). The first has lettuce, onions, tunny-fish, and eggs cut in slices; sausages with porridge, fresh cauliflower, bacon, and beans; pears and chestnuts, and, with the wine, olives, parched peas, and lupines. The second has mallows, onions, mint, ele-campane, ancho-vies with sliced eggs, and sow's udder in tunny sauce; the *cēna* was served in a single course (*ūna mēnsa*), kid, chicken, cold

FIG. 186
POMPEIAN MOSAIC SHOWING FISH
Now in the Museo Nazionale, Naples.

ham, haricot beans, young cabbage sprouts, and fresh fruits, with wine, inevitably. The last menu we owe to Macrobius (fifth century A.D.), who assigns it to a feast of the pontifices during the Republic, feasts proverbial for their splendor. The *antecēna* was served in two courses: first, sea-urchins, raw oysters, three kinds of sea-mussels, thrush on asparagus, a fat hen, panned oysters, and mussels; second, mussels again, shellfish, sea-nettles, figpeckers, loin of goat, loin of pork, fricasseed chicken, figpeckers again, two kinds of sea-snails. The number of courses in which the *cēna* was served is not given: sow's udder, head of wild boar, panned fish, panned

FIG. 187
JARS AND PANS FROM POMPEII
Now in the Museo Nazionale, Naples.

sow's udder, domestic ducks, wild ducks, hares, roast chicken, starch pudding, bread. Neither vegetables nor dessert is mentioned by Macrobius, but we may take it for granted that they corresponded to the rest of the feast, and the wine that the pontifices drank was famed as the best.

310. Serving the Dinner. The dinner hour marked the close of the day's work, as has been said (§ 301), and varied, therefore, with the season of the year and the social position of the family. In general the time may be said to have been not before the ninth and rarely after the tenth hour (§ 428). The dinner lasted usually until bedtime, that is,

for three or four hours at least, though the Romans went
to bed early because they rose early (§§ 79, 122). Sometimes even the ordinary dinner lasted until midnight, but,
when a banquet was expected to be unusually protracted,
it was the custom to begin earlier in order that there might
be time after it for the needed repose. Such banquets,
beginning before the ninth hour, were called *tempestīva
convīvia;* the word "early" here carried with it about the
same reproach as the word "late" in "late suppers." At the
ordinary family dinners the time was spent in conversation,
though in some good houses (notably that of Atticus:
§ 155) a trained slave read aloud to the guests. At "gentle-
men's dinners" other forms of entertainment were provided,
music, dancing, juggling, etc., by professional performers
(§ 153). At elaborate dinners souvenirs were sometimes
distributed.

311. When the guests had been ushered into the dining-
room the gods were solemnly invoked, a custom to which our
"grace before meat" corresponds. Then the guests took their
places on the couches (*accumbere, discumbere*) as these were
assigned them (§§ 305-306), their sandals were removed
(§ 250), to be cared for by their own attendants (§ 152), and
water and towels were carried around for washing the hands.
If napkins were used each guest brought his own. The meal
then began, and each course was placed upon the table on a
tray (*ferculum*), from which the various dishes were passed
in regular order to the guests. As each course was finished
the dishes were replaced on the *ferculum*, and removed,
and water and towels were again passed to the guests,
a custom all the more necessary because the fingers were
used for forks (§ 299). Between the chief parts of the
meal, too, the table was cleared and carefully wiped with a
cloth or soft sponge. Between the *cēna* proper and the
secunda mēnsa a longer pause was made, and silence was
preserved while wine, salt, and meal—perhaps also ordinary

articles of food—were offered to the *Larēs*.   The dessert was
then brought on in the same way as the other parts of the
meal.   When the diners were ready to leave the couches,
the guests called for their sandals (§ 250) and immediately
took their departure.

312. The *Cōmissātiō*. Cicero tells us of Cato the Elder
and his Sabine neighbors lingering over their dessert and

FIG. 188
END OF A DRINKING BOUT
From a Pompeian fresco now in the Museo Nazionale, Naples.

wine until late at night and makes them find the chief charm
of the long evening in the conversation.   For this reason Cato
is said to have declared the Latin word *convīvium*, "a living
together," a better word for such social intercourse than
the one the Greeks used, *symposium*, "a drinking together."
The younger men in the gayer circles of the capital inclined
rather to the Greek view and followed the *cēna* proper with
a drinking bout, or wine supper, called *cōmissātiō* or *com-*

pōtātiō. This differed from the form that Cato approved, not merely in the amount of wine consumed, in the lower tone, and in the questionable amusements, but also in the following of certain Greek customs unknown among the Romans until after the Second Punic War and never adopted in the regular dinner parties that have been described. These were the use of perfumes and flowers at the feast, the selection of a Master of the Revels, and the method of drinking.

313. The perfumes and flowers were used not entirely on account of the sweetness of their scent, much as the Romans enjoyed it, but because the Romans believed that the scent

Fig. 189
CUPIDS MAKING FLOWER GARLANDS
From a fresco in the House of the Vettii, Pompeii.

prevented, or at least retarded, intoxication. This is shown by the fact that they did not use the unguents and the flowers throughout the whole meal, but waited to anoint the head with perfumes and crown it with flowers until the dessert and the wine were brought on. Various leaves and flowers were used for the garlands (*corōnae convīvālēs*) according to individual tastes, but the rose was the most popular and came to be generally associated with the *cōmissātiō.* After the guests had assumed their crowns (sometimes garlands were worn also around the neck), each threw the dice, usually calling as he did so upon his sweetheart or upon some deity to help his throw. The one whose throw was the highest (§ 320) was forthwith declared the *rēx (magister, arbiter) bibendī.* Just what his duties and privileges were we are nowhere expressly told, but it can hardly be doubted that it was his province to determine the proportion of water to be added to the wine (§ 298), to lay down the rules for the drinking (*lēgēs īnsānae*, Horace calls them), to decide what each guest should do for the entertainment of his fellows, and to impose penalties and forfeits for breaking the rules.

FIG. 190
SILVER DRINKING CUP
Now in the Metropolitan
Museum of Art, New York.

314. The wine was mixed under the direction of the *magister* in a large bowl (*crātēr*), the proportions of the wine and water being apparently constant for the evening, and from the *crātēr* (Fig. 191), placed on the table in view of all, the wine was ladled by the slaves into the goblets (*pōcula:* Fig. 192) of the guests. The ladle (*cyathus*) held about one-twelfth of a pint, or, more probably, was graduated by twelfths. The method of drinking seems to have differed from that of the regular dinner chiefly in this: at the ordinary dinner each guest mixed his wine and water to suit his own taste and drank as little or as much as he pleased, while at the *cōmissātiō* all had to drink alike, regardless of differences in taste and capacity. The wine seems to have been drunk chiefly in "healths," but an odd custom regulated the size of the bumpers. Any guest might propose the health of any person he pleased to name; immediately slaves ladled into the goblet of each guest as many *cyathī* as there were letters in the name mentioned, and the goblets had to be drained at a draft. The rest of the entertainment was undoubtedly wild enough (§ 310); gambling seems to have

FIG. 191
MIXING BOWL
FROM POMPEII

been common, and Cicero, in his speeches against Catiline, speaks of more disgraceful practices. Sometimes the guests spent the evening roaming from house to house, playing host in turn, and, wearing their crowns and garlands, they staggered through the streets and made night hideous.

315. The Banquets of the Vulgar Rich. Little need be said of the banquets of the vulgar nobles in the last century of the Republic and of the rich parvenus (§ 181) who thronged the courts of the earlier emperors. They were arranged on the same plan as the dinners we have described, differing from them only in the ostentatious display of furniture, plate, and food. So far as particulars have reached us, they were, judged by the canons of today, grotesque and revolting rather than magnificent. Couches made of silver, wine instead of water for the hands, twenty-two courses to a single *cēna*, seven thousand birds served at another, a dish of livers of fish, tongues of flamingoes, brains of peacocks and pheasants mixed up together, strike us as vulgarity run mad. The sums spent upon these feasts do not seem so fabulous now as they did then. Every season in our great capitals sees social functions that surpass the feasts of Lucullus in cost as far as they do in taste and refinement. As signs of the times, however, as indications of changed ideals, of degeneracy and decay, they deserved the notice that the Roman historians and satirists gave them.

Fig. 192
GOBLETS

CHAPTER IX

AMUSEMENTS

REFERENCES: Marquardt, 269-297, 834-861, *Staatsverwaltung*, III, 482-566; Becker-Göll, III, 104-157, 455-480; Friedländer, II, 40-117; Pauly-Wissowa, under *amphitheātrum, calx, circus, Bäder;* Smith, Harper's, Rich, Walters, Daremberg-Saglio, under *balneum* or *balneae, circus, gladiātor, theātrum,* and other Latin words in the text of this book; *Encyclopaedia Britannica,* fourteenth edition, under "Bath," "Amphitheatre," "Circus," "Theatre"; Blümner, 420-441; Baumeister, 70-73, 241-244, 694, 1730-1758, 2089-2111; Sandys, *Companion,* 204-205, 501-521; Mau-Kelsey, 141-164, 186-211, 212-226; Cagnat-Chapot, I, 172-226, II, 204-228, 478-490; Jones, 115-141, 350-377; McDaniel, 141-167; Showerman, 308-365.

316. After the games of childhood (§§ 102-103), the Roman did not, as we do, pass on to an elaborate system

FIG. 193
A DISCUS THROWER
In the Vatican Museum, Rome.

of competitive games. Of sport in that sense he knew nothing. He played ball before dinner for the good of the exercise. He practiced riding, fencing, wrestling, hurling the discus (Fig. 193), and swimming for the skill in arms and the strength they gave him. In the country there might be hunting and fishing (§ 454). He played a few games of chance for the excitement the stakes afforded. But there was no national game for the young men, and there were no social amusements in which men and women took part together. The Roman made it hard and expensive, too, for others to amuse him. He cared more for farces (mimes and pantomimes) than for the drama, tragic or comic; but the one thing that really appealed to him was excitement, and this he found in gambling or in such amusements only as involved the risk of injury to life and limb—the sports of the circus and the amphitheater. We may describe first the games in which the Roman himself participated and then those at which he was a mere spectator. In the first class are field sports and games of hazard, in the second the public and private games (*lūdī pūblicī et prīvātī*).

FIG. 194
A BOXER
A bronze statue now in the Museo Nazionale, Rome.

317. Sports of the Campus Mārtius. The *Campus Mārtius*, often called simply the *Campus*, included all the level ground between the Tiber and the Capitoline and Quirinal Hills. The northwestern portion of this plain, bounded on two sides by the Tiber, which here sweeps abruptly to the west, was kept clear of public and private buildings and was for centuries the playground of Rome. Here the young men gathered to practice the athletic games mentioned above, naturally in the cooler parts of the day. Even men of graver years did not disdain a visit to the *Campus* after the *merīdiātiō* (§ 302), in preparation for the bath before dinner, instead of which the younger men preferred to take a cool plunge in the convenient river. The sports themselves were those that we are accustomed to group together as track and field athletics. The men ran foot races, jumped, threw the discus (Fig. 193), practiced archery, and had wrestling and boxing matches. These sports were carried on then much as they are now, if we may judge by Vergil's description in Book V of the *Aeneid*, but an exception must be made of the games of ball. These seem to have been very dull as compared with ours. It must be remembered, however (§ 316), that they were played more for the healthful exercise they furnished than for the joy of the playing, and by men of high position, too—Caesar, Maecenas, and even the Emperor Augustus.

FIG. 195
THE WRESTLERS
A statue in the Uffizi Gallery, Florence.

318. Games of Ball. Balls of different sizes, variously filled with hair, feathers, and air (*follēs:* Fig. 196), are known to have been used in the different games. Throwing and catching formed the basis of all the games; the bat was practically unknown. In the simplest game the player threw the ball as high as he could and tried to catch it before it struck the ground. Variations of this were what we should call juggling: the player kept two or more balls in the air, throwing and catching by turns with another player. Another game must have resembled our handball; it required a wall and smooth ground at its foot. The ball was struck with the open hand against the wall, allowed to fall back upon the ground and to bound, and then struck back against the wall in the same manner. The aim of the player was to keep the ball going in this way longer than his opponent could. Private houses and the public baths often had courts especially prepared for this amusement. A third game was called *trigōn*, and was played by three persons stationed at the angles of an equilateral triangle. Two balls were used, and the aim of the player was to throw the ball in his possession at the one of his opponents who would be the less likely to catch it. As two might throw at the third at the same moment, or as the thrower of one ball might have to receive the second ball at the very moment of throwing, both hands had to be used, and a good degree of skill with each hand was necessary. Other games, all of throwing and catching, are mentioned here and there, but none is described with sufficient detail to be clearly understood.

FIG. 196
FOLLĒS

319. Games of Chance. The Romans were passionately fond of games of chance, and gambling was so universally associated with such games that they were forbidden by law, even when no stakes were actually played for. A general indulgence seems to have been granted during the Saturnalia in December, and public opinion allowed old men to play at any time. The laws were hard to enforce, however, as such laws usually are, and large sums were won and lost, not merely at general gambling resorts, but also at private houses. Games of chance, in fact, with high stakes, were one of the greatest attractions at the men's dinners that have been mentioned (§ 314). The most common form of gambling was like our "heads or tails"; coins were used as with us, and the value of the stakes depended on the means of the player. Another common form was our "odd or even": each player guessed in turn whether the number of counters held by another player was odd or even, and in turn held counters concealed in his outstretched hand for his opponent to guess in like way. The stake was usually the contents of the hand, though side bets were not unusual. In a variation of this game the players tried to guess the actual number of the counters held in the hand. Of more interest, however, were the games of knucklebones and dice.

320. Knucklebones. Knucklebones (*tālī*) of sheep and goats, and imitations of them in ivory, bronze, and stone,

Fig. 197
GLASS TĀLĪ
In the Metropolitan Museum of Art,
New York.

were used as playthings by children and in gaming by men. Children played our game of jackstones with them: they threw five into the air at once and caught as many as possible on the back of the hand. The length of the *tālī* was greater than their width and they had, therefore, four long sides and two short ends. The ends were rounded off or pointed, so that the *tālī* could not stand on them. Of the four long sides two were broader than the others. Of the two broader sides one was concave, the other convex; of the narrower sides one was flat and the other indented. Since no two sides had the same shape, the *tālī* did not require marking as do our dice, but for convenience they were sometimes marked with the numbers 1, 3, 4, and 6; the numbers 2 and 5 were omitted. Four *tālī* were used at a time, either thrown into the air from the hand or thrown from a dice box (*fritillus*); the side on which the bone rested was counted, not that which came up. Thirty-five different throws were possible, each of which had its individual name and value. Four aces were the lowest throw, called the Vulture, while the highest, called the Venus, was when all the *tālī* lay differently. It was this throw that designated the *magister bibendī* (§ 313).

321. Dice. The Romans also had dice (*tesserae*) precisely like our own. The Roman dice were made of ivory, stone, or of close-grained wood, and each side was marked with dots, from one to six in number. Three of them, thrown from the *fritillus*, were used at a time, as were knuckle-bones, but the sides that came up counted. The highest possible throw was three

Fig. 198
DICE
Now in the Museo Nazionale, Naples.

sixes, the lowest was three aces. In ordinary gaming the aim of every player seems to have been to throw a higher

Fig. 199
PLAYING DICE
From a fresco at Pompeii.

number than his opponent, but there were also games played with dice on boards with counters, that must have been something like our backgammon, uniting skill with chance. Little more of these is known than their names, but a board used for some such game is shown in Figure 215. If one considers how much space is given in our newspapers to the game of baseball, and how impossible it would be for a person who had never seen a game of ball to get a correct idea of one from the newspaper descriptions only, it will not seem strange that we know so little of Roman games.

322. Public and Private Games.   With the historical development of the Public Games this book has no concern (§ 2).   It is sufficient to say that these free exhibitions, given at first in honor of some god, or gods, at the cost of the State and extended and multiplied for political purposes until all religious significance was lost, had come by the end of the Republic to be the chief pleasure in life for the lower classes in Rome; indeed Juvenal declares that free bread (§ 286) and the games of the circus (§ 328) were the people's sole desire.   Not only were these games free, but, when they were given, all public business was stopped and all citizens were forced to take a holiday.   These holidays became rapidly more and more numerous; by the end of the Republic sixty-six days were taken up by the games, and in the reign of Marcus Aurelius (161-180 A.D.) no less than one hundred thirty-five days out of the year were thus closed to business.[1]   Besides these standing games, others were often given for extraordinary events, and funeral games were common when great men died.   These last occasions were not made legal holidays.   For our purposes the distinction between public and private games is not important; games may be classified, according to the nature of the exhibitions, as *lūdī scaenicī*, dramatic entertainments given in a theater, *lūdī circēnsēs*, chariot races and other exhibitions given in a circus, and *mūnera gladiātōria*, shows of gladiators, given usually in an amphitheater.   It must be understood that there was no commercial theater, and that plays were shown only in connection with the games mentioned above.

323. Dramatic Performances.   The history of the development of the drama at Rome belongs, of course, to the history of Latin literature.   In classical times dramatic performances consisted of comedies (*cōmoediae*), tragedies

---

[1] There are about sixty holidays, including Sundays, annually in most of our states.

(*tragoediae*), farces (*mīmī*), and pantomimes (*pantomīmī*). The farces and pantomimes were used chiefly as interludes and after-pieces, though with the common people they were the most popular of all and outlived the others. Tragedy never had any real hold at Rome, and only the liveliest

Fig. 200
SCENE FROM A COMEDY
Masks were not used in the times of Plautus and Terence.
A relief now in the Museo Nazionale, Naples.

comedies gained favor on the stage. The only complete Roman comedies that have come down to us are those of Plautus and Terence, all adaptations from Greek originals, all depicting Greek life, and represented in Greek costumes (*fābulae palliātae*). They were a good deal more like our comic operas than our comedies; large parts were recited to the accompaniment of music and other parts were sung while the actors danced. Since Roman theaters were not provided with any means of lighting, the plays were always presented in the daytime. In the early period they were given after the noon meal (§ 301), but by Plautus's time they had come to be given in the morning. The average comedy must have required about two hours for its performance, if we make allowances for the occasional music between the scenes.

324. Staging the Play. The play, as well as the other sports, was under the supervision of the state officials in charge of the games at which it was given. They contracted for the production of the play with some recognized manager (*dominus gregis*), who was usually an actor of acknowledged ability and had associated with him a troupe (*grex*) of others inferior only to himself. The actors were all slaves (§ 143), and men took the parts of women. There was no fixed limit to the number of actors, but motives of economy would lead the *dominus* to produce each play with the smallest number possible, and two or even more parts were often assigned to one actor. The characters in the comedies mentioned above, the *fābulae palliātae*, wore the ordinary Greek dress of daily life, and the costumes (Fig. 200) were, therefore, not expensive. The only make-up required in the days of Plautus and Terence was paint for the face, especially for the actors who took women's parts, and wigs that were used conventionally to represent different characters, gray for old men, black for young men, red for slaves, etc. These and the few properties (*ōrnāmenta*) necessary were furnished by the *dominus*. It seems to have been customary also for him to feast the actors at his expense if their efforts to entertain were unusually successful.

325. The Early Theater. During the period when the best plays were being written (200-160 B.C.) by Plautus and Terence, very little was done for the accommodation of the actors or the audience. The stage was merely a temporary platform, the width of which was much greater than its depth; it was built at the foot of a hill or a grass-covered slope. There were few of the things that we are

accustomed to associate with a stage; there were no cur-
tains, no flies, no scenery that could be changed, not even a
sounding board to aid the actor's voice.   There was no way
to represent the interior of a house.   For a comedy the stage
represented a street.   At the back of the stage were shown,
usually, the fronts of two or three houses with windows and
doors that could be opened; sometimes there was an alley

Fig. 201
ROMAN THEATER AT ARLES, FRANCE
Part of the seats have been restored in modern times.   The tower is from
medieval fortifications.

or passageway between two of the houses.   This was the
regular setting for the play, and consequently the dramatist
was forced to place there scenes and conversations that might
normally be expected to take place indoors.[1]   An altar stood
on the stage, we are told, to remind the people of the religious
origin of the games.   No better provision was made for the
audience than for the actors.   The people took their places
on the slope before the stage, some reclining on the grass,
some standing, some, perhaps, sitting on stools which they

---

[1] Terence appears to ridicule this convention in *Andria*, 490-491.

had brought from home.   There were always din and confusion to try the actor's voice, pushing and crowding, dis-
puting and quarreling, wailing of children; and in the very
midst of the play the report of something livelier to be seen
elsewhere might draw the whole audience away.

326. The Later Theater.   Beginning about 145 B.C.,
however, efforts were made to improve upon this poor apology
for a theater, in spite of the opposition of those who con-

FIG. 202
THE SMALLER THEATER AT POMPEII

sidered the plays ruinous to morals.   In that year a wooden
theater provided with seats was erected on Greek lines, but
the senate caused it to be pulled down as soon as the games
were over.[1]   It became a fixed custom, however, for such a
temporary theater (with special and separate seats for senators and, much later, for the knights) to be erected as often
as plays were given at public games, until in 55 B.C. Pompeius

[1] It has been maintained recently that wooden seats were known as early as 200 B.C.

Magnus erected the first permanent theater at Rome. It was built of stone after the plans of one he had seen at Mytilene and could probably seat seventeen thousand people; Pliny the Elder says forty thousand.[1] This theater showed two noteworthy divergences from its Greek model. The Greek theaters were excavated out of the side of the hill, while the Roman theater was erected on level ground (that of Pompeius was erected in the *Campus Mārtius*) and gave,

Fig. 203
RUINS OF THE LARGER THEATER AT POMPEII
This shows the entrance to the orchestra, the foundations of the stage, and the slot into which the curtain was dropped at the opening of a play.

therefore, a better opportunity for exterior magnificence. The Greek theater had a space, usually circular, or larger than a semicircle, called the orchestra, before the *scaena* or scene building; this orchestra or dancing-place gave room for the choruses of the Greek drama. In the Roman theater the orchestra was not used for the chorus (there was seldom

[1] Huelsen thinks these figures too high, and estimates its capacity at not more than ten thousand, the theater of Balbus as seven or eight thousand, and the theater of Marcellus as fourteen thousand, six hundred.

a chorus in a Roman play); the orchestra in a Roman theater was therefore reduced in size until it became an exact semicircle.   The seats nearest the orchestra were assigned at Rome to the senators, in the country towns to the magistrates and town council.   The first fourteen rows of seats rising immediately behind them were reserved at Rome for the knights.   The seats back of these were occupied indiscriminately by the people, on the principle, apparently, of first come, first served.   No other permanent theaters were erected at Rome until 13 B.C., when two were constructed. The smaller, that of Balbus,[1] is said to have had room for

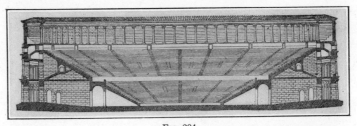

Fig. 204
SECTION OF THE THEATER OF MARCELLUS
(A restoration.)
This illustration shows the stairways and passages beneath the seats.

eleven thousand spectators, the larger, erected in honor of Marcellus, the nephew of Augustus, for twenty thousand.[1] These improved playhouses made possible spectacular elements in the performances that the rude scaffolding of early days had not permitted, and these spectacles proved the ruin of the legitimate drama.   To make realistic the scenes representing the pillaging of a city, Pompeius is said to have furnished troops of cavalry and bodies of infantry, hundreds of mules laden with real spoils of war, and three thousand mixing bowls (§ 314).   In comparison with these three thousand mixing bowls, the avalanches,

[1] See the footnote on page 249.

runaway locomotives, airplane crashes, and cathedral scenes of modern times seem poor indeed.

327. The general appearance of these theaters, the type of many erected later throughout the Roman world, may be gathered from Figure 205, the plan of a theater on lines laid down by Vitruvius (§ 187). *GH* is the back line of the stage (*prōscaenium*); between *GH*

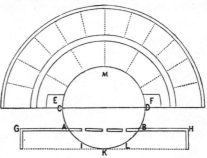

Fig. 205
PLAN OF A ROMAN THEATER, ACCORDING TO VITRUVIUS

and *CD* is the *scaena*, devoted to the actors; beyond *CD* is the *cavea*, devoted to the spectators. Opposite *IKL* are the positions of three doors, for those of the three houses mentioned in § 325. The first four rows of seats closest to the stage, in the semicircular orchestra *CMD*, constitute the part appropriated to the senators. The seats behind these front rows, rising in concentric semicircles, are divided by five passageways into six portions (*cuneī*); in a similar way the seats above the semicircular passage (*praecīnctiō*) are divided by eleven passageways into twelve *cuneī*. Access to the seats of the

Fig. 206
PART OF THE SMALLER THEATER AT POMPEII

senators was afforded by passageways under the seats at the
right and the left of the stage, one of which may be seen in
Figure 206, which represents a part of the smaller of the
two theaters uncovered at Pompeii, built about 80 B.C. Over
the vaulted passage will be noticed what must have been the

FIG. 207
EXTERIOR OF THE THEATER AT ORANGE

best seats in the
theater, which
correspond in
some degree to
the boxes of
modern times.
Those on one
side were re-
served for the
emperor, if he
should be pres-
ent, or for the
officials who su-

perintended the games; those on the other side were reserved
for Vestals. These reserved seats were reached only by private staircases on the stage side of the auditorium. Access to
the upper tiers of the *cavea* was given by passageways constructed under the seats and running up to the passageways
between the *cuneī*. These are shown in Figure 204, a theoretical restoration of the theater of Marcellus, already mentioned. Above the highest seats were broad colonnades,
affording shelter in case of rain, and above them were tall
masts from which awnings (*vēla*) were spread to protect the
people from the sun. The appearance of the stage end may
be gathered from Figure 207, which shows the remains of a
Roman theater still existing at Orange,[1] in the south of France.
The great width of the Roman stage, sometimes forty or sixty
yards, made practicable certain dramatic devices that seem

---

[1] This theater has been restored and used for reproductions of the classical drama.
It is supposed to have been erected in the reign of Marcus Aurelius (161-180 A.D.).
It was allowed to fall into ruins in the fourth century A.D.

forced or unnatural on the modern stage, such as asides and
dialogues on one part of the stage unheard at another, and the
length of time sometimes allowed for crossing the stage. In the
later theater changes in scenery were possible; the extant
Roman plays, however, seldom require change of scenery.
It should be noticed that the stage was connected with the

Fig. 208
A RESTORATION OF THE CIRCUS OF MAXENTIUS

auditorium by the seats over the vaulted passages to the
orchestra, and that the curtain was raised from the bottom,
to hide the stage, not lowered from the top as ours is now.
The slot through which the curtain was dropped can still
be seen in some theaters, as at Pompeii. Vitruvius suggested
that rooms and porticos be built behind the stage, like the
colonnades that have been mentioned, to afford space for
the actors and properties, and shelter for the people in case
of rain.

328. The Circus. The games of the circus were the
oldest of the free exhibitions at Rome and always the most
popular. The word *circus* means simply a "ring"; the *lūdī*

circēnsēs were, therefore, any shows that might be given in a ring. We shall see below (§ 343) that these shows were of several kinds, but the one most characteristic, the one that is always meant when no other is specifically named, is the chariot race. For these races the first and really the only

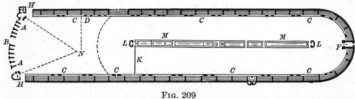

Fig. 209
PLAN OF THE CIRCUS OF MAXENTIUS

necessary condition was a large and level piece of ground. This was furnished by the valley between the Aventine and Palatine Hills, and here in prehistoric times the first Roman race course was established. This remained *the* circus, the one always meant when no descriptive term was added, though, when others were built, it was called sometimes, by way of distinction, the Circus Maximus. None of the others ever approached it in size, in magnificence, or in popularity.

329. The second circus to be built at Rome was the Circus Flaminius, erected in 221 B.C. by the Caius Flaminius who built the Flaminian Road. It was located in the southern part of the Campus Martius (§ 317), and like the Circus Maximus, was exposed to the frequent overflows of the Tiber. Its position is fixed beyond question—it was near the Capitoline Hill—but the actual remains are very scanty, so that little is known of its size or appearance. The third to be established was erected in the first century A.D. It was named after Caius (Caligula) and Nero, the two emperors who had to do with its construction. It lay at the foot of the Vatican Hill, where St. Peter's now stands, but we know little more of it than that it was the smallest of the three. These three were the only circuses within the city. In the immediate neighborhood, however, were three others. Five miles out on the *Via Portuēnsis* was the Circus of the Arval Brethren. About three miles out on the Appian Way was the Circus of Maxentius, erected in 309 A.D. The Circus of Maxentius is the best preserved of all; a restoration and a plan of it are shown in Figures 208 and 209, respectively. On the same road, some twelve miles from the city, in the old town of Bovillae, was a third, making six within easy reach of the people of Rome.

330. Plan of the Circus. All the Roman circuses known to us had the same general arrangement, which will be readily understood from the plan of the Circus of Maxentius shown in Figure 209. The long and comparatively narrow stretch

Fig. 210
OPPIDUM OF A CIRCUS
(A restoration.)

of ground which formed the race course (*harēna;* English, "arena") is almost surrounded by the tiers of seats, running in two long parallel lines uniting in a semicircle at one end. In the middle of this semicircle is a gate, marked *F* in the plan, by which the victor left the circus when the race was over. It was called, therefore, the *porta triumphālis.* Opposite this gate at the other end of the arena was the station for the chariots (*AA* in the plan), called *carcerēs,* "barriers," flanked by two towers at the corners (*II*), and divided into two equal sections by another gate (*B*), called the *porta pompae*, by which processions entered the circus. There are also gates (*HH*) between the towers and the seats.   The exterior appearance of the towers and barriers, called together the *oppidum*, is shown in Figure 210.

331. The arena is divided for about two-thirds its length by a fence or wall (*MM*), called the *spīna*, "backbone." Beyond the ends of this were fixed pillars (*LL*), called *mētae*, marking the ends of the course.   Once around the *spīna* was a lap (*spatium, curriculum*), and a fixed number of laps,

FIG. 211
ROMAN ARENA AT PARIS

usually seven to a race, was called a *missus*. The last lap, however, had but one turn, that at the *mēta prīma*, the one nearest the *porta triumphālis;* the finish was a straightaway dash to the *calx*. This was a chalk line drawn on the arena far enough away from the second *mēta* to keep it from being obliterated by the hoofs of the horses as they made the turn, and far enough also from the *carcerēs* to enable the driver to stop his team before dashing into them.   The dotted line (*DN*) is the supposed location of the *calx*.   It will be noticed that the important things about the developed circus are the *arēna, carcerēs, spīna, mētae,* and the seats, all of which will be more particularly described in succeeding paragraphs.

332. The Arena. The arena is the level space surrounded by the seats and the barriers. The name was derived from the sand used to cover its surface to spare as much as possible the unshod feet of the horses. A glance at the plan will show that speed could not have been the important thing with the Romans that it is with us. The sand, the shortness of the stretches, and the sharp turns between them were all against great speed. The Roman found his excitement in the danger of the race. In every representation of the race course that has come down to us may be seen broken chariots, fallen horses, and drivers under wheels and hoofs. The distance was not a matter of very close measurement, but varied in the several circuses, the Circus Maximus being fully 300 feet longer than the Circus of Maxentius. All seem, however, to have had a constant number of laps, seven to the race, and this also goes to prove that the danger was the chief element in the popularity of the contests. The distance actually traversed in the Circus of Maxentius may be very closely estimated. The length of the *spīna* is about 950 feet. If we allow fifty feet for the turn at each *mēta,* each lap makes a distance of 2000 feet, and six laps, 12,000 feet. The seventh lap had but one turn in it, but the final stretch to the *calx* made it perhaps 300 feet longer than one of the others, say 2300 feet. This gives a total of 14,300 feet for the whole *missus,* or about 2.7 miles. Jordan calculates the *missus* of the Circus Maximus at 8.4 kilometers, which would be about 5.2 miles, but he seems to have taken the whole length of the arena into account, instead of considering merely that of the *spīna.*

333. The *Carcerēs.* The *carcerēs* were the stations of the chariots and teams when ready for the races to begin. They were a series of vaulted chambers entirely separated from one another by solid walls, and closed behind by doors through which the chariots entered. The front of each chamber was formed by double doors of grated bars admitting the only

light which it received. From this arrangement the name *carcer* was derived. Each chamber was large enough to hold a chariot with its team, and, as a team was composed sometimes of as many as ten horses, the "prison" must have been

FIG. 212
THE CARCERĒS
From a relief in the British Museum, London.

nearly square. There was always a separate chamber for each chariot. Up to the time of Domitian the highest number of chariots was eight, but after his time as many as twelve sometimes entered the same race, and twelve *carcerēs* had, therefore, to be provided. The usual number of chariots had been four, one from each syndicate (§ 339), though each syndicate might enter more than one. Half of these chambers lay to the right, half to the left of the *porta pompae*. The appearance of a section of the *carcerēs* is shown in Figure 212.

FIG. 213
BOX OF THE DATOR LŪDŌRUM
From a relief at Rome.

334. It will be noticed from the plan (Fig. 209) that the *carcerēs* were arranged in a curved line. This is supposed to have been drawn in such a way that all the chariots, no matter which of the *carcerēs* one happened to occupy,

would have the same distance to travel in order to reach the
beginning of the course proper at the nearer end of the *spīna*.
There was no advantage in position, therefore, at the start,
and places were assigned by lot. In later times a starting
line (*līnea alba*) was drawn with chalk between the second
mēta and the seats to the right, but the line of *carcerēs* remained curved as of old. At the ends of the row of *carcerēs*,
towers were built which seem to have been the stands for the
musicians; over the *porta pompae* was the box of the chief
state official of the games (*dator lūdōrum*), and between his
box and the towers were seats
for his friends and persons
connected with the games.
The *dator lūdōrum* gave the
signal for the start with a
white cloth (*mappa*). In Figure 213 is shown a victor

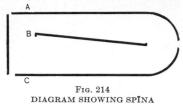

Fɪɢ. 214
DIAGRAM SHOWING SPĪNA

pausing before the box of the *dator* to receive a prize before
riding in triumph around the arena.

335. The *Spīna* and the *Mētae*. The *spīna* divided the
race course into two parts, and thus measured a minimum
distance to be run. Its length was about two-thirds that
of the arena, but it started only the width of the track (plus
the *mētae*) from the *porta triumphālis;* a much larger space
at the end near the *porta pompae* was left entirely free. It
was perfectly straight, but did not run precisely parallel to
the rows of seats; at the end *B* in the exaggerated diagram
(Fig. 214) *BC* is greater than the distance *AB*, in order to
allow more room at the starting line (*līnea alba*, § 334),
where the chariots would be side by side, than farther along
the course, where they would be strung out. The *mētae*, so
named from their shape (§ 284), were pillars erected beyond
the two ends of the *spīna* and architecturally related to it,
though there was a space between the *mēta* and the *spīna*.
In Republican times the *spīna* and the *mētae* must have been

made of wood and movable, in order to afford free space for
the shows of wild beasts and the exhibitions of cavalry that
were originally given in the circus. After the amphitheater
was devised, the circus came to be used primarily for races,

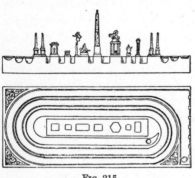

and the *spīna* became permanent. It was built up,
of massive proportions,
on foundations of concrete (§§ 210-211) and
was usually adorned with
magnificent works of art
that must have entirely
concealed horses and
chariots when they
passed to the other side
of the arena (§ 336).

FIG. 215
BOARD-GAME SHOWING SPĪNA

336. A representation
of a circus has been preserved to us in a board-game of some
sort found at Bovillae (§ 329), which gives an excellent idea
of the *spīna* (Fig. 215). We know from various reliefs and
mosaics that the *spīna* of the Circus Maximus was covered
with a series of statues and ornamental structures, such as
obelisks, small temples or shrines, columns surmounted by
statues, altars, trophies, and fountains. Augustus was the
first to erect an obelisk in the Circus Maximus; it was restored in 1589 A.D., and now stands in the Piazza del Popolo;
without the base it measures about seventy-eight feet in
height. Constantius erected another in the same circus,
which now stands before the Lateran Church; it is 105 feet
high. The obelisk of the Circus of Maxentius now stands in
the Piazza Navona. Besides these purely ornamental features, every circus had on each end of its *spīna* a pedestal,
one supporting seven large eggs (*ōva*) of marble, the other
seven dolphins. One of each was taken down at the end of
each lap, in order that the people might know just how

many laps remained to be run. Another and very different idea for the *spīna* is shown in Figure 216 from a mosaic at Lyons. This is a canal filled with water, with an obelisk in the middle. The *mētae* in their developed form are shown very clearly in this mosaic, three conical pillars of stone set on a semicircular plinth, all of the most massive construction.

337. The Seats. The seats around the arena in the Circus Maximus were originally of wood, but accidents owing to decay and losses by fire had led by the time of the Empire to reconstruction in marble, except perhaps in the very highest rows. The seats in the later circuses seem from the first to

Fig. 216
A CANAL AS SPĪNA
A mosaic at Lyons.

have been of stone. At the foot of the tiers of seats was a marble platform (*podium*) which ran along both sides and the curved end; it was therefore coextensive with them. On this *podium* were erected boxes for the use of the more important magistrates and officials of Rome, and here Augustus placed the seats of the senators and others of high rank. He also assigned seats throughout the whole *cavea* to various classes and organizations, separating the women from the men, though up to his time they had sat together. Between the *podium* and the track was a metal screen of openwork. When Caesar showed wild beasts in the circus, he had a canal ten feet wide and ten feet deep dug next the *podium* and filled

with water as an additional protection. Access to the seats
was provided from the rear; numerous broad stairways ran
up to the *praecīnctiōnēs* (§ 327), of which there were probably
three in the Circus Maximus. The horizontal sections between the *praecīnctiōnēs* were called *maeniāna*. Each of
these sections was divided by stairways into several *cuneī*
(§ 327); the rows of seats in the *cuneī* were called *gradūs*.

Fig. 217
RESTORATION OF THE CIRCUS MAXIMUS

The sittings in the row do not seem to have been marked
off any more than they are now in the bleachers at our
baseball grounds. When sittings were reserved for a number
of persons, they were described as so many feet in such a
row (*gradus*) of such a wedge (*cuneus*) of such a section
(*maeniānum*).

338. The number of sittings testifies to the popularity of
the races. The little circus at Bovillae had seats for at least
8000 people, according to Huelsen, that of Maxentius for
about 23,000, while the Circus Maximus, accommodating
60,000 in the time of Augustus, was enlarged to a capacity of

nearly 200,000 in the time of Constantius. The seats themselves were supported upon arches of massive masonry; an idea of their appearance from the outside may be had from the exterior view of the Coliseum shown in Figure 231. Every third vaulted chamber under the seats seems to have been used for a staircase; the others were used for shops and booths, and in the upper parts, as rooms for the employees of the circus, who must have been very numerous. Galleries seem to have crowned the seats, as in the theaters (§ 327), and balconies for the emperors were built in conspicuous places, but we are not able, from the ruins, to fix precisely their positions. A general idea of the appearance of the

Fig. 218
CHARIOT RACE WITH CUPIDS AS DRIVERS
From a sarcophagus now in the Vatican Museum, Rome.

seats from within the arena may, however, be had from an attempted reconstruction of the Circus Maximus (Fig. 217), although the details are uncertain.

339. The _Factiōnēs_ of the Circus. There must have been a time, of course, when the races in the circus were open to all who wished to show their horses or their skill in driving them, but by the end of the Republic no persons of repute took part in the games, and the teams and drivers were furnished by racing syndicates (_factiōnēs_), which practically controlled the market so far as trained horses and trained men were concerned. With these syndicates the giver of the games contracted for the number of races that he wanted (ten or twelve a day in Caesar's time, later twice the number, and even more on special occasions), and they furnished everything needed.   These syndicates were named from the colors worn by their drivers.   We hear at first of two only, the red (*russāta*) and the white (*albāta*); the blue (*veneta*) was added in the time of Augustus, probably, and the green (*prasina*) soon after his reign; finally Domitian added two more, the purple and the gold.   Great rivalry existed between these organizations.   They spent immense sums of money on

Fig. 219
BĪGA
Marble group in the Vatican Museum, Rome.

their horses, importing them from Greece, Spain, and Mauritania, and even larger sums, perhaps, upon the drivers. They maintained training stables on as large a scale as any of which modern times can boast; a mosaic found in one of these establishments in Algeria names among the attendants jockeys, grooms, stableboys, saddlers, doctors, trainers, coaches, and messengers, and shows the horses covered with blankets in their stalls.   This rivalry spread throughout the city; each *factiō* had its partisans, and vast sums of money were lost and won as each *missus* (§ 331) was finished.   All

the tricks of the ring were skillfully practiced; horses were
"doped," drivers hired from rival syndicates or bribed, and
even poisoned, we are told, when they were proof against
bribes. Further, the aid of magicians was invoked to work
a spell that should prevent a team from winning.

340. The Teams. The chariot used in the races was low
and light, closed in front, open behind, with long axles and

FIG. 220
RACING CHARIOT AND TEAM

low wheels to lessen the risk of turning over. The driver
seems to have stood well forward in the car, as shown in
Figure 220; there was no standing-place behind the axle.
The teams consisted of two horses (*bīgae*), three (*trīgae*),
four (*quadrīgae*), and in later times six (*sēiugēs*) or even seven
(*septeiugēs*), but the four-horse team was the most common
and may be taken as the type. Two of the horses were yoked
together, one on each side of the tongue; the others were attached to the car merely by traces. Of the four the horse to
the extreme left was the most important, because the *mēta* lay
always on the left and the highest skill of the driver was

shown in turning it as closely as possible. The failure of the horse nearest it to respond promptly to the rein or the word might mean the wreck of the car (by going too close) or the loss of the inside track (by going too wide), and in either case the loss of the race. Inscriptions sometimes give the names

Fig. 221
A VICTORIUS AURIGA
A statue now in the Vatican
Museum, Rome.

of all the horses of the team; sometimes only the horse on the left is mentioned. Before the races began, lists of the horses and drivers in each were published for the guidance of those who wished to stake their money. Though no time was kept, the records of horses and men were followed as eagerly as now. From the nature of the course (§ 332) it is evident that strength and courage and, above all, lasting qualities were more essential than speed. The horses were almost always stallions (mares are very rarely mentioned), and were never raced under five years of age. Considering the length of the course and the great risk of accidents, it is surprising how long the horses lasted. It was not unusual for a horse to figure in a hundred victories (such a horse was called *centēnārius*); Diocles, who was himself a famous driver, owned a horse that had won two hundred (*ducēnārius*).

341. The Drivers. The drivers (*agitātōrēs, aurīgae*) were slaves or freedmen, some of whom had won their freedom by their skill and daring in the course. Only in the most corrupt days of the Empire did citizens of any social position take actual part in the races. The dress of the driver is shown in Figures 220, 221, and in the frontispiece; especially to be noticed are the close-fitting cap, the short tunic (always of the color of his *factiō*), laced around the body with leather thongs, the straps of leather around the thighs, the shoulder pads, and the heavy leather protectors for the legs. Our football players wear like defensive armor. The reins were knotted together and passed around the driver's body. In his belt he carried a knife to cut the reins in case he should be thrown from the car, or to cut the traces if a horse should fall and become entangled in them. The races gave as many opportunities then as now for skillful driving, and required even more strength and daring. What we should call "fouling" was encouraged. The driver might turn his team against another, or might upset the car of a rival if he could; having gained the inside track, he might drive out of the straight course to keep a swifter team from passing his. The rewards were proportionately great. The successful *aurīga*, though his social station was low, was the pet and pride of the race-mad crowd, and under the Empire, at least, he was courted and fêted by high and low. The pay of successful drivers was extravagant, since the rival syndicates bid against one another for the services of the most popular. Rich presents were given the drivers when they won their races, not only by their *factiōnēs*, but also by outsiders who had backed them and profited by their skill.

342. Famous *Aurīgae*. The names of some of the victors have come down to us in inscriptions (§ 13) composed in their honor or to their memory by their friends. Among these may be mentioned: Publius Aelius Gutta Calpurnianus (§ 59) of the late Empire (1127 victories); Caius Apuleius Diocles, a Spaniard (in twenty-four years 4257 races, 1462 victories; he won the sum of 35,863,120 sesterces, about $1,800,000); Flavius Scorpus (2048 victories by the age of twenty-seven); Marcus Aurelius Liber (3000 victories); Pompeius Muscosus

(3559 victories). To these may be added Crescens, an inscription[1] in whose honor (found at Rome in 1878) is shown in Figure 222.

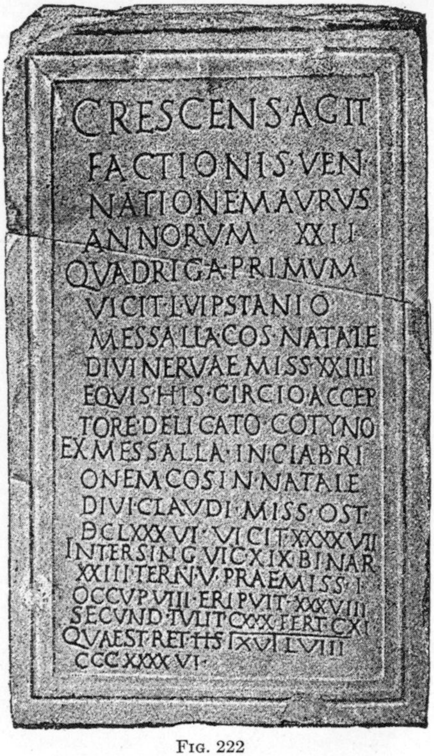

Fig. 222
INSCRIPTION IN HONOR OF CRESCENS[1]

343. Other Shows of the Circus. The circus was used less frequently for exhibitions other than chariot races. Of these may be mentioned the performances of the *dēsultōrēs*, men who rode two horses and leaped from one to the other while they were going at full speed, and of trained horses that performed various tricks while standing on a sort of wheeled platform which gave a very unstable footing. There were also exhibitions of horsemanship by citizens of good standing, riding under leaders in squadrons, to show the evolutions of the cavalry.

---

[1] "Crescens, a driver of the blue syndicate, of the Moorish nation, twenty-two years of age. He won his first victory as a driver of a four-horse chariot in the consulship of Lucius Vipstanius Messalla, on the birthday of the deified Nerva, in the twenty-fourth race, with these horses: Circius, Acceptor, Delicatus, and Cotynus. From Messalla's consulship to the birthday of the deified Claudius in the consulship of Glabrio he was sent from the barriers six hundred and eighty-six times and was victorious forty-seven times. In races between chariots with one from each syndicate, he won nineteen times; with two from each, twenty-three times; with three from each, five times. He held back purposely once, took first place at the start eight times, took it from others thirty-eight times. He won second place one hundred and thirty times, third place one hundred and eleven times. His winnings amounted to 1,558,346 sesterces [about $78,000]."

The *lūdus Trōiae* was also performed by young men of the nobility; this game is described in the *Aeneid*, Book V. More to the taste of the crowd were the hunts (*vēnātiōnēs*); wild beasts were turned loose in the circus to slaughter one another or be slaughtered by men trained for the purpose. We read of panthers, bears, bulls, lions, elephants, hippopotamuses, and even crocodiles (in artificial lakes made in the arena) exhibited during the Republic. In the circus, too, combats of gladiators sometimes took place, but these were more frequently held in the amphitheater.

One of the most brilliant spectacles must have been the procession (*pompa circēnsis*) which formally opened some of the public games. It started from the Capitol and wound its way down to the Circus Maximus, entering by the *porta pompae* (named from it: § 330), and passed entirely around the arena. At the head in a car rode the presiding magistrate, wearing the garb of a triumphant general and attended by a slave who held a wreath of gold over his head. Next came a crowd of notables on horseback and on foot, then the chariots and horsemen who were to take part in the games. Then followed priests, arranged by their colleges, and bearers of incense and of the instruments used in sacrifices, and statues of deities on low cars drawn by mules, horses, or elephants, or else carried on litters (*fercula*) on the shoulders of men. Bands of musicians headed each division of the procession. A feeble reminiscence of all this is seen in the parade through the streets that for many years has preceded the performance of the modern circus.

344. Gladiatorial Combats. Gladiatorial combats seem to have been known in Italy from very early times. We hear of them first in Campania and Etruria. In Campania the wealthy and dissolute nobles, we are told, made slaves fight to the death at their banquets and revels for the entertainment of their guests. In Etruria the combats go back in all probability to the offering of human sacrifices

at the burial of distinguished men, in accordance with the
ancient belief that blood is acceptable to the dead. The
victims were captives taken in war, and it became the
custom gradually to give them a chance for their lives by

Fig. 223
GLADIATOR'S HELMET
Now in the Toronto Museum.

supplying them with weapons and
allowing them to fight one another
at the grave, the victor being
spared, at least for the time. The
Romans were slow to adopt the
custom; the first exhibition was
given in the year 264 B.C., almost
five centuries after the assumed
date of the founding of the city.
That they derived it from Etruria
rather than from Campania is
shown by the fact that the exhibitions were at funeral games,
the earliest at those of Brutus Pera in 264 B.C., Marcus
Aemilius Lepidus in 216 B.C., Marcus Valerius Laevinus
in 200 B.C., and Publius Licinius in 183 B.C.

345. For the first one hundred years after their introduction the exhibitions were infrequent, as the dates just given
show; those mentioned are all of which we have any knowledge during the period. But after that time they were
given more and more frequently, with increasing elaboration.
During the Republic, however, they remained in theory at
least private games (*mūnera*), not public games (*lūdī*), that is,
they were not celebrated on fixed days recurring annually,
and the givers of the exhibitions had to find a pretext for them
in the deaths of relatives or friends, and to defray the expenses
from their own pockets. In fact we know of but one instance
in which actual magistrates (the consuls P. Rutilius Rufus
and C. Manlius, 105 B.C.) gave such exhibitions, and we know
too little of the attendant circumstances to warrant us in
assuming that they acted in their official capacity. Even

under the Empire the gladiators did not fight on the days of the regular public games. Augustus, however, provided funds for "extraordinary shows" under the direction of the praetors. Under Domitian the aediles-elect were put in charge of the exhibitions which were given regularly in December, the only instance known of fixed dates for the *mūnera gladiātōria*. All others of which we read are to be considered the freewill offerings to the people of emperors, magistrates, or private citizens.

346. Popularity of the Combats. The Romans' love of excitement (§ 316) ultimately made the exhibitions immensely popular. At the first exhibition mentioned in § 344, that in honor of Brutus Pera, only three pairs of gladiators were shown, but in the three that followed, the number of pairs rose in order to twenty-two, twenty-five, and sixty. By the time of Sulla, politicians had found in the *mūnera* the most effective means to win the favor of the people, and vied with one another in the frequency of the shows and the number of the combatants. Besides this, the politicians made these shows serve as a pretext for surrounding themselves with bands of professional fighters; these fighters were called gladiators whether they were destined for the arena or not. With these they started riots in the streets, broke up public meetings, over-awed the courts, and even directed or prevented the elections. Caesar's preparations for an exhibition when he was canvasing for the aedileship (65 B.C.) caused such general fear that the senate passed a law limiting the number of gladiators which a private citizen might employ, and he was allowed to exhibit only 320 pairs. The bands of Clodius and Milo made the city a slaughterhouse in 54 B.C., and order was not restored until late in the following year when Pompey as "sole consul" put an end to the battle of the bludgeons with the swords of his soldiers. During the Empire the number of gladiators exhibited almost surpasses belief. Augustus gave eight *mūnera*, in which no less than ten thousand men fought, but these were distributed through the whole period of his reign. Trajan exhibited as many in four months only of the year 107 A.D., in celebration of his conquest of the Dacians. The first Gordian, emperor in 238 A.D., gave *mūnera* monthly in the year of his aedileship, the number of pairs running from 150 to 500. These exhibitions did not cease until the fifth century of our era.

FIG. 224
A WOUNDED GLADIATOR
From a fresco in Pompeii.

347. Sources of Supply. In the early Republic the gladiators were captives taken in war, naturally men practiced in the use of weapons (§ 161), who thought death by the sword a happier fate than the slavery that awaited them otherwise (§§ 135, 140). Captives always remained the chief source of supply, though it became inadequate as the demand increased. From the time of Sulla, training schools were established in which slaves with or without previous experience in war were fitted for the business. These were naturally slaves of the most intractable and desperate character (§ 170). From the time of Augustus criminals (in all cases non-citizens) were sentenced to the arena (later "to the lions"), for the most heinous crimes, treason, murder, arson, and the like. Finally, in the late Empire the arena became the last desperate resort of the dissipated and prodigal, and these volunteers were numerous enough to receive as a class the name *auctōrātī*.

348. As the number of the exhibitions increased, it became harder and harder to supply the gladiators demanded, for it must be remembered that there were exhibitions in many of the cities of the provinces and in the smaller towns of Italy as well as at Rome. In order to supply this increasing demand, thousands died miserably in the arena whom only the most glaring injustice could number in the classes mentioned above. In Cicero's time provincial governors were accused of sending unoffending provincials to be slaughtered in Rome and of forcing Roman citizens, obscure and friendless, of course, to fight in the provincial shows. Later, when the supply of real criminals had run short, it was common enough to send to the arena men sentenced for the pettiest offenses, and to trump up charges against the innocent for the same purpose. The persecution of the Christians was largely due to the demand for more gladiators. So, too, the distinction was lost between actual prisoners of war and peaceful non-combatants; after the fall of Jerusalem all Jews over seventeen years of age were condemned by Titus to work in the mines or fight in the arena. Wars on the border were sometimes waged for the sole purpose of taking men who could be made gladiators; in default of men, women and children were sometimes made to fight.

349. Schools for Gladiators. The training schools for gladiators (*lūdī gladiātōriī*) have been mentioned already. Cicero speaks of one at Rome during his consulship, and there were others before his time at Capua and Praeneste. Some of these were set up by wealthy nobles for the purpose of preparing their own gladiators for *mūnera* which they expected to give; others were the property of regular dealers in gladiators, who kept and trained them for hire. The business was at first almost as disreputable as that of the *lēnōnēs* (§ 139). During the Empire, however, training schools were maintained at public expense and under the direction of state officials, not only in Rome, where there were four at least of these schools, but also in other cities of Italy, where exhibitions were frequently given, and even in the provinces. The purpose of all the schools, public and private alike, was the same, to make the men trained in them as effective fighting machines as possible. The gladiators were in charge of competent training masters (*lanistae*); they were subject to the strictest discipline; their diet was carefully looked after, and a special food (*sagīna gladiātōria*) was provided for them; regular gymnastic exercises were prescribed, and lessons in the use of the various weapons were given by recognized experts (*magistrī, doctōrēs*).   In their fencing bouts, wooden

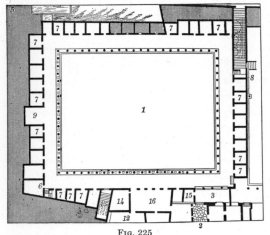

swords (*rudēs*) were used. The gladiators associated in a school were collectively called a *familia*.

350.   These schools had also to serve as barracks for the gladiators between engagements, that is, practically as houses of detention.   It was

FIG. 225
PLAN OF A SCHOOL FOR GLADIATORS IN POMPEII

from the school of Lentulus at Capua that Spartacus had escaped, and the Romans needed no second lesson of the sort. The general arrangement of these barracks may be understood from the ruins of one uncovered at Pompeii, though in this case the buildings had been originally planned for another purpose, and the rearrangement may not be typical in all respects.   A central court, or exercise ground (Fig. 225), is surrounded by a wide colonnade, and this in turn by rows of buildings two stories in height; the general arrangement is not unlike that of the peristyle of a house (§ 202).   The dimensions of the court are nearly 120 by 150 feet.   The buildings are cut up into rooms, nearly all small (about twelve feet square), disconnected and opening upon the court; those in the first story are reached from the colonnade, those in the second from a gallery to which ran several stairways. These small rooms are supposed to be the sleeping rooms of the gladiators; each accommodated two persons. There are seventy-one of them (marked *7* on the plan), affording room for one hundred forty-two men. The uses of the larger rooms are purely conjectural. The entrance is supposed to have been at *3*, with a room (*15*) for the watchman or sentinel. At *9* was an *exedra*, where the gladiators may have waited in full panoply for their turns in the exercise ground (*1*). The guard room (*8*) is identified by the remains of stocks, in which the refractory were fastened for punishment or safe-keeping. The stocks permitted the culprits to lie only on their backs or to sit in a very uncomfortable position. At *6* was the armory or property room, if we may judge from articles found in it. Near it in the corner was a staircase leading to the gallery before the rooms of the second story. The large room (*16*) was the mess-room, with the kitchen (*12*) opening into it. The stairway (*13*) gave access to the rooms above kitchen and mess-room, possibly the apartments of the trainers and their helpers.

351. Places of Exhibition. During the Republic the combats of gladiators took place sometimes at a grave or in the circus, but regularly in the Forum. None of these places was well adapted to the purpose, the grave least of all. The circus had seats enough, but the *spīna* was in the way (§ 335) and the arena too vast to give all the spectators a satisfactory view of a struggle that was confined practically to a single spot. In the Forum, on the other hand, the seats could be arranged very conveniently; they would run parallel with the sides, could be curved around the corners, and would leave free only sufficient space to afford room for the combatants. The inconvenience here was due to the fact

that the seats had to be erected before each performance
and removed after it, a delay to business if they were constructed carefully and a menace to life if they were put up
hastily. These considerations finally led the Romans, as
they had led the Campanians half a century before, to

provide permanent
seats for the *mūne-*
ra, arranged as they
had been in the
Forum, but in a
place where they
would not interfere
with public or pri-
vate business. To
these places for
shows of gladiators
came in the course
of time to be exclu-
sively applied *am-*
phitheātrum, a word
which had been pre-
viously given in its
general sense to any
place, the circus for

FIG. 226
OUTER WALLS OF THE AMPHITHEATER
AT VERONA

example, in which the seats ran all the way around, as
opposed to the theater, in which the rows of seats were
broken by the stage.

352. Amphitheaters at Rome. Just when the first amphitheaters, in the special sense of the word, were erected at
Rome cannot be determined with certainty. We are told that
Caesar erected a wooden amphitheater in 46 B.C., but we have
no detailed description of it, and no reason to think that it
was anything more than a temporary structure. In the year
29 B.C., however, an amphitheater was built by Statilius
Taurus, partly at least of stone, that lasted until the great

conflagration in the reign of Nero (64 A.D.). Nero himself erected one of wood in the *Campus.* Finally, by 80 A.D., was completed the structure known at first as the *amphi-theātrum Flāvium,* later as the *Colossēum* or *Colisēum,* which was large enough and durable enough to make forever unnecessary the erection of similar structures in the city. Remains of amphitheaters have been found in many cities throughout the Roman world. Those at Nîmes (*Nemausus*), and at Arles (*Arelas*), France, for instance, have been cleared and partly restored in modern times and are still in use, though bullfights have taken the place of the gladiatorial combats. The amphitheater at Verona, too (Fig. 226), in northern Italy, has been partly restored. "Buffalo Bill" gave exhibitions there.

Fig. 227
EXTERIOR OF THE AMPHITHEATER AT POMPEII
This shows the double stairway referred to on page 278.

353. The Amphitheater at Pompeii. The essential features of an amphitheater may be most easily understood from the ruins of the one at Pompeii, erected about 75 B.C., almost half a century before the first permanent structure of the sort at Rome (§ 352), and the earliest known to us from either literary or monumental sources. The exterior is shown in Figure 227 (see also Overbeck, 176-184; Mau-Kelsey, 212-226). It will be seen in Figure 228 that the arena and most of the seats lie in a great hollow excavated for the purpose, so that there was needed for the exterior a wall of hardly

more than ten to thirteen feet in height. Even this wall
was necessary on only two sides, as the amphitheater was
built in the southeast corner of the city and its south and
east sides were bounded by the city walls. The shape is
elliptical; the major axis is 444 feet long, the minor 342.

FIG. 228
INTERIOR OF AMPHITHEATER AT POMPEII
This shows the entrance from one underground passageway.

The arena occupies the middle space. It was encircled by
thirty-five rows of seats arranged in three divisions; the
lowest (*infima* or *ima cavea*) had five rows, the second
(*media cavea*) twelve, and the highest (*summa cavea*) eighteen.
A broad terrace ran around the amphitheater at the height
of the topmost row of seats. Access to this terrace was
given from without by the double stairway on the west,
shown in Figure 227, and by single stairways next the city
walls on the east and south (*10* in Fig. 229). Between the
terrace and the top seats was a gallery, or row of boxes,
each about four feet square, probably for women. Beneath

the boxes persons could pass from the terrace to the seats.
The amphitheater had seating capacity for perhaps 20,000
spectators.

354. The arena is shown in Figure 228, its plan in Figure
229. It was an ellipse with axes of 228 and 121 feet. Around

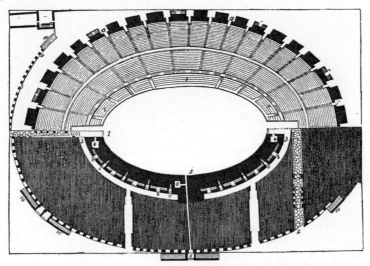

FIG. 229
PLAN OF ARENA IN THE AMPHITHEATER AT POMPEII

it ran a wall a little more than six feet high, on a level with
the top of which were the lowest seats. For the protection of
the spectators when wild animals were shown, a grating of
iron bars was put up on the top of the arena wall. Access to
the arena and to the seats of the *cavea īma* and the *cavea
media* was given by the two underground passageways, (*1*)
and (*2*) in Figure 229, of which *2* turns at right angles on account of the city wall on the south. From the arena ran also
a third passage (*5*), low and narrow, leading to the *porta
Libitīnēnsis*, through which the bodies of the dead were
dragged with ropes and hooks. Near the mouths of these

Fig. 230
INTERIOR OF THE COLISEUM

passages were small chambers or dens, marked *4, 4, 6,* the purposes of which are not known.   The floor of the arena was covered with sand, as in the circus (§ 332), but in this case to soak up the blood as well as to give a firm footing to the gladiators.

355. Of the part of this amphitheater set aside for the spectators, only the *cavea īma* was supported upon artificial foundations.   All the other seats were constructed in sections as means were obtained for the purpose; the people in the interim found places for themselves on the sloping banks as in the early theaters (§ 325).   The *cavea īma* was, in fact, not supplied with seats all the way around; a considerable section on the east and west sides was arranged with four low, broad ledges of stone, rising one above the other, on which the members of the city council could place the seats of honor (*bisellia*) to which their rank entitled them.   In the middle of the section on the east the lowest ledge is made of double width for some ten feet; this was the place set apart for the giver of the games and his friends. In the *cavea media* and the *cavea summa* the seats were of stone resting on the bank of earth. It is probable that all the places in the lowest section were reserved for people of distinction, that seats in the middle section were sold to the well-to-do, and that admission was free to the less desirable seats of the highest section.

356. The Coliseum. The Flavian Amphitheater (§ 352) is the best known of all the buildings of ancient Rome, because to so large an extent it has survived to the present day. For our purpose it is not necessary to give its history

FIG. 231
EXTERIOR OF THE COLISEUM

or to describe its architecture; it will be sufficient to compare its essential parts with those of its modest prototype in Pompeii. The latter was built in the outskirts of the city, in a corner, in fact, of the city walls (§ 353); the Coliseum lay near the center of Rome, and was easily accessible from all directions. The interior of the Pompeian structure was reached through two passages and by three stairways only, while eighty numbered entrances made it easy for the Roman multitudes to find their appropriate places in the Coliseum. Much of the earlier amphitheater was below ground level; all the corresponding parts of the Coliseum were above street level, the walls rising to a height of nearly 160 feet. This gave opportunity for the same architectural magnificence that had distinguished the Roman theater from that of the Greeks (§ 326). The general effect is shown in Figure 231, an exterior view of the ruins as they exist today.

357. The interior form of the Coliseum (Fig. 230) is an ellipse with axes of 620 and 513 feet; the building covers nearly six acres of ground. The arena is also an ellipse, its axes measuring 287 and 180 feet. The width of the space appropriated for the spectators is, therefore, 166½ feet all around the arena. It will be noticed, too, that subterranean chambers were constructed under the whole building, including the arena. These furnished room for the regiments of gladiators, the dens of wild beasts, the machinery for the transformation scenes that Gibbon has described in the twelfth chapter of his *Decline and Fall of the Roman Empire*, and above all for the vast number of water and drainage pipes that made it possible to turn the arena into a lake at a moment's notice and as quickly to get rid of the water. The wall that surrounded the arena was fifteen feet high; it was faced with rollers and was defended, like the one at Pompeii, by a grating or network of metal above it. The top of the wall was level with the floor of the lowest range of seats, called the *podium*, as in the circus (§ 337), and had room for two, or at the most three, rows of marble chairs. These were for the use of the emperor and the imperial family, the giver of the games, the magistrates, senators, Vestal Virgins, ambassadors of foreign states, and other persons of consequence.

358. The arrangement of the seats with the method of reaching them is shown in the sectional plan, Figure 232. The seats were arranged in three tiers (*maeniāna*, § 337), one

above the other, separated by broad passageways and rising
more steeply the farther they were from the arena, and were
crowned by an open gallery. In the plan the *podium* is
marked *A*. Twelve feet above it begins the first *maeniānum*
(*B*), with fourteen rows of seats reserved for members of the
equestrian order. Then came a broad *praecīnctiō* (§ 327)
and after it the second *maeniānum* (*C*), intended for ordinary
citizens. Back of this was a wall of considerable height, and

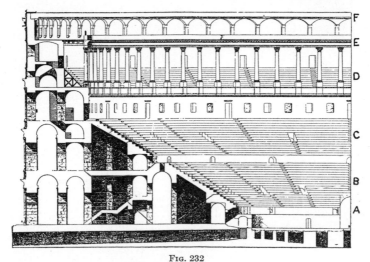

Fig. 232
SECTION OF THE COLISEUM
(A restoration.)
This section shows the vaulted passageways supporting the tiers of seats.

above it the third *maeniānum* (*D*), supplied with rough
wooden benches for the lowest classes, foreigners, slaves, and
the like. The row of pillars along the front of this section
made the distant view all the worse. Above this was an
open gallery (*E*), in which women found an unwelcome place.
No other seats were open to them unless they were of sufficient distinction to claim a place upon the *podium*. At the
very top of the outside wall was a terrace (*F*), in which were

fixed masts to support the awnings that could be spread to give protection to those sections lying in the sun. The seating capacity of the Coliseum was said to have been eighty thousand, with standing room for twenty thousand more, but Huelsen thinks that it can have provided seats for not more than forty or fifty thousand (see note 1, page 249).

Fig. 233
RĒTIĀRIUS AND SECŪTOR
Roman Mosaic at Madrid.

359. Styles of Fighting. Gladiators fought usually in pairs, man against man, but sometimes in masses (*gregātim, catervātim*). In early times they were actually soldiers, captives taken in war (§ 347), and so naturally fought with the weapons and equipment to which they were accustomed. When the professionally trained gladiators came in, they received the old names, and were called "Samnites," "Thracians," etc., according to their arms and tactics. In much later times victories over distant peoples were celebrated with combats in which the weapons and methods of war of the conquered were shown to the people of Rome; thus, after the conquest of Britain *essedāriī* exhibited in the arena the tactics of chariot fighting which Caesar had described several generations before in his *Commentaries*. It was natural enough, too, for the people to want to see different arms and different tactics tried against one another, and so the Samnite was matched against the Thracian, the heavy-armed against the light-armed. This became under the Empire the favorite style of combat. Finally, when people had tired of the regular shows, novelties were introduced that seem to us grotesque; men fought blindfold (*andabatae*), or armed with two swords (*dimachaerī*), or with the lasso (*laqueātōrēs*), or with a heavy net (*rētiāriī*). There were also battles of dwarfs and of dwarfs with women. Of these the *rētiārius* became immensely popular. He carried a huge net in which he tried to entangle his opponent, always a *secūtor* (see § 360), dispatching him with a dagger if the throw was successful. If unsuccessful he took to flight while preparing his net for another throw; or if he had lost his net, he tried to keep his opponent off with a heavy three-pronged spear (*fuscina*), his only weapon besides the dagger (Fig. 233).

360. Weapons and Armor. The armor and weapons used in these combats are known from pieces found in various places, and from paintings and sculpture, but we are not always able to assign them to definite classes of gladiators. The oldest class of gladiators were the Samnites. They had belts, thick sleeves on the right arm (*manicae*), helmets with visors (shown in Figure 223, § 345), greaves on the left leg, short swords, and the long shield (*scūtum*). Under the Empire the name Samnite was gradually lost, and gladiators with equivalent equipment were called

Fig. 234
A THRAEX

hoplomachī (heavy-armed), when they were matched against the lighter-armed Thracians, and *secūtōrēs*, when they fought with the *rētiāriī*. The Thracians (Fig. 234) had much the same equipment as the Samnites; the marks of distinction were the small shield (*parma*) in place of the *scūtum* and, to make up the difference, greaves on both legs. They carried a curved sword. The Gauls were heavy-armed, but we do not know how they were distinguished from the Samnites. In later times they were called *murmillōnēs*, perhaps from an ornament on their helmets shaped like a fish (*mormyr*). The *rētiāriī* had no defensive armor except a leather protec-

tion for the shoulder, shown in Figure 233. Of course, the
same man might appear by turns as Samnite, Thracian, etc.,
if he was skilled in the use of the various weapons (see the
inscription in § 363).

361. Announcements of the Shows. The games were ad-
vertised in advance by means of notices painted on the walls
of public and private houses, and even on the tombstones that
lined the approaches to the towns and cities. Some are
worded in very general terms, announcing merely the name
of the giver of the games with the date:

A · Svetti · Certi

AEDILIS · FAMILIA · GLADIATORIA · PUGNAB · POMPEIS

PR · K · Ivnias · Venatio · et · vela · erunt[1]

Others promise, in addition to the awnings, that the dust
will be kept down in the arena by sprinkling. Sometimes
when the troop was particularly good the names of the gladiators were announced in pairs as they would be matched
together, with details as to their equipment, the school in
which each had been trained, the number of his previous
battles, etc. To such a notice on one of the walls in Pompeii
someone added after the show the result of each combat.
The following gives part only of this announcement:

MVNUS · N. . . · IV · III

Prid · Idus · Idibus · Mais

T   M   O   T

v. Pugnax · Ner · III   *v.* Cycnvs · Ivl · VIII

p. Mvrranvs · Ner · III   *m.* Atticvs · Ivl · XIV[2]

The letters in italics before the names of the gladiators
were added after the exhibition by some interested spectator,

---

[1] "On the last day of May the gladiators of the Aedile Aulus Suettius Certus will
fight at Pompeii. There will also be a hunt, and awnings will be used." *Corpus Inscriptionum Latinarum*, IV, 1189.

[2] "The games of N. . . from the twelfth to the fifteenth of May. The Thracian
Pugnax, of the gladiatorial school of Nero, who has fought three times, will be matched
against the *murmillō* Murranus, of the same school and the same number of fights.
The *hoplomachus* Cycnus, from the school of Julius Caesar, who has fought eight
times, will be matched with the Thracian Atticus of the same school and of fourteen
fights." *Corpus Inscriptionum Latinarum*, IV, 2508.

and stand for *vīcit, periit,* and *missus* ("beaten, but spared"). To such particulars as those given above, other announcements added the statement that pairs other than those mentioned would fight each day; these were meant to excite the curiosity and interest of the people.

362. The Fight Itself. The day before the exhibition a banquet (*cēna lībera*) was given to the gladiators, and they received visits from their friends and admirers. The games took place in the afternoon. After the *ēditor mūneris* had taken his place (§ 355), the gladiators marched in procession around the arena, pausing before him to give the famous greeting: *Moritūrī tē salūtant.* All then retired from the arena to return in pairs, according to the published program. The show began with a series of sham combats, the *prōlūsiō,* with blunt weapons. When the people had had enough of this, the trumpets gave the signal for the real exhibition to begin. Those reluctant to fight were driven into the arena with

Fig. 235
VOTIVE GALĒRUS

whips or hot iron bars. If one of the combatants was clearly overpowered without being actually killed, he might appeal for mercy by holding up his finger to the *ēditor.* It was customary to refer the plea to the people, who signaled in some fashion not known to us to show that they wished it to be granted, or gesticulated *pollice versō,* apparently with the arm out and thumb down, as a signal for death. The gladiator to whom release (*missiō*) was refused received without resistance the death blow from his opponent. Combats where all must fight to the death were said to be *sine missiōne,* but these were forbidden by Augustus. The body of the dead man was dragged away through the *porta Libitīnēnsis* (§ 354), sand was sprinkled or raked over the blood, and the contests were continued until all had fought.

363. The Rewards. Before making his first public appearance, the gladiator was technically called a *tīrō*. When after many victories he had proved himself to be the best of his class, or second best, in his *familia*, he received the title of *prīmus*, or *secundus, pālus*. When he had won his freedom, he received a wooden sword (*rudis*). From this the title *prīma rudis* and *secunda rudis* seem to have been given to those who were afterwards employed as training masters (*doctōrēs*, § 349) in the schools. The rewards given to famous gladiators by their masters and backers took the form of valuable prizes and gifts of money. These may not have been so generous as those given to the *aurīgae* (§ 341), but they were enough to enable them to live in luxury the rest of their lives. The class of men, however, who became professional gladiators probably found their most acceptable reward in the immediate and lasting notoriety that their strength and courage brought them. That they did not shrink from the *īnfāmia* that their lives entailed is shown by the fact that they did not try to hide their connection with the amphitheater. On the contrary, their gravestones record their classes and the number of their victories, and have often cut upon them their likenesses with the *rudis* in their hands.

D · M · ET · MEMORIAE
AETERNAE · HYLATIS
DYMACHAERO · SIVE
ASSIDARIO · P · VII · RV · I
ERMAIS · CONIVX
CONIVGI · KARISSIMO
P · C · ET · S · AS · D[1]

364. Other Shows in the Amphitheater. Of other games that were sometimes given in the amphitheaters something has been said in connection with the circus (§ 343). The most important were the *vēnātiōnēs*, hunts of wild beasts. These

---

[1] Inscription on the tomb of a gladiator. "To the Gods Manes and the lasting memory of Hylas, a dimachaerus or essedarius of seven victories and head trainer. His wife Ermais erected this monument to her beloved husband and dedicated it, reserving the usual rights." *Corpus Inscriptionum Latinarum*, XIII, 1997.

were sometimes killed by men trained to hunt them, sometimes made to kill one another. As the amphitheater was primarily intended for the butchery of men, the *vēnātiōnēs* given in it gradually became fights of men against beasts. The victims were condemned criminals, some of them guilty of crimes that deserved death, some of them sentenced on trumped-up charges, some of them (among these were women and children) condemned "to the lions" for political or religious convictions. Sometimes they were supplied with weapons; sometimes they were exposed unarmed, even fettered or bound to stakes; sometimes the ingenuity of their executioners found additional torments for them by making them play the parts of the sufferers in the tragedies of mythology.

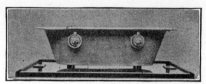

Fig. 236
BRONZE BATHTUB FROM BOSCOREALE
In the Field Museum of Natural History, Chicago.

The arena could be adapted, too, for the maneuvering of boats, when it had been flooded with water (§ 357). Naval battles (*naumachiae*) were often fought, as desperate and as bloody as some of those that have given a new turn to the history of the world. The very earliest exhibitions of this sort were given in artificial lakes, also called *naumachiae*. The first of these was dug by Caesar, for a single exhibition, in 46 B.C. Augustus had a permanent basin constructed in 2 B.C., measuring 1800 by 1200 feet, and four others at least were built by later emperors.

365. The Daily Bath. To the Roman of early times the bath had stood for health and decency only. He washed his arms and legs every day, for the ordinary costume left them exposed (§ 239); he washed his body once a week. He bathed at home, using a primitive sort of wash-room; it was situated near the kitchen (§ 203) in order that the water heated on the kitchen stove might be carried into it with

the least inconvenience. By the last century of the Republic
all this had changed, though the steps in the change cannot
now be followed. The bath had become a part of the daily
life as momentous as the *cēna* itself, which it regularly preceded. It was taken, too, by preference, in one of the public
bathing establishments which were by this time operated
on a large scale in all parts of Rome, in the smaller towns
of Italy, and even in the provinces. They were often built
where hot or mineral springs were found. These public establishments offered all sorts of baths, plain, plunge, douche,
and with massage (Turkish); in many cases they offered
features borrowed from the Greek gymnasia, exercise
grounds, courts for various games, reading and conversation
rooms, libraries, gymnastic apparatus, everything in fact
that our athletic clubs now provide for their members. The
accessories had become really of more importance than the
bathing itself and justify the description of the bath under
the head of amusements. In places where there were no
public baths, or where they were at an inconvenient distance, the wealthy fitted up bathing places in their houses,
but no matter how elaborate they were, the private baths
were merely a makeshift at best.

366. Essentials for the Bath. The ruins of the public and
private baths found all over the Roman world, together with
an account of baths by Vitruvius, and countless allusions in
literature, make very clear the general construction and
arrangement of the bath, but show that the widest freedom
was allowed in matters of detail. For the luxurious bath of
classical times four things were thought necessary: a warm
anteroom, a hot bath, a cold bath, and the rubbing and
anointing with oil. All these might have been provided in
one room, as all but the last are furnished in every modern
bathroom, but as a matter of fact we find at least three
rooms set apart for the bath in very modest private houses,
and often five or six, while in the public establishments this

number might be multiplied several times. In the better
equipped baths were provided: (1) a room for undressing
and dressing (*apodȳtērium*), usually unheated, but furnished
with benches and often with compartments for the clothes;
(2) the warm anteroom (*tepidārium*), in which the bather
waited long enough for the perspiration to start, in order to

FIG. 237
GREAT HALL IN THE BATHS OF CARACALLA
(A restoration.)

guard against the danger of passing too suddenly into the
high temperature of the next room (*caldārium*); (3) the hot
room (*caldārium*) for the hot bath; (4) the cold room
(*frīgidārium*) for the cold bath; (5) the room for the rubbing
and anointing with oil that finished the bath (*ūnctōrium*),
from which the bather returned into the *apodȳtērium* for
his clothes.

367. In the more modest baths space was saved by using

one room for several purposes. The separate *apodȳtērium* might be dispensed with, as the bather could undress and dress in either the *frīgidārium* or *tepidārium* according to the weather; or the *ūnctōrium* might be dispensed with by using

FIG. 238
STRIGILS FROM POMPEII
Now in the Museo Nazionale, Naples.

the *tepidārium* for this purpose as well as for its own. In this way the suite of five rooms might be reduced to four or three.   On the other hand, private baths had sometimes an additional hot room without water (*lacōnicum*), used for a sweat bath, and a public bathhouse would be almost sure to have an exercise ground (*palaestra*) with a pool at one side (*piscīna*) for a cold plunge and a room adjacent (*dēstrictārium*) in which the sweat and dirt of exercise were scraped off with the *strigilis* (Fig. 238) before and after the bath. It must not be supposed that all bathers went the round of all the rooms in the order given above, though that was common enough.   Some dispensed with the hot bath altogether, taking instead a sweat in the *lacōnicum*, or if that was lacking, in the *caldārium*, removing the perspiration with the strigil (*strigilis*), following this with a cold bath (perhaps merely a shower or douche) in the *frīgidārium* and the rubbing with linen cloths and anointing with oil. Young men who deserted the *Campus* and the Tiber (§ 317) for the *palaestra* and the bath would content themselves with removing the effects of their exercise with the scraper, taking a plunge in the open pool, and then a second scraping and the oil. Much would depend on the time and the tastes of individuals. Physicians, too, laid down strict rules for their patients to follow.

368. Heating the Bath. The arrangement of the rooms, were they many or few, depended upon the method of heating.

This in early times must have been by stoves placed in the
rooms as needed, but by the end of the Republic the furnace
had come into use, heating the rooms as well as the water
with a single fire. The hot air from the furnace was not conducted into the rooms directly, as it is with us, but was made
to circulate under the floors and through spaces around the
walls, the temperature of the room depending upon its
proximity to the furnace (§ 218). The *lacōnicum*, if there was
one, was put directly over the furnace, next to it came the
caldārium and then the *tepidārium;* the *frīgidārium* and the

apodȳtērium, hav-
ing no need of heat,
were at the greatest
distance from the
fire and without
connection with it.
If there should be
two sets of baths in
the same building,
as there sometimes
were for the accom-
modation of men
and women at the

FIG. 239
SUSPĒNSŪRA

same time, the two *caldāria* were put on opposite sides of
the furnace (see the plan: Fig. 242) and the other rooms
were connected with them in the regular order; the two
entrances were at the greatest distance apart. The method
of conducting the air under the floors is shown in Figure 239.
There were really two floors; the first was even with the
top of the firepot, the second (*suspēnsūra*) with the top
of the furnace. Between them was a space of about two
feet into which the hot air passed.[1] On the top of the fur-

---

[1] This method of heating has been revived in the construction of the great new
cathedral in Liverpool. See *The Classical Weekly*, XVIII, 64.

nace, just above the level, therefore, of the second floor, were two kettles for heating the water. One was placed well back, where the fire was not so hot, and contained water that was kept merely warm; the other was placed directly over the fire and the water in it, received from the former, was easily kept intensely hot. Near them was a third kettle containing cold water. From these three kettles the water was piped as needed to the various rooms. The arrangement will be easily understood after a study of the plans in §§ 376-378.

369. The *Caldārium*. The hot-water bath was taken in the *caldārium* (*cella caldāria*), which served also as a sweat bath when there was no *lacōnicum*. It was a rectangular room. In the public baths its length exceeded its width; Vitruvius says the proportion should be 3:2. One end was rounded off like an apse or bay window. At the other end stood the large hot-water tank (*alveus*), in which the bath was taken by a number of persons at a time. The *alveus* was built up two steps from the floor of the room, its length equal to the width of the room and its breadth at the top not less than six feet. At the bottom it was not nearly so wide; the back sloped inward, so that the bathers could recline against it, and the front had a long broad step, for convenience of descent into it, upon which, too, the bathers sat. The water was received hot from the furnace, and was kept hot by a metal heater (*testūdō*), which opened into the *alveus* and extended beneath the floor into the hot-air chamber. Near the top of the tank was an overflow pipe, and in the bottom was an escape pipe which allowed the water to be emptied on the floor of the *caldārium*, to be used for scrubbing it. In the apse-like end of the room was a tank or large basin of metal (*lābium*, *solium*), which seems to have contained cool water for the douche. In private baths the room was usually rectangular, and then the *lābrum* was placed in a corner. For the accommodation of those using the room for the sweat bath only, there were benches along the wall.

The air in the *caldārium* would, of course, be very moist, while that of the *lacōnicum* would be perfectly dry, so that the effect would not be precisely the same.

370. The *Frīgidārium* and the *Ūnctōrium*. The *frīgidārium* (*cella frīgidāria*) contained merely the cold plunge bath, unless it was made to do duty for the *apodȳtērium*, when there would be lockers on the walls for the clothes (at least in a

Fig. 240
RUINS OF THE BATHS OF CARACALLA IN ROME

public bath) and benches for the slaves who watched them. Persons who found the bath too cold would resort instead to the open swimming pool in the *palaestra*, which would be warmed by the sun. In one of the public baths at Pompeii a cold bath seems to have been introduced into the *tepidā-rium*, for the benefit, probably, of invalids who found even the *palaestra* too cool for comfort. The final process, that of scraping, rubbing, and oiling, was exceedingly important. The bather was often treated twice, before the warm bath and after the cold bath; the first might be omitted, but the second never. The special room, *ūnctōrium*, was furnished with benches and couches. The scrapers and oils were brought by the bathers; they were usually carried along with the towels for the bath by a slave (*capsārius*). The bather might scrape (*dēstringe-re*) and oil (*dēun-gere*) himself, or he might receive a regular massage at the hands of a trained slave. It is probable that in the large baths expert operators could be hired, but we have no direct testimony on the subject. When there was no special *ūnctō-rium*, the *tepidā-rium* or *apodȳtē-rium* was made to serve instead.

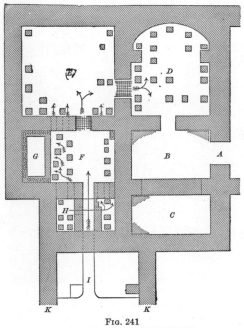

Fig. 241
PLAN OF BATH AT CAERWENT

371. A Private Bathhouse. Figure 241 shows the plan of a private bath in Caerwent, Monmouthshire, England, the ruins of which were discovered in the year 1855. The bath dates from about the time of Constantine (306-333 A.D.), and, small though it is, gives a clear notion of the arrangement of the rooms. The entrance (*A*) leads into the *frīgidārium* (*B*), 10′6″×6′6″ in size, with a plunge (*C*), 10′6″×3′3″. Off *B* is the *apodȳtērium* (*D*),

$10'6'' \times 13'3''$, which has the apse-like end that the *caldārium* ought to have. Next is the *tepidārium* (*E*), $12' \times 12'$, which, contrary to all the rules, is the largest instead of the smallest of the four main rooms. Then comes the *caldārium* (*F*), $12' \times 7'6''$, with its *alveus* (*G*), $6' \times 3' \times 2'$, but with no sign of its *lābrum* left, perhaps because the basin was too small to require any special foundation. Finally comes the rare *lacōnicum* (*H*), $8' \times 4'$, built over one end of the furnace (*I*), which was in the basement room (*KK*). The hot air passed as indicated by the arrows, escaping through openings near the roof in the outside walls of the *apodўtērium*. It should be noticed that there was no direct passage from the *caldārium* (*F*) to the *frīgidārium* (*B*), no special entrance to the *lacōnicum* (*H*), and that the *tepidārium* (*E*) must have served as the *ūnctōrium*. The dimensions of the Caerwent bath as a whole are 31×34 feet.

372. The Public Baths. To the simpler bathhouse of the earlier times as well as to the bath itself was given the name *balneum* (*balineum*), used often by the dactylic poets in the plural, *balnea*, for metrical convenience. The more complex establishments of later times were called *balneae*, and to the very largest, which had features derived from the Greek gymnasia (§ 365), the name *thermae* was finally given. These words, however, were loosely used and often interchanged in practice. Public baths are first heard of after the Second Punic War. They increased in number rapidly; 170 at least were operated in Rome in the year 33 B.C., and later there were more than eight hundred. With equal rapidity they spread through Italy and the provinces;[1] all the towns and even many villages had at least one. They were public only in the sense of being open to all citizens who could pay the modest fee demanded for their use. Free baths did

---

[1] See Walters, H. B., *A Classical Dictionary of Greek and Roman Antiquities*, under *Aquae Sulis*, for illustration and account of a Roman bath in Bath, England.

not exist, except when some magistrate or public-spirited citizen or candidate for office arranged to relieve the people of the fees for a definite time by meeting the charges himself. So Agrippa in the year 33 B.C. kept open free of charge 170 establishments at Rome. The rich sometimes in their wills provided free baths for the people, but always for a limited time.

373. Management. The first public baths were opened by individuals for speculative purposes. Others were built by wealthy men as gifts to their native towns, as such men give hospitals and libraries now; the administration was lodged with the town authorities, who kept the buildings in repair and the baths open by means of the fees collected. Other baths were built by the towns out of public funds, and others were credited to the later emperors. However they were started, the management was practically the same for all. They were leased for a definite time and for a fixed sum to a manager (*conductor*), who paid his expenses and made his profits out of the fees which he collected. The fee (*balneāticum*) was hardly more than nominal. The regular price at Rome for men seems to have been a *quadrāns*, quarter of a cent; the bather furnished his own towels, oil, etc., as we have seen (§ 370). Women paid more, perhaps twice as much, while children up to a certain age, unknown to us, paid nothing. Prices varied, of course, in different places. It is likely that higher prices were charged in some baths than in others in the same city, either because they were more luxuriously equipped or to make them more exclusive and fashionable than the rest, but we have no positive knowledge that this was done.

374. Bathing Hours. The bath was regularly taken between the *merīdiātiō* and the *cēna;* the hour varied, therefore, within narrow limits in different seasons and for different classes (§ 310). In general it may be said to have been taken about the eighth hour, and at this hour all the *conductōrēs* were bound by their contracts to have the baths open and all things in readiness. As a matter of fact many persons preferred to bathe before the *prandium* (§ 302), and some, at least, of the baths in the larger places must have been open then. All were regularly kept open until sunset, but in the smaller towns, where public baths were fewer, it is probable that they were kept open later; at least the lamps found in large numbers in the Pompeian baths seem to point to evening hours. It may be taken for granted that the managers would keep the doors open as long as was profitable.

375. Accommodations for Women. Women of respectability bathed in the public baths, as they bathe in public places now, but with women only, enjoying the opportunity to meet their friends as much as did the men. In the large cities there were separate baths devoted to their exclusive use. In the larger towns separate rooms were set apart for them in the baths intended generally for men. Such a combination bath is discussed in the next paragraph. It will be noted that the rooms intended for use of the women are smaller than those for the men. On combination baths something has been said, too, in § 368. In the very small places the bath was opened to men and women at different hours. Late in the Empire we read of men and women bathing together, but this was true only of women who had no claim to respectability at all.

376. *Thermae.* In Figure 242 is shown a plan of the so-called Stabian Baths at Pompeii, which gives a correct idea of the smaller *thermae* and serves at the same time to illustrate the combination of baths for men and women under the same roof. In the plan the unnumbered rooms opening upon the surrounding streets were used for shops and stores independent of the baths; those opening within were for the use of the attendants or for purposes that cannot now be deter-

mined. The main entrance (*1*), on the south, opened upon
the *palaestra* (*2*), which was inclosed on three sides by
colonnades and on the west by a bowling alley (*3*), where
large stone balls were found. Behind the bowling alley was
the *piscīna* (*6*) open to the sun, with a room on either side
(*5*, *7*) for douche baths and a *dēstrictārium* (*4*) for the use

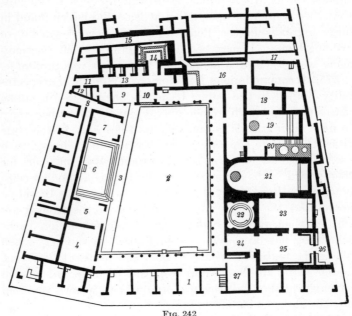

Fig. 242
PLAN OF THE STABIAN BATHS AT POMPEII

of the athletes. There were two side entrances (*8*, *11*) at the
northwest, with the porter's room (*12*) and manager's office
(*10*) within convenient reach. The room (*9*) at the head of
the bowling alley was for the use of the players and may be
compared with the similar room for the use of the gladiators
marked *9* in Figure 225. Behind the office was the *lātrīna*,
marked *14*.

377. On the east are the baths proper, the men's to the south. There were two *apodȳtēria* (*24, 25*) for the men. Each had a separate waiting-room for the slaves (*26, 27*); (*26*) had a door to the street. Then come in order the *frīgidārium* (*22*), the *tepidārium* (*23*), and the *caldārium* (*21*). The *tepidārium*, contrary to custom, had a cold bath, as explained in § 370. The main entrance to the women's bath was at the northeast (*17*), but there was also an entrance from the northwest through the long corridor (*15*); both opened into the *apodȳtērium* (*16*). This contained in one corner a cold bath, as there was no separate *frīgidārium* in the baths for women. Then come in the regular position the *tepidārium* (*18*) and *caldārium* (*19*). The furnace (*20*) was between the two *caldāria*, and the position of the three kettles (§ 368) which furnished the water is clearly shown. It should be noticed that there was no *lacōnicum*. It is possible that one of the two rooms marked *24* and *25* was used as an *ūnctōrium*. The ruins show that the rooms were most artistically decorated, and there can be no doubt that they were luxuriously furnished. The colonnades and the large waiting-rooms gave ample space for the lounge after the bath, with his friends and acquaintances, which the Roman prized so highly.

378. The Baths of Diocletian. The irregularity of plan and the waste of space in the Pompeian *thermae* just described are due to the fact that the baths were rebuilt at various times with all sorts of alterations and additions. Nothing can be more symmetrical than the *thermae* of the later emperors, as a type of which is shown in Figure 243 the plan of the Baths of Diocletian, dedicated in 305 A.D. They lay in the northeastern part of the city and were the largest and, with the exception of those of Caracalla, the most magnificent of the Roman baths. The plan shows the arrangement of the main rooms, all in the line of the minor axis of the building; the uncovered *piscīna* (*1*), the *apodȳtērium* and *frīgidārium*

(*2*), combined as in the women's baths at Pompeii, the *tepidārium* (*3*), and the *caldārium* (*4*), projecting beyond the other rooms for the sake of the sunshine. The uses of the surrounding halls and courts cannot now be determined, but it is clear from the plan that nothing known to the luxury of the time was omitted. In the sixteenth century Michelangelo restored the *tepidārium* as the Church of S. Maria degli Angeli, one of the largest in Rome. The cloisters that he built in the east part of the building are now a museum. One of the corner domed halls of the Baths is now a church, and a number of other institutions occupy the site of part of the ruins. An idea of the magnificence of the central room may be had from Figure 237, showing a restoration of the corresponding room in the Baths of Caracalla.

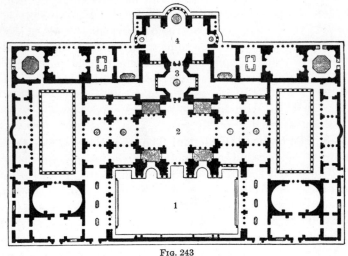

FIG. 243
THE BATHS OF DIOCLETIAN

CHAPTER X
TRAVEL AND CORRESPONDENCE. BOOKS.

REFERENCES: Marquardt, 469-474, 731-738, 799-833; Blümner, 442-474; Becker-Göll, II, 418-462, 469-474, III, 1-45;
Friedländer, I, 268-428; Sandys, *Companion*, 208-210, 237-242,
421-435; Cagnat-Chapot, I, 246-249, 41-56, II, 285-296; Pauly-
Wissowa, under *carpentum, cisium, charta, Brief, Buch, Buch-
handel, Bibliotheken, cursus pūblicus;* Smith, Harper's, Rich,
Walters, Daremberg-Saglio, under *via, tabula* or *tabulae, liber,
bibliothēca,* and other Latin words in the text of the book; Baumeister, 2079-2083, 354-356, 361-364; Jones, *Companion*, 40-51;
McDaniel, 168-178. See, also, Hall, 1-21, 53-69; Johnston, 13-26,
27-47; Showerman, 485-502, 235-236; Gest, 108-169.

379. For our knowledge of the means of traveling employed by the Romans we have to rely upon indirect sources
(§ 12), because, if any books of travel were written by
Romans they have not come down to us. We know, however, that while no distance was too great to be traversed, no
hardships too severe to be surmounted, the Roman in general
cared little for travel in itself, for the mere pleasure, that is,
of sight-seeing as we enjoy it now. This was partly due to
his blindness to the charms of nature in its wilder aspects,
more perhaps to the feeling that to be out of Rome was
to be forgotten. He made once in his life the grand tour
(§ 116), when he visited famous cities and strange or historic
sites; he spent a year abroad, in the train of some general
or governor (§ 117), but, this done, only the most urgent
private affairs or public duties could draw him from Italy.
And Italy meant to him only Rome and his country estates
(§ 145). These he visited when the hot months had closed ·
the courts and adjourned the senate; he roamed restlessly
from one estate to another, enjoying the beauty of the
Italian landscape, but impatient for his real life to begin

again.   Even when public or private business called him
from Rome, he kept in touch with affairs by correspondence; he expected his friends to write him voluminous letters,
and was ready himself to return the favor when positions
should be reversed.   So, too, the proconsul kept as near to
Rome as the boundaries of his province would permit.

380. Travel by Water.   The means of travel were the

Fig. 244
A ROMAN BOAT
From a relief at Rome.

same as our ancestors used
a century ago.   By water
the Roman used sailing
vessels, rarely canal boats;
by land, vehicles drawn by
horses or mules; for short
distances sedan chairs or
litters.   There were, however, few transportation
companies, few lines of
boats or vehicles, that is,
few running between cer-
tain places and prepared to carry passengers at a fixed price
on a regular schedule.   The traveler by sea whose means
did not permit him to buy or charter a vessel for his
exclusive use had often to wait at the port until he found
a boat going in the desired direction and then make
such terms as he could for his passage.   And there were
other inconveniences.   The boats were small, and this
made them uncomfortable in rough weather; the lack of
the compass caused them to follow the coast as much as
possible, and this often increased the distance; in winter
navigation was usually suspended.   Traveling by water was,
therefore, avoided as much as possible.   Rather than sail
to Athens from Ostia or Naples, for example, the traveler
would go by land to Brundisium, by sea across to Dyrrachium, and continue the journey by land.   Between
Brundisium and Dyrrachium boats were constantly passing, and the only delay to be feared was that caused by

bad weather. The short voyage, only 100 miles, was usually made within twenty-four hours. For a detailed and easily accessible account of an ancient voyage, see *Acts*, xxvii-xxviii.

381. Travel by Land. The Roman who traveled by land was distinctly better off than Americans of the time of the Revolution. His inns were not so good, it is true, but his

FIG. 245
AN ARCH OVER A ROMAN ROAD

vehicles and horses were fully equal to theirs, and his roads were the best that have been built until very recent times. Horseback riding was not a recognized mode of traveling (the Romans had no saddles), but there were vehicles, covered and uncovered, with two wheels and with four, for one horse and for two or more. These were kept for hire outside the gates of all important towns, but the price is not known. To save the trouble of loading and unloading the baggage it is probable that persons going great distances took their own vehicles and merely hired fresh horses from time to time. There were, however, no post-routes and no places where horses were changed at the end of regular stages for ordinary travelers, though there were such arrangements for couriers and officers of the government, especially in the provinces. For short journeys and when haste was not necessary, travelers would naturally use their own horses as well as their own carriages. Of the pomp which often accompanied such journeys something has been said in § 152.

Fig. 246
A ROMAN CARRIAGE
From a tombstone in Verona.

382. The Vehicles. The streets of Rome were so narrow that wagons and carriages were not allowed upon them at hours when they were likely to be thronged with people. Through many years of the Republic, and for at least two centuries afterwards, the streets were closed to all vehicles during the first ten hours of the day, with the exception of four classes only: market wagons, which brought produce into the city by night and were allowed to leave empty the next morning, transfer wagons (*plaustra*) conveying material for public buildings, the carriages used by the Vestals, *flāminēs*, and *rēx sacrōrum* in their priestly functions, and the chariots driven in the *pompa circēnsis* (§ 343) and in triumphal processions. Similar regulations were in force in almost all Italian towns. This, in imperial times, made general the use within the walls of the *lectīca* and its bearers (§ 151). (See illustration in Walters under *lectīca*, and Sandys, *Companion*, page 209.) Besides the litter in which the passenger reclined, a sedan chair in which he sat erect was common. Both were covered and curtained. The *lectīca* was sometimes used for short journeys, and in place of the six or eight bearers, mules were sometimes put between the shafts, one before and one behind, but not until late in the Empire. Such a litter was called *basterna*.

383. Carriages. The monuments show us rude representations of several kinds of vehicles and the names of at least eight have come down to us, but we are not able positively to connect the representations and the names, and have, therefore, only very general notions of the form and

Fig. 247
A FAMILY TRAVELING IN THE CARPENTUM
From a relief now in the Louvre, Paris.

construction of even the most common. Some, of ancient design, were retained wholly, or chiefly, for use as state carriages in the processions that have been mentioned. Such were the *pīlentum* and the *carpentum*, the former with four wheels, the latter with two, both covered, both drawn by two horses, both used by the Vestals and priests. The *carpentum* is rarely spoken of as a traveling carriage; its use for such a purpose was a mark of luxury. According to Livy, the first Tarquin came from Etruria to Rome in a *carpentum*, and the one shown in Figure 247 is a carriage of this kind. The *petōritum* also was used in the triumphal processions, but only for the spoils of war. It was essentially a baggage wagon and was occupied by the servants in a traveler's train. The *carrūca* was a luxurious traveling van, of which we hear first in the late Empire. It was furnished with a bed on which the traveler reclined by day and slept by night.

Fig. 248
THE CISIUM

384. The *Raeda* and *Cisium*.

The usual traveling vehicles, however, were the *raeda* and the *cisium*. The former was large and heavy, covered, had four wheels, and was drawn by two or four horses. It was regularly used by persons accompanied by their families or having baggage with them, and was kept for hire for this purpose. For a rapid journey, when a man had no traveling companions and little baggage, the two-wheeled and uncovered *cisium* was the favorite vehicle. It was drawn by two horses, one between shafts and the other attached by traces; it is possible that three were sometimes used. The *cisium* had a single seat, broad enough to accommodate a driver also. It is very likely that the cart on a monument found near Trèves (Fig. 248) is a *cisium*, but the identification is not certain. Cicero speaks of these carts making fifty-six miles in ten hours, probably with one or more changes of horses. Other vehicles of the cart type that came into use during the Empire were the *essedum* and the *covīnus*, but we do not know how they differed from the *cisium*. These carts had no springs, but the traveler took care to have plenty of cushions. It is worth noticing that none of the vehicles mentioned has a Latin name; the names, with perhaps one exception (*pīlentum*), are Celtic. In like manner, most of our own carriages had foreign names, and many French terms came in with the automobile.

385. The Roads. The engineering skill of the Romans and the lavish outlay of money made their roads the best that the world has known until very recent times (§ 386). They were strictly military works, built for strategic purposes, intended to facilitate the dispatching of supplies to the frontier and the massing of troops in the shortest possible time. Beginning with the first important acquisition of territory in Italy (the *Via Appia* was built in 312 B.C.) they kept pace with the expansion of the Republic and the

FIG. 249
THE APPIAN WAY, NEAR ROME
This shows ancient paving and curbstones and the ruins of ancient
tombs which line the road.

Empire, so that a great network of roads covered the Roman world, all indeed leading to Rome, as the proverb has it. In Britain, for instance, the roads, some of which are still in use, converged at Londinium (London). They ran as far north as the wall of Antoninus Pius, and out to points on the coast. After crossing the Channel one found the highway again as it may still be traced, running down through Gaul and on to Rome. In the fourth century of our era nineteen great roads, it is said, went out from Rome through the fifteen gates of the Wall of Aurelian. In Italy

roads were built at the cost of the State; in the provinces
the conquered communities bore the expense of construction
and maintenance, but the work was done under the direction
of Roman engineers and often by the legions between cam-

Fig. 250
A ROMAN BRIDGE IN SOUTHERN FRANCE

paigns.   Roads ran in lines as straight as possible between
the towns they were to connect, with frequent crossroads and
branch roads only less carefully constructed.   The grade
was always easy, because hills were cut through, gorges and
rivers were crossed on arches of solid stone, and valleys and
marshes were spanned by viaducts of the same material.

386. The surface of the roads was rounded, and there
were gutters at the sides to carry off rain and melted snow.

Milestones showed the distance from the starting-point of the road and often that to important places in the opposite direction, as well as the names of the consuls or emperors under whom the roads were built or repaired (Fig. 251). The roadbed was wide enough to permit the meeting and passing, without trouble, of the largest wagons. For the pedestrian there was a footpath on either side, sometimes paved, and seats for him to rest upon were often built by the milestones. The horseman found blocks of stone set here and there for his convenience in mounting and dismounting. Where springs were discovered, wayside fountains for men and watering-troughs for cattle were constructed. Such roads often went a hundred years without repairs, and some portions of them have endured the traffic

FIG. 251
A MILE-STONE

of centuries and are still in good condition today. It might be noted that in the United States good roads finally came into existence and milestones and crossroad signs were revived neither for military nor business purposes, but for pleasure driving, with the increased use of the automobile.

387. Construction. Our knowledge of the construction of the military roads is derived from a treatise of Vitruvius on pavements and from existing remains of the roads themselves. The Latin phrase for building a road, *mūnīre viam*, epitomizes the process exactly, for *mūnīre* means "to build a wall" (*moenia*); and throughout its full length, whether carried above the level of the surrounding country (Fig. 252) or in a cut below it, the road was a solid wall averaging

L · CAECILI · Q · F
METEL · COS
CXIX
ROMA[1]

---

[1]Inscription on a milestone of the *Via Salaria*. "Erected by the consul [117 B.C.] Lucius Caecilius Metellus, etc. One hundred nineteen (miles) from Rome."

fifteen feet in width and perhaps three feet in height. The method followed will be easily understood from Figure 253.

FIG. 252
EMBANKMENT AND CROSS SECTION

A cut (*fossa*) was first made of the width of the intended road and of a depth sufficient to hold the filling, which varied with the nature of the soil. The earth at the bottom of the cut (*E*) was leveled and made solid with heavy rammers (§ 213). Upon this was spread the *statūmen* (*D*), a foundation course of stones not too large to be held in the hand; the thickness of the layer varied with the porosity of the soil. Over this came the *rūdus* (*C*), a nine-inch layer of coarse concrete or rubble (§ 210) made of broken stones and lime. Over this was laid the *nucleus* (*B*), a six-inch bedding of fine concrete made of broken potsherds and lime, in which was set the final course (*A*) of blocks of lava or of other hard stone furnished by the adjacent country. This last course (*dorsum*) made the roadway (*agger viae*) and was laid with the greatest care so as to leave no seams or fissures to admit water or to jar the wheels of vehicles. In the diagram the stones are represented with the lower

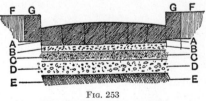

FIG. 253
CONSTRUCTION OF A ROAD

surface flat, but they were commonly cut to a point or edge, as in Figure 252, in order to be held more firmly by the *nucleus*. The *agger* was bounded on the sides by *umbōnēs* (*G,G*), curbstones, beyond which lay the footpaths (*F, F*), *sēmitae* or *marginēs*. On a subsoil of rocky character the foundation course or even the first and second courses might be unnecessary. On the less traveled branch roads the *agger* seems to have consisted of a thick course of gravel (*glārea*), well rounded and compacted, instead of the blocks of stone, and the crossroads may have been of still cheaper materials.

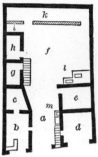

FIG. 254
PLAN OF AN INN,
POMPEII

388. The Inns. There were numerous lodging houses and restaurants in all the cities and towns of Italy, but all were of the meanest character. Respectable travelers avoided them scrupulously; they either had stopping-places of their own (*dēversōria*) on roads that they used frequently, or claimed entertainment from friends (§ 303) and *hospitēs* (§ 184), whom they would be sure to have everywhere. Nothing but accident, stress of weather, or unusual haste could drive them to places of public entertainment (*tabernae dēversōriae, caupōnae*). The guests of such places were, therefore, of the lowest class, and innkeepers (*caupōnēs*) and inns bore the most unsavory reputations. Food and beds were furnished the travelers, and their horses were accommodated under the same roof and in unpleasant proximity. The plan of an inn at Pompeii (Fig. 254) may be taken as a fair sample of all such houses. The entrance (*a*) is broad enough to admit wagons into the wagon-room (*f*), behind which is the stable (*k*). In one corner is a watering-trough (*l*), in another a *lātrīna* (*i*). On either side of the entrance is a wine-room (*b, d*), with the room of the proprietor (*c*) opening off one of them. The small rooms (*e, g, h*) are bedrooms, and other bedrooms in the second story over the wagon-room were reached by the back stairway. The front stairway has an entrance of its own from the street; the rooms reached by it had probably no connection with the inn. Behind this stairway on the lower floor was a fireplace (*m*) with a water heater. An idea of the moderate prices charged in such places may be had from a bill which has come down to us in an inscription preserved in the Museum at Naples:

Fig. 255
A WEARY TRAVELER
A relief in the Uffizi Gallery, Florence.

a pint of wine with bread, one cent; other food, two cents; hay for a mule, two cents. The corners of streets, especially at points close to the city walls, were the favorite sites for inns, and they had signs (the elephant, the eagle, etc.) like those of much later times.

389. Speed. The lack of public conveyances running on regular schedules (§ 380) makes it impossible to tell the speed ordinarily made by travelers. Speed depended upon the total distance to be covered, the degree of comfort demanded by the traveler, the urgency of his business, and the facilities at his command. Cicero speaks of fifty-six miles in ten hours by cart (§ 384) as something unusual, but on Roman roads it ought to have been possible to go much faster, if fresh horses were provided at the proper distances, and if the traveler could stand the fatigue. The sending of letters gives the best standard of comparison. There was no public postal service, but every Roman of position had among his slaves special messengers (*tabellāriī*), whose business it was to deliver important letters for him. They covered from twenty-six to twenty-seven miles on foot in a day, and from forty to fifty in carts. We know that letters were sent from Rome to Brundisium, 370 Roman miles, in six days, and on to Athens in fifteen more. A letter from Sicily would reach Rome on the seventh day, from Africa on the twenty-first day, from Britain on the thirty-third day, and from Syria on the fiftieth day.

Fig. 256

A TRAVELER STARTING OUT
Grave relief from Aesernia,
now at Naples.

In the time of Washington it was no unusual thing for a letter to take a month to go from the eastern to the southern states in winter.

390. Sending Letters. For long distances, especially over seas, sending letters by special messengers was very expensive, and, except for the most urgent matters, recourse was had to traders and travelers going in the desired direction. Persons sending messengers or intending to travel themselves made it a point of honor to notify their friends in time for letters to be prepared; they also carried letters for entire strangers, if requested to do so. There was great danger, of course, that letters sent in this way might fall into the wrong hands or be lost. It was customary, therefore, to send a copy of an important letter (*litterae eōdem exemplō, ūnō exemplō*), or at least an abstract of its contents, by another person and, if possible, by a different route. It was also possible to disguise the meaning by the use of fictitious names known to the correspondents only or by the employment of regular cipher codes. Suetonius tells us that Caesar simply substituted for each letter the one that stood three places lower in the alphabet (D for A, E for B, etc.), but elaborate and intricate systems were also in use.

391. Writing the Letter. The extensive correspondence carried on by every Roman of position (§ 379) made it impossible for him to write with his own hand any but the most important of his letters or those to his dearest friends.

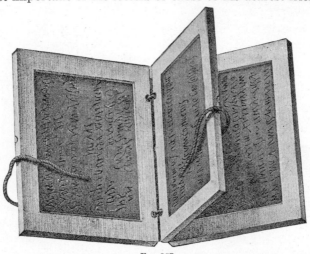

Fig. 257
CŌDICILLĪ

The place of the stenographer and writing machine of to-day was taken by slaves or freedmen, often highly educated (§ 154), who wrote at his dictation. Such slaves were called in general terms *librāriī*, more accurately *servī ab epistulīs, servī ā manū,* or *āmanuēnsēs.* Notes and short letters were written on tablets (*tabellae:* Fig. 49, page 87) of firwood or ivory of various sizes, often fastened together in sets of two or more by wire hinges (*cōdicillī, pugillārēs:* Fig. 257). The inner faces were slightly hollowed out, and the depression was nearly filled with wax, so as to leave a raised rim about the edges, much like the frame of an old-fashioned slate. Upon the wax the letters were traced with an ivory, bone, or metal tool (*stilus, graphium*) which had one end

pointed, like a pencil, for writing, and the other broad
and flat, like a paper cutter, for smoothing the wax
(Fig. 258). With the flat end mistakes could be
corrected or the whole letter erased and the tablets
used again, often for the reply to the letter itself.
Such tablets were used not only for letters, but also
for the schoolboy's exercises (§ 110) and for business documents. For longer communications the
Romans used a coarse "paper" (*papȳrus*), the making of which is described in § 394. Upon it they
wrote with pens made of split reeds and with a
thick ink made of soot (lampblack) mixed with res-
inous gums. Paper, pens, and ink were poor, and
papyrus expensive, and the bulky tablets, which
could be used again, were preferred for all but the
longest letters. Parchment did not come into general use until the fourth or
fifth century of our era.

**392. Sealing and Opening
of Letters.** For sealing the
letter, thread (*līnum*), wax
(*cēra*), and a seal (*signum*)
were necessary. The seal (§ 255)
not only secured the letter against
improper inspection, but also at-
tested the genuineness of those
written by the *librāriī;* autograph
signatures seem not to have been
thought of. The tablets were put
together face to face with the writing on the inside, and the thread
was passed around them and through
small holes bored through them, and was then securely tied.
Upon the knot softened wax was dropped and to this the seal

Fig. 258
BRONZE
STILUS

Fig. 259
A LETTER WRITTEN ON
PAPYRUS

was applied.   Letters written on sheets of papyrus (*schedae*) were rolled longitudinally and then secured in the same way.   On the outside was written the name of the person addressed, with, perhaps, the place where he was to be found,

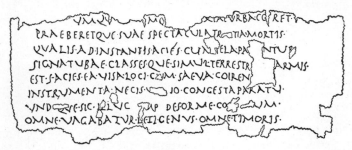

Fig. 260
FRAGMENT OF A PAPYRUS ROLL FROM HERCULANEUM

if the letter was not sent by a special messenger.   When the letter was opened, care was taken not to break the seal; the cutting of the thread gave access to the contents.   If the letter was preserved, the seal was kept attached to it in order to attest its authenticity.   In the fifth chapter of the *Third Oration against Catiline* Cicero describes the opening of a letter.

393. Books.   Almost all the materials used by the ancients to receive writing were known to the Romans and used by them for one purpose or another, at different times.   For the publication of works of literature, however, during the period when the great classics were produced, the only material was "paper" (*papȳrus*), the only form the roll (*volūmen*).   The book of modern form (*cōdex*), written on parchment (*membrānum*), played an important part in the preservation of the literature of Rome, but did not come into use for the purpose of publication until long after the canon of the classics had been completed and the great masters had passed away.   The Romans adopted the papyrus roll from the Greeks; the Greeks had received it from the Egyptians.   When the Egyptians first used it we do not know, but we have in museums Egyptian papyrus rolls that were written at least twenty-five hundred years before the Christian era.   The oldest Roman books of this sort that have been preserved were found in Herculaneum, badly charred and broken.   Those that have

Fig. 261
PAPYRUS PLANTS GROWING

been deciphered contain no Latin author of any value.   A specimen of the writing on one of these, a mere fragment by an unknown author, is shown in Figure 260.   At the time it was buried, there were still to be seen rolls in the hand-writing of the Gracchi, and autograph copies of works of Cicero, Vergil, and Horace must have been common enough. All these have since perished, so far as we know.

394. Manufacture of Papyrus. The papyrus reed (Fig. 261) had a triangular stem which reached a maximum height of perhaps fourteen feet with a thickness of four or five inches. The stem contained a pith of which the paper was made by a process substantially as follows. The stem was cut crosswise, and the rind removed. The pith was cut into thin lengthwise strips as evenly as possible. The first cut seems to have been made from one of the angles to the middle of the opposite side, and the others parallel with it to the right and to the left. The strips were then assorted according to width, and enough of them were arranged side by side as closely as possible upon a board to make their combined width almost equal to the length of the single strip. Across these was laid another layer at right angles, with perhaps a coating of glue or paste between them. The mat-like sheet that resulted was then soaked in water and pressed or hammered into a substance not unlike our paper, called by the Romans, *charta*. After the sheets (*schedae*) had been dried and bleached in the sun, they were freed of rough places by scraping and trimmed into uniform sizes, depending upon the length of the strips of pith. The fewer the strips that composed each sheet, or in other words the greater the width of each strip, the closer the texture of the *charta* and the better its quality. It was possible, therefore, to grade the paper by its size, and the width of the sheet rather than its height was taken as the standard. The best quality was sold in sheets about ten inches wide; the poorest that could be used to write upon came in sheets about six inches wide. The height in each case was perhaps one inch to two inches greater. It has been calculated that a single papyrus plant would make about twenty sheets, and this number seems to have been made the commercial unit of measure (*scāpus*) by which the paper was sold, a unit corresponding roughly to our quire.

395. Pens and Ink. Usually only the upper surface of the sheet—formed by the horizontal layer of strips—was used for writing. These strips, which showed even after the process of manufacture, served to guide the pen of the writer. In the case of books where it was important to keep the number of lines constant to the page, lines were ruled with a circular piece of lead. The pen (*calamus*) was made of a reed brought to a point and cleft in the manner of a quill pen. For the black ink (*ātrāmentum:* § 391) was occasionally substituted the liquid of the cuttlefish. Red ink was much used for headings, ornaments, and the like, and in pictures the inkstand is generally represented with two compartments (Fig. 263), presumably one for black ink, one for red ink. The ink was more like paint than modern ink, and, when fresh, could be wiped off with a damp sponge. It could be washed off even when it had become dry and hard.

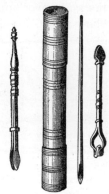

FIG. 262
PENS, PENCASE,
AND CRAYON
HOLDER

To wash sheets in order to use them a second time was a mark of poverty or niggardliness, but the reverse side of *schedae* that had served their purpose was often used for scratch paper, especially in the schools (§ 110).

396. Making the Roll. A single sheet might serve for a

FIG. 263
A DOUBLE INKSTAND

letter or other brief document, but for literary purposes many sheets might be required. These were not fastened side by side in a back, as are the separate sheets in our books, or numbered and laid loosely together, as we arrange sheets in our letters and manuscripts, but, after the writing was done, they were glued together at the sides (not at the tops) into a long, unwieldy strip, with the lines on each sheet running parallel with the length of the strip, and with the writing on each sheet forming a column perpendicular to the length of the strip. On each side of the sheet, therefore, a margin was left as the writing was done, and these margins, overlapping and glued together, made a thick blank space, a double thickness of paper, between every two

Fig. 264
WRITING INSTRUMENTS

sheets in the strip. Very broad margins, too, were left at the top and bottom, where the paper would suffer from use a great deal more than in our books. When the sheets had been securely fastened together in the proper order, a thin slip of wood might be glued to the left (outer) margin of the first sheet, and a second slip (*umbilīcus*) to the right (also outer) margin of the last sheet, much as a wall map is mounted today. When not in use, the volume was kept tightly rolled about the *umbilīcus*. Some authorities think that the *umbilīcī* were not always attached to the rolls, but that they might be slipped in when the books were in use.[1]

397. A roll intended for permanent preservation was always finished with greatest care. The top and bottom (*frontēs*) were trimmed perfectly smooth, polished with pumice-stone, and often painted black. The back of the roll was rubbed with cedar oil to defend it from moths and mice. To the ends of the *umbilīcus* were added knobs (*cornua*), sometimes gilded or painted a bright color. The first sheet would be used for the dedication, if there was one, and on the back of it were frequently written a few words giving a clue to the contents of the roll; sometimes a pen-and-ink portrait of the author graced this page. In many books the full title and the name of the author were written only at the end of the roll on the last sheet, but in any case to the top of this

[1] For a discussion of the *umbilicus* see *The Classical Weekly*, VI, 169-170.

sheet was glued a strip of parchment (*titulus*) with the title and author's name upon it; the strip projected above the edge of the roll. For every roll a parchment cover was made, cylindrical in form, into which it was slipped from the top; the *titulus* alone was visible. If a work was divided into several volumes (see § 398), the rolls were put together in a bundle (*fascis*) and kept in a wooden box (*capsa, scrīnium*) like a modern hat box. When the cover was removed, the *titulī* were visible, and the roll desired could be taken without disturbing the others (Fig. 265). The rolls were kept sometimes in cupboards (*armāria*: § 230), where they were laid lengthwise on the shelves with the *titulī* to the front, as shown in the figure in the next paragraph.

FIG. 265
CAPSA

398. Size of the Rolls. When a volume was consulted, the roll was held in both hands and unrolled column by column with the right hand, while with the left the reader rolled up the part he had read on the slip of wood fastened to the margin of the first sheet (Fig. 266), or around the *umbilicus*. When he had finished reading, he rolled the volume back upon the *umbilicus*, usually holding it under his chin and turning the *cornua* with both hands. In the case of a long roll this turning backward and forward took much time and patience and must have sadly soiled and damaged the roll itself. The early rolls were always long and heavy. There was theoretically no limit to the number of sheets that might be glued together, and consequently

FIG. 266
READING A ROLL
Relief from a sarcophagus.

none to the size or length of the roll. It was made as long as was necessary to contain the given work. In ancient Egypt rolls were put together of more than fifty yards in length, and in early times rolls of corresponding length were used in Greece and Rome. From the third century B.C., however, it had become customary to divide works of great length into two or more volumes. The division at first was purely arbitrary and made wherever it was convenient to end the roll, no matter how much the unity of thought was interrupted. A century later authors had begun to divide their works into convenient parts, each part having a unity of its own, such as the five "books" of Cicero's *Dē Fīnibus*, and to each of these parts, or "books," a separate roll was allotted. An innovation so convenient and sensible quickly became the universal rule. It even worked backward; some ancient works, which had not been divided by their authors, e.g., Herodotus, Thucydides, and Naevius, were now divided into books. About the same time, too, it became the custom to put upon the market the sheets already glued together, to the amount at least of the *scāpus* (§ 394). It was, of course, much easier to glue two or three of these together, or to cut off the unused part of one, than to work with the separate sheets. The ready-made rolls, moreover, were put together in a most workmanlike manner. Even sheets of the same quality (§ 394) would vary slightly in toughness or finish, and the manufacturers of the roll were careful to put the very best sheets at the beginning, where the wear was the most severe, and to keep for the end the less perfect sheets, which might sometimes be cut off altogether.

399. Multiplication of Books. The process of publishing the largest book at Rome differed in no important respect from that of writing the shortest letter. Every copy was made by itself, the hundredth or the thousandth taking just as much time and labor as the first had done.

The author's copy would be distributed for reproduction among a number of *librāriī*, his own, if he were a man of wealth, a Caesar or a Sallust; his patron's, if he were a poor man, a Terence or a Vergil. Each of the *librāriī* would write and rewrite the portions assigned to him, until the required number of copies had been made. The sheets were then arranged in the proper order, if the ready-made rolls were not used, and the rolls were mounted as has been described (§ 396). Finally the books had to be looked through to correct the errors that were sure to be made, a process much more tedious than the modern proofreading, because every copy had to be corrected separately, as no two copies would show precisely the same errors. Books made in this way were almost exclusively for gifts, though friends would exchange books with friends and a few might find their way into the market. Up to the last century of the Republic there was no organized book trade, and no such thing as commercial publication. When a man wanted a book, instead of buying it at a bookstore he borrowed a copy from a friend and had his *librāriī* make him as many more as he desired. In this way Atticus made for himself and Cicero copies of all the Greek and Latin books on which he could lay his hands, and distributed Cicero's own writings everywhere.

400. Commercial Publication. The publication of books at Rome as a business began in the time of Cicero. There was no copyright law and no protection therefore for author or publisher. The author's pecuniary returns came in the form of gifts or grants from those whose favor he had won by his genius; the publisher depended, in the case of new books, upon meeting the demand before his rivals could market their editions, and, in the case of standard books, upon the accuracy, elegance, and cheapness of his copies. The process of commercial publication was essentially the same as the method already described, except that larger numbers of *librāriī* would be employed. The pub-

lisher would estimate as closely as possible the demand for
any new work that he had secured, would put as large a
number of scribes upon it as possible, and would take care
that no copies should leave his establishment until his whole
edition was ready. After the copies were once on sale, they
could be reproduced by anyone. The best houses took all
possible pains to have their books free from errors; they had
competent correctors to read them copy by copy, but in
spite of their efforts blunders were legion. Authors sometimes corrected with their own hands the copies intended
for their friends. In the case of standard works purchasers
often hired scholars of reputation to revise their copies for
them, and copies of known excellence were borrowed or
hired at high prices for the purpose of comparison.

401. Rapidity and Cost of Publication. Cicero tells us
of Roman senators who wrote fast enough to take evidence
verbatim, and the trained scribes must have far surpassed
them in speed. Martial tells us that his second book could
be copied in an hour. It contains five hundred and forty
verses, which would make the scribe equal to nine verses
to the minute. It is evident that a small edition, consisting
of copies not more than twice or three times as numerous as
the scribes, could be put upon the market more quickly than
it could be produced now. The cost of the books varied,
of course, with their size and the style of their mounting.
Martial's first book, containing eight hundred twenty
lines and covering thirty-nine pages in Teubner's text,
sold at thirty cents, fifty cents, and one dollar; his *Xenia*,
containing two hundred and seventy-four verses and covering fourteen pages in Teubner's text, sold at twenty cents,
but cost the publisher less than ten. Such prices would
hardly be considered excessive now. Much would depend
upon the reputation of the author and the consequent demand. High prices were put on certain books. Autograph copies—Gellius (late in the second century, A.D.)

says that one by Vergil cost the owner one hundred dollars
—and copies whose correctness was vouched for by some
recognized authority commanded extraordinary prices.

402. Libraries. The gathering of books in large private
collections began to be general only toward the end of the
Republic.   Cicero had considerable libraries not only in
his house at Rome, but also at his countryseats.   Probably the bringing to Rome of whole libraries from the East
and Greece by Lucullus and Sulla started the fashion of
collecting books; at any rate collections were made by
many persons who knew and cared nothing about the
contents of the rolls, and every town house had its library
(§ 206) lined with volumes.   In these libraries were often
displayed busts of great writers and statues of the Muses.
Public libraries date from the time of Augustus.   The first
to be opened in Rome was founded by Asinius Pollio (died 4
A.D.), and was housed in the *Ātrium Lībertātis.*   Augustus
himself founded two others, and the number was brought
up to twenty-eight by his successors.   The most magnificent
of these was the *Bibliothēca Ulpia,* founded by Trajan.
Smaller cities had their libraries, too, and even the little
town of Comum boasted one founded by Pliny the Younger
and supported by an endowment that produced thirty
thousand sesterces annually.   The public baths often had
libraries and reading-rooms attached to them (§ 365).

Fig. 267
LIBRĪ

CHAPTER XI

SOURCES OF INCOME AND MEANS OF LIVING.
THE ROMAN'S DAY

REFERENCES: Friedländer, I, 98-206; Sandys, *Companion*, 202-208, 358-362; Blümner, 372-385, 589-656, and *Technologie*, throughout; Marquardt, 607-634; Jones, 316-337; Pauly-Wissowa, under *collēgium;* Harper's under *commerce, collēgium;* Daremberg-Saglio, under *collēgium, mercātūra;* Smith, under *mercātūra, collēgia,* and other Latin words in the text of this book; Mau-Kelsey, 383-404; Fowler, *Social Life*, 24-134, 263-284; Dill, 100-195, 251-286; Abbott, *The Common People*, 205-234; Waltzing; Frank, *An Economic History*, 219-345; Rostovtzeff, 38-74, 75-100, 101-124; McDaniel, 106-140; Showerman, 137-147, 225-233, 234-250, 251-266; Davis; Charlesworth; Knapp, "Roman Business Life as Seen in Horace," *The Classical Journal*, 3 (1907), 111-122.

403. It is evident from what has been said that abundant means were necessary to support the state in which every Roman of position lived. It will be of interest also to see how the great mass of the people made the scantier living with which they were forced to be content. For the sake of the inquiry it will be convenient, if not very accurate, to divide the people of Rome into the three great classes of nobles, knights, and commons into which political history has distributed them. The "nobles" during the Republic had come to be the descendants of those men who had held curule office. As the senate was composed of those men who had held the higher magistracies, the nobles and the senatorial families were practically the same, for the political influence of this group was so strong that it was very difficult for a "new man" (*novus homō*) to be elected to office. At the same time it must be remembered that for a long time there was no hard and fast line drawn between the classes; a noble might, if he pleased, associate himself with the knights, provided the noble possessed the $20,000 which one must have to be a knight, and during the Republic any free-born citizen might aspire to the highest offices of the State, however poor in pocket or talent he might be. The drawing of definite lines that under the later Empire fixed citizens in hereditary castes began under Augustus, when he limited eligibility for the curule offices to those whose ancestors had held such offices. This regulation formed a hereditary nobility, to which additions were made at the emperor's pleasure. The emperor also revised the lists of the knights, and so controlled admission to that Order.

404. Careers of the Nobles. The nobles inherited certain of the aristocratic notions of the old patriciate. These limited their business activities and had much to do with the corruption of public life in the last century of the Republic. Men in their

FIG. 268
AMPHORA OF GLAZED TERRA COTTA
In the Metropolitan Museum of Art, New York.

position were held to be above all manner of work, with the hands or with the head, for the sake of gain. Agriculture alone was free from debasing associations, as it has been in England until recent times, and statecraft and war were the only careers fit to engage the energies of these men. Even as statesmen and generals, too, they served their fellow citizens without material reward, for no salaries were drawn by the senators, no salaries attached to the magistracies or to positions of military command. This theory had worked well enough in the time before the Punic Wars, when every Roman was a farmer, when the farmer produced all that he needed for his simple wants, when he left his farm only to serve as a soldier in his young manhood or as a senator in his old age, and returned to his fields, like Cincinnatus, when his services were no longer required by his country. Under the aristocracy of later times, however, the theory subverted every aim that it was intended to secure.

405. Agriculture. The farm life that Cicero has described so eloquently and praised so enthusiastically in his *Catō Maior* would have scarcely been recognized by Cato himself and, long before Cicero wrote, had become a memory or a dream. The farmer no longer tilled his fields, even with the help of his slaves. The yeoman class had largely disappeared from Italy. Many small holdings had been absorbed in the vast estates of the wealthy landowners, and the aims and methods of farming had wholly changed. This is discussed elsewhere (§§ 146, 434), and it will be sufficient here to recall the fact that in Italy grain was no longer raised for the market, simply because the market could be supplied more cheaply from overseas. The grape and the olive had become the chief sources of wealth, and Sallust and Horace complained that for them less and less space was being left by the parks and pleasure grounds (§ 145). Still, the making of wine and oil under the direction of a careful steward (§ 148) must have been very profitable in Italy, and many of the nobles had plantations in the provinces as well, the revenues of which helped to maintain their state at Rome. Further, certain industries that naturally arose from the soil were considered proper enough for a senator, such as the development and management of stone quarries, brickyards, tile works, and potteries (§ 146).

406. Political Office. During the Republic politics must have been profitable only for those who played the game to the end. No salaries were attached to the offices, and the indirect gains from one of the lower magistracies would hardly pay the expenses necessary to secure the next office in order. Spending great sums of money on the public games had been an obvious way to win popularity so long as the people voted at elections; it continued to be a heavy obligation even when under the Empire this right to vote was taken from the people. The gain came through positions in the provinces. The quaestorship might be spent in a province; the praetorship and consulship were sure to be followed by a year abroad. To honest men the places gave the opportunity to learn of profitable investments. A good governor was often selected by a community to look after its interests in the capital, and this meant an honorarium paid in the form of valuable presents from

Fig. 269
ROMAN POTTERY JARS
Now in the Toronto Museum.

time to time. Cicero's justice and moderation as quaestor in Sicily earned him a rich reward when he came to prosecute Verres for plundering that province, and when he was in charge of the grain supply during his aedileship. To corrupt officials the provinces were gold mines. Every sort of robbery and extortion was practiced, and the governor was expected to enrich not merely himself but also the *cohors* (§ 118) that had accompanied him. Catullus complains bitterly of the selfishness of Memmius, who prevented his staff from plundering a poor province. The story of Verres may be read in any history of Rome; it differs from that of many governors only in the fate that overtook the offender. Though in the Imperial period there were great reforms in the administration of the provinces, the salaries then paid the governors did not always save the provincials from extortion.

407. The Law. Closely connected with the political career then, as now, was that of the law, at all periods the obvious way to prominence and political success, and the only way to such advancement for persons without family influence. There were no conditions imposed for practicing in the courts. Anyone could bring suit against anyone else on any charge that he pleased, and it was no uncommon thing for a young politician to use this license for the purpose of gaining prominence, even when he knew there were no grounds for the charges he brought. On the other hand, the lawyer had been forbidden by law to accept pay for his services. In olden times the client had of his right gone to his patron for legal advice (§ 179); the lawyer of later times was theoretically at the service of all who applied to him. Men of the highest character made it a point of honor to put their technical knowledge at the disposal of their fellow citizens. At the same time the statutes against fees were easily evaded. Grateful clients could not be prevented from making valuable presents, and it was a very common thing for generous legacies to be left to successful advocates. Cicero had no other source of addition to his income, so far as we know, but while he was never a rich man he owned a house on the Palatine (§ 222, note) and half a dozen countryseats (§ 448), lived well, and spent money lavishly on works of art that appealed to his tastes, and on books (§ 206). Finally the statutes against fees came to be so generally disregarded that the Emperor Claudius fixed the fees that might be asked. Corrupt judges (*praetōrēs*) could find other sources of income then as now, of course, but we hear more of this in relation to the jurors (*iūdicēs*) than in relation to the judges, probably because with a province before him the *praetor* did not think it worth his while to stoop to petty bribe-taking.

408. The Army. The spoils of war went nominally into the treasury of the State. Practically they passed first through the hands of the commanding general, who kept what he pleased for himself, his staff (§ 118), and his soldiers, and sent the rest to Rome. The opportunities were magnificent, and the Roman general understood how to use them all.

Some of them were legitimate enough according to the usages of the time: the plunder of the towns and cities that were taken, the ransom exacted from those that were spared, the sale of captives as slaves (§ 134). Entirely illegitimate, of course, were the fortunes made by furnishing supplies to the army at extravagant prices or diverting these supplies to private uses. The reconstruction of the conquered territory brought in returns equally rich; it is safe to say that the Aedui paid Caesar well for the supremacy in central Gaul that he assured them after his defeat of the Helvetii. The civil wars that cost the best blood of Italy made the victors

Fig. 270
ROMAN GLASS FROM POMPEII
Now in the Museo Nazionale, Naples.

immensely rich. Besides the looting of the public treasury, the estates of men in the opposing party were confiscated and sold to the highest bidder. The proceeds went nominally to the treasury of the new government, but the proceeds were infinitesimal in comparison with the profits. After Sulla had established himself in Rome, the names of friends and foes alike were put on the proscription lists, and if powerful influence was not exerted in their behalf they lost lives and fortunes. For such influence they had to pay dearly. One example may be cited. The estate of one Roscius of Ameria, valued at $300,000, was bid in for one hundred dollars by Lucius Chrysogonus, a freedman of Sulla, because no one dared bid against the creature of the dictator. The settling of the soldiers on grants of land made good business for the three commissioners who superintended the distribution of the land. The grants were always of farms owned and occupied by adherents of the beaten party, and the bribes came from both sides.

409. Careers of the *Equitēs*. The name of knight (*eques*) had lost its original significance long before the time of

Fig. 271
PORTRAIT BUST OF L.
CAECILIUS JUCUNDUS, A
POMPEIAN BANKER
Now in the Museo Nazionale,
Naples.

Cicero. The *equitēs* had become the class of capitalists who found in financial transactions the excitement and the profit that the nobles found in politics and war. Under the Empire certain important administrative posts were turned over to the *equitēs*, and there came to be a regular equestrian *cursus honōrum*, but the *equitēs* continued to be on the whole the business class. It was the immense scale of their operations that relieved them from the stigma that attached to working for gain, just as in modern times the wholesale dealer may have a social position entirely beyond the hopes of the small retailer. From early times their syndicates had financed and carried on great public works of all sorts, bidding for the contracts let by the magistrates. Though "big business" never exerted the power at Rome attributed to it in modern times, in the later years of the Republic the *equitēs* as a body exerted considerable political influence, holding in fact the balance of power between the senatorial and the democratic parties. As a rule they exerted this influence only so far as was necessary to secure legislation favorable to them as a class, and to insure as governors for the provinces men that

would not look too closely into their transactions there. For
in the provinces the knights as well as the nobles found
their best opportunities. Their chief business in the provinces was collecting the revenues on a contract basis. For
this purpose syndicates were formed, which paid into the
public treasury a lump sum fixed by the senate, and reim-
bursed themselves by collecting what they could from the
province. While the system lasted, the profits were far beyond all reason, and the word "publican" became a synonym
for "sinner." Besides farming the revenues, the *equitēs*
"financed" provinces and allied states, advancing money to
meet the ordinary or extraordinary expenses. Sulla levied a
contribution of 20,000 talents (about $20,000,000) in Asia.
The money was advanced by a syndicate of Roman capitalists, and they had collected the amount six times over, when
Sulla interfered, for fear that there would be nothing left for
him in case of future needs. More than one pretender was
set upon a puppet throne in the East in order to secure the
payment of sums previously lent to him by the capitalists.
The operations of the *equitēs* as individuals were only less
extensive and less profitable. The grain in the provinces,
the wool, and the products of mines and factories could be
moved only with the money advanced by them. They
ventured also to engage in commercial enterprises abroad
that were barred against them at home, doing the buying
and selling themselves, not merely supplying the money to
others. They lent money to individuals, too, though at
Rome money-lending was discreditable. The usual rate of
interest was twelve per cent, but Marcus Brutus was lending
money at forty-eight per cent in Cilicia, and trying to collect
compound interest, too, when Cicero went there as governor
in 51 B.C., and he expected Cicero to enforce his demands
for him.

410. Business and Commerce. Roman commerce covered
all known lands and seas, though Italy had little export

trade. Pliny the Elder tells us that the trade with India and
China took from Rome $5,000,000 yearly. The West sent
more raw materials than the East, and fewer finished articles.
Bankers (*argentāriī*) united money-changing with money-
lending. Money-changing was very necessary in a city into
which came all the coins of the known world; money-lending
was never looked upon as entirely respectable for a Roman,

Fig. 272
SHOPPING SCENE
The salesmen are showing cloth to two seated customers, while the latter's slaves look on.
From a relief now in the Uffizi Gallery, Florence.

but there can be no doubt that many a Roman of the highest
respectability drew large profits from this business, carried
on discreetly in the name of a freedman. The bankers took
deposits, paid interest, and made payments on written
orders. They helped their clients to find investments, and
through their foreign connections could supply letters of
credit to travelers.

411. The wholesale trade was to a large extent in the hands
of the capitalists (*equitēs*); the retail business was conducted
chiefly by freedmen and foreigners. The supplying of food to
the city must have given employment to thousands, but the

producer seems to have dealt directly with the retailer, as a rule, and there were few middlemen.   The clothing trade has been mentioned already (§ 271).   No factory system seems to have developed there.   The spinning and weaving were probably done at home by women who may have contracted for the disposition of their work with the large dealers, the fullers, perhaps, as the cloth had to go through their hands

FIG. 273
SEWING UTENSILS
These are much like the sewing utensils in common use today.

for finishing (§ 271).   There are not many traces of a regular factory system, but something of the sort seems to have been developed in iron at Puteoli, in fine copper and bronze work at Capua, perhaps also in silverware and in glass, and at Rome in brick and tile.

412. Building operations were carried on to an immense scale and at an immense cost.   Public buildings and many of the important private buildings were erected by contract.

There can be little doubt that the letting of the contracts for the public buildings was made very profitable for the officers who had it to do, but it must be admitted on the other hand that the building was well done. Crassus seems to have done a sort of salvage business. When buildings seemed certain to be destroyed by fire, he would buy their contents at a nominal sum, and then fight the flames with gangs of slaves that he had trained for the purpose. The slave trade itself, though disreputable, was very considerable, and large fortunes were

FIG. 274
ROMAN BUILDING TOOLS
In the British Museum, London.

amassed in it (§ 139). The heavy work of ordinary laborers was performed almost entirely by slaves (§ 143), and much work was then done by hand that is now done by machinery. The book business has been mentioned (§ 400).

413. Professions and Trades. The professions and trades, between which the Romans made no distinction, in the last years of the Republic were practically given over to the *libertīnī* (§ 175) and to foreigners. Of these something has been said already. Some occupations were considered unsuitable for a gentleman. Undertakers and auctioneers were disqualified for office by Caesar. Architecture was considered respectable. Cicero put it on a level with medicine.[1] Teachers were poorly paid and were usually looked upon with contempt (§ 121). Vespasian first endowed professorships in the liberal arts. The place of the modern newspaper was taken by letters written as a business by persons who collected all the news, scandal, and gossip of the city, had it copied by slaves, and sent it to persons away from the city who did not wish to trouble their friends (§ 379) and who were willing to pay for the news.

Fig. 275

PORTRAIT OF HATERIUS, A PHYSICIAN
Grave relief in the Museo Laterano, Rome.

414. Physicians. Some physicians were well paid in the Imperial period, if we may judge by those attached to the court. Two of these left a joint estate of $1,000,000, and another received from the Emperor Claudius a yearly stipend of $25,000. In knowledge and skill in both medicine and surgery they do not seem to have been much behind the practitioners of two centuries ago. Surgery seems to have developed in early times chiefly in connection with the necessary treatment of wounds in warfare. Medicine, apart from religious rites to gods of health or disease, must have been limited for a long period to such household remedies and charms as Cato describes in his work on farming.

---

[1]For a most important passage relating to the Roman attitude toward trade and business see Cicero, *De Officiis*, I, 150-151.

415. The first foreign surgeon, a Greek, came to Rome in 219 B.C. Physicians and surgeons were as a rule slaves, freedmen, or foreigners, especially Greeks. The great number of Greek medical terms in use today testifies to Greek influence in the history of medicine. Caesar gave citizenship to Greek physicians who settled in Rome, and Augustus granted them certain privileges. The great houses were apt to

have carefully trained physicians among their own slaves. We can judge of ancient medical and surgical methods from books on the subject that have come down to us, such as those of Celsus, a Roman who wrote in the first century of our era, and Galen, the great Greek physician who came to Rome in the reign of Hadrian. Surgical instruments, too, have been found at Pompeii and elsewhere. Galen says that by his time surgery (*chīrurgia*) and medicine (*medicīna*) had been carefully distinguished. There were oculists, dentists, and other specialists, and occasionally women physicians. In the second century of our era many cities had regularly salaried medical officers for the treatment of the poor, and gave them rooms for offices. By Trajan's time there were regular army doctors attached to the legions, as there probably had been before, though we know little of them. There were no medical schools. Physicians took pupils, and let them go with them on their rounds. Martial complains of the many cold hands that felt his pulse when a doctor called with a train of pupils.

416. The Soldiers. The free-born citizens of Rome below the nobles and the knights may be roughly divided into two classes, the soldiers and the proletariat. The civil wars had driven them from their farms or had unfitted them for the work of farming, and the pride of race or the competition of slave labor had closed against them the other avenues of industry, numerous as these must have been in the world's capital. The best of these free-born citizens turned to the army, which had ceased to be composed of citizen-soldiers, called out to meet a special emergency for a single campaign, and disbanded at its close. From the time of the reorganization by Marius, at the beginning of the first century before our era, this was what we should call a regular army, the soldiers enlisting for a term of twenty years, receiving stated pay and certain privileges after an honorable discharge. In time of peace—when there *was* peace—they were employed on public works (§ 385). The pay was small, perhaps forty or fifty dollars a year with rations in Caesar's time, but this was as much as a laborer could earn by the hardest kind of toil, and the soldier had the glory of war to set over against the stigma of work, and hopes of presents from his commander and the privilege of occasional pillage and plunder. After he had completed his time, he might, if he chose, return to Rome, but many had formed connections in the communities where their posts were fixed and preferred to make their homes there on free grants of land, an important instrument in spreading Roman civilization.

417. The Proletariat. In addition to the idle and the profligate attracted to Rome by the free grain and by the other allurements that bring a like element into our cities now, large numbers of the industrious and the frugal had been forced into the city by the loss of their property during the civil wars and the failure to find employment elsewhere. No exact estimate of the number of these unemployed people can be given, but it is known that before Caesar's time it had passed the mark of 300,000. Relief was occasionally given by the establishing of colonies on the frontiers

—in this manner Caesar put as many as 80,000 in the way of
earning their living again, short as was his administration
of affairs at Rome—but it was the least harmful element that
was willing to emigrate. The dregs were left behind. Aside
from beggary and petty crimes the only source of income

Fig. 277
AN ANCIENT FOOD SHOP
Food and hot drinks were served from such places. Kettles containing hot food
were set in the holes in the masonry counters as described on page 343.

for such persons was the sale of their votes; this made them a
real menace to the Republic. Under the Empire their
political influence was lost, and the State found it necessary
to make distributions of money occasionally to relieve their
want. Some of them played client to the upstart rich (§ 181),
but most of them were content to be fed by the State and
amused by the shows and games (§ 322).

418. Small Tradesmen. Little is to be found in literature
about the small tradesman or the free laborer. From the
excavations at Pompeii, however, we may form some idea of
the shops and the business done in them. It has been said
already that the street sides of residences might be rows of
small shops, most of which were not connected with the
house within (§§ 193, 208, 209). Such a shop was usually a
small room with a counter across the front, closed with heavy

shutters at night. The goods sold over the counter were often made directly behind it. The shoemaker (*sūtor*) had his workbench and his case of lasts (*fōrmae*), and made, sold, and repaired shoes. Some masonry counters show the kettles sunk in them, where the hot food prepared in the shop was kept for sale. In one case change was found lying on the counter as it was left in alarm at the time of the eruption. Locksmiths, goldsmiths, and other craftsmen had the necessary equipment and sold their own goods. There were also retail shops where goods were sold that were produced elsewhere on a larger scale, as the

Fig. 278
A SHOEMAKER
A grave relief in the Palazzo
dei Conservatori, Rome.

red glazed Arretine ware (§ 307) from Arretium and Puteoli, the copper and bronze utensils from Capua, and so on. The shopkeeper might work alone in his small room by day and sleep there at night. The plan of the house of Pansa (§ 208) shows that there were also larger establishments of several rooms, as the bakery, for instance, which, as usual, included mills for grinding the grain (§ 283, Fig. 166), because there were no separate mills. Some shops have stairways leading to a room

Fig. 279
THE TOMB OF A WHOLESALE BAKER
This tomb is outside the Porta Maggiore
at Rome.

or two in the floor above, where the family, we may suppose, lived over the shop. Shoppers drifted along the streets
from counter to counter, buying, bargaining, or "just looking." Martial describes a dandy in the fashionable shopping
district at Rome going from one shop to another. He demands that the covers be taken off expensive table-tops and
that their ivory legs be brought down for his inspection,

FIG. 280
SHOPPING FOR BELTS AND PILLOWS IN ROMAN DAYS
From a bas-relief in the Uffizi Gallery, Florence.

he criticizes objects of art and has certain ones laid aside,
and, leaving at last for luncheon, buys two cups for a penny
and carries them home himself!

419. Free Laborers. Literature has little to say about the
free laborer. Inscriptions, particularly those that deal with
the guilds (§ 420), tell us more. In spite of the increase of
slave labor (§ 131) and the decrease of the native Italian
stock (§ 129), there continued to be free laborers working in
many lines, their numbers constantly swelled by the manumission of slaves (§ 175). They worked at many trades, at

heavy labor, in the cities, and even on the farms (§ 434).
They were not always as well off as many of the slaves or
freedmen, as they were dependent on their own efforts and
the labor market and were without owner or patron on
whom they might fall back. It is difficult to learn anything
about wages, but they cannot have been high. The free distribution of grain helped the poor citizen at Rome, and vegetables, fruits, and cheese made the rest of his diet. He
could nearly always afford a little cheap wine to mix with
water (§ 298). If he married, his wife helped by spinning or
weaving (§ 411). He lived in a cheap tenement, and in that
mild climate there was no fuel problem. His dress was a

FIG. 281
CUPIDS AS GOLDSMITHS
From a fresco in the House of the Vettii, Pompeii.

rough tunic (§ 268); if shoes were worn they were wooden
shoes or cheap sandals. The public games gave him amusement on the holidays, and the baths were cheap, when not
free (§ 373). The guild gave him his social life (§ 422), and
decent burial was provided by membership in guild or burial
society (§ 475).

420. Guilds. The trades were early organized at Rome
into guilds (*collēgia*), but the original purpose of the guilds
seems to have been to hand down and perfect the technique
of the crafts; at least there was no obstacle in the way of the
workmen who did not belong to the guilds, and there were no
such things as patents or special privileges in the way of
work. Eight of these guilds were older than history, those of

the tanners, cobblers, carpenters, goldsmiths, coppersmiths, potters, dyers, and, oddly enough, the flute-blowers. These all traced their organization to Numa. Numerous others were formed as knowledge of the arts advanced or the division of labor proceeded. Special parts of the city seem to have been appropriated by special classes of workmen, as in our cities, like businesses are apt to be carried on in the

FIG. 282
CUPIDS AS PERFUMERS
From a fresco in the House of the Vettii, Pompeii.

same neighborhood; Cicero speaks of a street of the scythe-makers. The use of guilds and clubs for political purposes in the later years of the Republic led to the suppression of most of them, and from that time the formation of new ones was carefully limited.[1] There seems however to have been no restriction on the formation of the burial societies described in Chapter XIV.

421. Most of our information in regard to the guilds comes from inscriptions of the Imperial age. These organizations differed from both the medieval guilds and the modern trades-unions. There was no system of apprenticeship, and the members did not use their organizations to make demands for better wages or working conditions. As the necessity for competition with slave labor made such demands useless, there were no strikes. The guilds became largely social organizations for men engaged in the same line of work. The drift to specialization shows in the guilds, for,

[1] Government opposition to Christianity was due in large part to the fear that Christian organizations were, or might become, political in character.

whereas in early times there had been only the guild of the cobblers (*sūtōrēs*), there came to be guilds of those who made each kind of shoe, the *calceolāriī*, the *soleāriī*, and so on through the list (§§ 250-251).

422. The guild gave the poor man his best opportunity for social life, and offered to the freedman and occasionally the slave the right to hold office and manage affairs therein that was denied to him outside. Its organization was based on that of the towns (§ 456); the guilds had their magistrates, decurions, and plebs. When there was a distribution of money, the members shared in proportion to their rank in the guild. Each guild had a patron, or patrons, chosen for reputed wealth and generosity. The members of a guild had their regular times and places for meetings of business and festivity, and if prosperous or blessed with a generous patron might own their own hall (*schola*). They filled their treasuries by means of initiation fees, dues, and fines. On the great holidays they marched in processions with their banners. Each guild had its patron deity and common religious rites. Even when a guild was not organized as a funerary association, it often maintained a common burial ground.

423. The Freedman. The process of manumission and the relation of patron to freedman have been described (§ 175). It is impossible to estimate the number of freedmen at any given period of Roman history, but the practice of manumission had grown general enough to cause alarm by the end of the Republic, and Augustus limited it in some degree by legislation. In certain respects the effects of manumission were good. The prospect served to make the slave ambitious and industrious. The practice greatly increased the number of the free laboring class. On the other hand, as the slaves came from all parts of the world (§ 136), a constantly increasing cosmopolitan population was thus added to the native citizen-body, which had been impoverished and weakened by the civil wars. The Greeks and Orientals, clever and industrious, were particularly successful in adapting themselves to the conditions of their slavery and in working their way to freedom. The large Oriental admixture changed the character of the free population in many respects, and for the worse, as the new citizens thus added did not have the same

FIG. 283
ROMAN KEYS
Now in the Museum at Saint-Germain.

political traditions as the native Italians, and had no knowledge and understanding of Roman institutions. The freedmen filled the ranks of many of the trades and professions (§ 413), particularly those despised by the freeborn. Some were highly trained and educated (§ 143); many were masters of a craft or trade learned in slavery (§ 144). A great many became wealthy, and, though many such were often generous and highly useful citizens in their communities, the self-made man, vulgar, purse-proud, and ostentatious, was a ready subject for the satirists. Petronius, who died in Nero's reign, has left us in "Trimalchio's Dinner" a brilliant sketch of the wealthy and vulgar freedmen. In any case neither the freedman nor his son could attain true social equality with the free citizen. The freedmen reached their greatest wealth and power as officials in the Imperial household in the first century, holding important administrative offices that later were transferred to the equestrian order.

424. The "Civil Service." The free persons employed in the offices of the various magistrates were mostly *libertini*. They were paid by the State, and, though appointed nominally for a year only, they seem to have held their places practically during good behavior.   This was largely due to the shortness of the term of the regular magistrates and the rarity of re-election.   Having no experience themselves in conducting their offices, the magistrates would have all the greater need of thoroughly trained and experienced assistants. The highest class of these officials formed an *ōrdō*, the *scrībae*, whose name gives no adequate notion of the extent and importance of their duties.   All that is now done by cabinet officers, secretaries, department heads, bureau chiefs, auditors, comptrollers, recorders, and accountants, down to the work of the ordinary clerks and copyists, was done by these "scribes."   Below them came others almost equally necessary but not equally respected, the lictors, messengers, etc.   These civil servants had special places at the theater and the circus.   The positions seem to have been in great demand, as such places are now in France, for example. Horace is said to have been a clerk in the treasury department.

425. The Roman's Day.[1]   The way in which a Roman spent his day depended, of course, upon his position and business, and varied greatly with individuals and with the particular day.   The ordinary routine of a man of the higher class, the man of whom we read most frequently in Roman literature, was something like this.   He rose at a very early hour—he began his day before sunrise, because it ended so early.   After a simple breakfast (§ 302) he devoted such time at home as was necessary to his private business, looking over accounts, consulting with his managers, giving directions, etc.   Cicero and Pliny the Elder found these early hours the best for their literary work.   Horace tells of lawyers giving free advice at three in the morning.   After his private business was dispatched, the man took his place in the *ātrium*

---

[1] An interesting detailed account is found in *The Classical Weekly*, XVII (1923), 91–95, "The Daily Life of a Roman Gentleman in the First Century A. D.," by J. W. Spaeth, Jr.

(§ 198) for the *salūtātiō* (§ 182), when his clients came to pay their respects, perhaps to ask for the help or advice that he was bound to furnish them (§ 179). All this business of the early morning might have to be dispensed with, however, if the man was asked to a wedding (§ 79), or to be present at the naming of a child (§ 97), or to witness the coming of age (§ 128) of the son of a friend, for all these semi-public functions took place in the early morning. But after them or after the levee the man went to the Forum, attended by his clients and

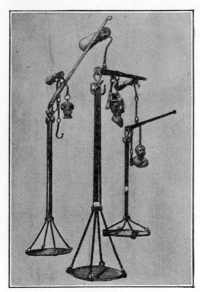

carried in his litter (§ 151) with his *nōmenclātor* (§ 151) at his elbow. The business of the courts and of the senate began about the third hour, and might continue until the ninth or tenth; that of the senate was bound to stop at sunset. Except on extraordinary occasions all business was pretty sure to be over before eleven o'clock, and at this time the lunch was taken (§ 302).

FIG. 284
ROMAN SCALES
Now in the Museo Nazionale, Naples.

426. Then came the midday siesta (*merīdiātiō*, § 302), so general that the streets were as deserted as at midnight; one of the Roman writers fixes upon this as the proper time for a ghost story. Of course there were no sessions of the courts or meetings of the senate on the public holidays; on such days the hours generally given to business might be spent at the theater or the circus or other games.   As a matter of fact some Romans of the better class rather avoided these shows, unless they were officially connected with them, and many of them devoted the holidays to visiting their country estates.   After the siesta, which lasted for an hour or more, the Roman was ready for his regular athletic exercise and bath, either in the *Campus* (§ 317), and the Tiber (§ 317) or in one of the public bathing establishments (§ 365).   The bath proper (§ 367) was followed by the lounge (§ 377), or perhaps by a promenade in the court, which gave a chance for a chat with a friend, or an opportunity to hear the latest news, to consult business associates, in short to talk over any of the things that men now discuss at their clubs.   After this came the great event of the day, the dinner (§ 303), at one's own house or at that of a friend, followed immediately by retirement for the night.   Even on the days spent in the country this program would not be materially changed, and the Roman took with him into the provinces, so far as possible, the customs of his home life.

427. Hours of the Day. The daylight itself was divided into twelve hours (*hōrae*); each was one-twelfth of the time between sunrise and sunset and varied therefore in length with the season of the year.   The length of the day and hour at Rome at different times of the year is shown in the following table:

Month and Day	Length of Day	Length of Hour	Month and Day	Length of Day	Length of Hour
Dec. 23	8° 54′	44′ 30″	June 25	15° 6′	1° 15′ 30″
Feb. 6	9° 50′	49′ 10″	Aug. 10	14° 10′	1° 10′ 50″
March 23	12° 00′	1° 00′ 00″	Sept. 25	12° 00′	1° 00′ 00″
May 9	14° 10′	1° 10′ 50″	Nov. 9	9° 50′	49′ 10″

428. Taking the days of June 25 and December 23 as respectively the longest and shortest of the year, the following table gives the conclusion of each hour for summer and winter:

Time Sunrise	Summer 4° 27′ 00″	Winter 7° 33′ 00″	Time Sunrise	Summer 4° 27′ 00″	Winter 7° 33′ 00″
1st Hour	5° 42′ 30″	8° 17′ 30″	7th Hour	1° 15′ 30″	12° 44′ 30″
2nd Hour	6° 58′ 00″	9° 2′ 00″	8th Hour	2° 31′ 00″	1° 29′ 00″
3rd Hour	8° 13′ 30″	9° 46′ 30″	9th Hour	3° 46′ 30″	2° 13′ 30″
4th Hour	9° 29′ 00″	10° 31′ 00″	10th Hour	5° 2′ 00″	2° 58′ 00″
5th Hour	10° 44′ 30″	11° 15′ 30″	11th Hour	6° 17′ 30″	3° 42′ 30″
6th Hour	12° 00′ 00″	12° 00′ 00″	12th Hour	7° 33′ 00″	4° 27′ 00″

In the same way the hours may be calculated for any given day, if the length of the day and the hour of sunrise are known, but for all practical purposes the old couplet will serve:

> The English hour you may fix,
> If to the Latin you add six.

When the Latin hour is above six it will be more convenient to subtract than to add.

FIG. 285
ROMAN SILVER SPOONS

CHAPTER XII

FARMING AND COUNTRY LIFE

REFERENCES: Blümner, 67-89, 533-589; Sandys, *Companion*, 66-84, 211-217; Daremberg-Saglio, under *rūstica rēs, vīlla, hortus;* Smith, Walters, Harper's, under *agricultūra, hortus, vīlla;* Pauly-Wissowa, under *Ackerbau, Gartenbau, Gemüsebau, Getreide;* Cagnat-Chapot, II, 295-308; Friedländer, II, 193-202; Mau-Kelsey, 355-366; Jones, 170-184, 304-315; Showerman, 251-266. See, also, Heitland, 131-335; Frank, *An Economic History,* 1-15, 55-68, 96-107, 219-274; Rostovtzeff, 180-194; "The Crooked Plow," by Fairfax Harrison, *The Classical Journal,* 11 (1916), 323-332; *Roman Farm Management;* Tanzer.

429. In addition to casual references in literature our sources of information about Roman farming include treatises on the subject by the Elder Cato, who wrote in the second century B.C., Varro and Vergil, at the beginning of our era, Columella and Pliny the Elder in the first century A.D., and Palladius in the fourth. Works of art occasionally show something of the implements used. Excavations have brought to light remains of villas in different parts of the Roman world, and occasionally metal parts of implements have been found.

430. Agriculture was the industry of early Italy. The great number of rural festivals in the calendar testifies to its dominating influence. The interests of the Romans of all times were agricultural rather than commercial. Agriculture was the proper business of the senatorial class (§ 404). Writers of all periods looked back to the days when a Roman citizen-farmer tilled his own land with the help of a slave or two and when a dictator might be called from the plow.

431. Something has been said already (§ 272) of the varied climatic and geographic conditions of Italy and the possi-

bility of varied production. There was deep alluvial soil in
the valley of the Po. The volcanic ash that formed the plain
of Latium gave a subsoil rich in potash and phosphate, but
the surface soil was thin and easily exhausted. Great forests
once grew on plains and hills that have been bare for centuries. Cutting the timber from the hills caused erosion and
rendered much land unproductive. With the lack of forests
on the hills to retain moisture the seasons in the lowland
were affected.

Fig. 286
A VILLA BY THE WATER
From a Pompeian fresco.

432. An Ideal Farm. Cato discusses carefully the purchase of an estate (*fundus*). He thought that an ideal farm
would lie at the foot of a hill facing south. It was important
to choose a healthful locality and make sure of the water
supply. The soil should be good, rich, not too heavy. The
land should not be too nearly level, for that made drainage
difficult. The farm should be in a prosperous neighborhood
near a good market town, and on a good road if not near a
river or the sea. Cato advised buying a farm in good condition and with good buildings. There should be a local supply
of labor to be hired for the harvest or other times of extra
work. He recommends a farm of 240 *iūgera*, about 160 acres,

suitable for diversified farming. Pliny the Younger, when discussing land which joined his, says "The farms are productive, the soil rich, the water supply good; they include pastures, vineyards, and timberland that gives a small but regular return." He speaks of the saving in equipment, supervision, and skilled service gained by the concentration of holdings—a good concrete instance of the rise of the great estates (*lātifundia*) as small-scale farming became less profitable (§ 434). On the other hand, he says, to own much land in one neighborhood is to be exposed too much to the same climatic risks.

433. Small Farms. Evidence of farm life before 200 B.C. is chiefly traditional. The early farms were very small. We read of holdings of two *iūgera* (about an acre and a half). These seem too small for the support of a family unless they were accompanied with rights in community land. Holdings of seven *iūgera* (a little over five acres) are frequently mentioned, and were assigned when allotments were made of the public land in 393 B.C. Such a farm could be worked by the owner with a hired man or a slave or two. The houses were grouped together in villages, and the men went out to their work each day. Thus there was not the loneliness of farm life so often complained of in this country. With hand labor and simple tools the Romans did intensive farming indeed, or rather, gardening.

434. Various conditions led to the decrease in the number of small farms and the increase of the large estates (*lātifundia*). The devastation of Italy by Hannibal led to the ruin of many farmers and the abandonment of much land. The loss of life in that war brought a great decrease in free labor. The richer citizens bought large tracts of land or leased them from the government and worked them with slaves. The small farmer naturally found competition increasingly difficult (§ 129). And when the importation of grain made wheat-growing in Italy no longer profitable (§ 282), or when the ex-

haustion of the surface soil in Latium forced the small farmer
to give up the struggle, the wealthy landowner could afford
to plant his lands with vines or olives, or to turn large tracts
into pasture, and wait for his investment to become profitable. However, in parts of Italy, particularly in the remote
or hilly sections, small farms were worked at all periods. The
lātifundia were regularly worked by slaves under a *vīlicus*
(§ 145). Tenant farmers (*colōnī*) are rarely referred to during
the Republic but become increasingly common later. Horace
had five tenants on part of his Sabine farm; he worked the rest
himself, through his *vīlicus*. Free labor on the farms did not
entirely disappear, for we read that extra hands were hired
at times.

435. Drainage and Fencing. The land was drained
with care. Open ditches were used in heavy soils, covered
ones in light. The covered drains were filled halfway with
stones, gravel or brush, and then filled to the top with soil.
Open furrows were left across the fields to drain into the
ditches. Careful drainage produced thriving farms in sections that are now marshes where people cannot live or work
on account of the malaria. On the other hand, most careful
conservation of water and the building of aqueducts, dams,
and cisterns made land productive in Africa where we now
find ruins of Roman cities in wastes of sand.

436. Four kinds of fencing are described: hedges, fences of
pickets interlaced with brush or of posts pierced with holes for
the connecting rails, the "military fence" of ditch and bank,
and walls of stone, burned or sun-dried brick, or concrete.
Trees were often planted along roads, property lines, and
fence rows, sometimes, of course, for windbreaks.

437. Plowing and Manuring. Cato said that the first and
second rules of good farming were to plow well, and the third
to manure well. Farmyard manure was stored in piles, old
and new separately. Ancient writers advised that, where
stock was not kept, the farmer should make such a compost

heap as one does now for gardening, piling together leaves, weeds, straw, and the like, with the ashes from burning hedge clippings and other rubbish that does not decay readily. The Romans understood green manuring, and though they had no knowledge of nitrogen-fixing bacteria, they did understand planting legumes and plowing them under, green. Without litmus paper they knew how to test soil for sourness.

FIG. 287
PEASANT WITH OX TEAM AND PRIMITIVE PLOW
Bronze figurines in the Museo di Villa Giulia, Rome.

438. Plows (*arātra*) were small and light. Some were of iron, some of wood. A wooden plow is still in use in Italy where the surface soil is thin and light and the ground stony. Some plows were straight, some curved. Heavy plowing was done with the straight plow. The field was plowed twice; the first time the plow was held straight, the second, sloping. The modern plow does the same work with one operation. Oxen were used for plowing, and 120 Roman feet, the length that the oxen were supposed to plow without resting, was a traditional land measure. The plowing was done in close furrows, and the ground was stirred until it was as fine as dust. The mark of good plowing was to leave no sign of the plow. The ancient Romans thought that harrowing after sowing was an evidence of bad plowing. Pliny the Younger tells of land that had to be plowed nine times.

439. Calendar. The traditional knowledge of astronomy was important to the farmer, as a basis for the calendar of operations. The beginning and ending of the seasons was fixed by the positions of stars or constellations, and the heliacal rising and setting of certain stars indicated the seasons even to the day. This was the more important because of the confusion of the calendar before it was regulated by Caesar.

FIG. 288
ROMAN FARM IMPLEMENTS
Now in the Museum at Saint-Germain.

440. Farm Implements. Farm slaves (*familia rūstica*) have already been discussed (§§ 145-146), and something has been said of the work they were called upon to do. On the great estates skilled craftsmen of all sorts were kept. The smaller farmer might arrange to hire them, when needed, of his neighbor. Implements included different sorts of hoes and rakes, spades and forks. There were pruning knives, sickles, scythes, and similar implements. The plow has been mentioned already (§ 438), and there were primitive forms of the harrow. Where grapes or olives were grown, presses and storage jars were part of the permanent equipment.

441. Crops. The Roman farmer understood something of

seed selection and practiced rotation of crops.   He followed
wheat with rye, barley, or oats.   The second or fourth year
beans or peas might be planted, sometimes to be plowed
under green as stated above (§ 437), or alfalfa was put in.
Alfalfa (*mēdica*) was well established in Italy before the
beginning of our era; according to Pliny the Elder, it was
brought from Greece, having come there from Asia.   In
other cases the land was left fallow every second or third year.
Sometimes it was left fallow the year before wheat was
planted.   It was then plowed in the spring and summer as
well as in the fall.

442. Cato lists farm crops in the order of their importance
in his time.   First he puts the vineyard, then the vegetable
garden, willow copse, olive grove, meadow, grain fields,
wood lot, orchard, and oak grove.   It is to be noted that he
puts grain in the sixth place (§ 282).   The transportation
problem was also a factor here, for, as moving grain overland
was difficult and expensive, it was cheaper to import it from
the provinces by sea.   Vine-growing has been discussed in detail, as have the growing of the olive and processes pertaining to it (§§ 289-292, 293-298).

443. The vegetables grown by the Romans and their
importance in the diet have been mentioned (§ 275).   The
farm garden contained the commonest of these for home
consumption, with herbs for seasoning and for the home
remedies (§ 414), bee plants, and garland flowers   These last
were not for garlands at banquets, unless the farm lay near
a town and they were grown for sale, but for garlands to
deck the hearth in honor of the household gods on festival
days (§ 492).   Near the towns market-gardening was profitable, and vegetables, fruits, and flowers were grown.   In
early days a garden had lain behind each house, and the
excavations at Pompeii show occasional traces of small
gardens even behind large town houses (§§ 202, 208).

444. Wheat was sown in the fall (§ 282) and cultivated by hand with the hoe in the spring. At harvest time it was generally cut by hand. Sometimes the reapers cut close to the ground, and after the sheaves were piled in shocks cut off the heads for the threshing. Sometimes they cut the heads first and the standing straw later. There was a simple form of a header pushed by an ox, but this could be used only where the ground was level. Threshing was done by hand on the threshing floor, or the grain was trodden out by cattle, or beaten out by a simple machine. It was winnowed by hand, by the process of tossing it in baskets, or by shovels so that the chaff flew out or away.

FIG. 289
BRONZE FIGURES OF PLOW, CART, AND FARM ANIMALS
The plow is drawn by oxen.
Now in the Metropolitan Museum of Art, New York.

445. Reeds and willows were planted in damp places. Willows were useful for baskets, ties for vines, and other farm purposes. The wood made a quick, hot fire in the kitchen. Vergil knew the willow as a hedge plant, whose early blossoms were loved by the bees. The word *arbustum*, translated by the word "orchard," does not refer to an orchard as we understand the term, but to regular rows of trees, elm, poplar, fig, or mulberry, planted for the training of vines (§ 295), with grass, alfalfa, or vegetables between. Pigs were pastured in the oak groves to feed on the acorns.

446. Varro advised keeping stock and game on all farms. Oxen were used for plowing (§ 438), though that was slow work, but cattle-raising produced milk and cheese and beef (§§ 277, 281). Sheep were valuable for the wool, to be worked up by the women, as well as for the milk and cheese and meat (§ 281). Where olives were grown, the sheep could be pastured on the grass in the groves. When the lowland pastures burned in the summer the flocks were driven to the hills. Goats were kept for the milk. The importance of pork has been mentioned (§ 278), but it must be remembered that the Roman in general ate less meat than we do (§ 273). Fowls were kept at the *vīlla*. Cato says that it is the business of the *vīlica* to see that there are eggs in plenty. In addition to the chickens, geese, ducks, and guinea fowl familiar to us now, pigeons, thrushes, peafowl, and other birds were often raised for market (§ 279). On some of the great estates game was bred in great variety (§ 279). Bees were kept, of course, for honey was used where we use sugar (§ 281).

447. Farmhouses. The ordinary farmhouse (*vīlla rūstica*) was built for use. It was not merely a house, but included the farm buildings gathered around a court (*cohors*) or courts, and was more or less regular in plan. Remains of a number have been discovered near Pompeii, and of others in various parts of the Roman world. They varied, of course, with the size and needs of the farm, its locality, and the taste and needs of the owner. Where the working farmer tilled his own land they must have been small and simple. On the large estates the *vīlla* included quarters for the master's use when he came for inspection or rest. These might be in the second story. Cato recommends that the master's quarters be comfortable, that he may spend the more time on the farm, and Columella adds that they should please the mistress. The room for the *vīlicus* must be near the gate, so that he could keep watch of comings and goings. There were quarters for the slaves (*cellae familiae*), and an *ergastulum*, partly underground and heavily barred, if there were any slaves worked in chains (§ 170). The kitchen was large and the slaves got their breakfast there in the morning and might gather there after work in the evening, if there were not the servants' hall that Varro advises. Vitruvius says that the bath should be near the kitchen (§ 203); we find it so in some of the villas near

Fig. 290
A ROMAN VILLA
From a fresco now in the Museo Nazionale, Naples.

Pompeii. The press-rooms and storage-rooms for the wine were supposed to face north, the rooms for the oil south. There were tool-rooms and wagon-sheds, and Varro's remarks show that there were farmers then who had to be urged to keep their implements under cover. There were stables and a granary, and whatever else was needed for each particular farm. In the court there might be a pool, and if there were no spring or well there were cisterns. If the villa were suitably located on a main-traveled road, part of it was sometimes used for a wineshop or tavern.

448. Country Houses. It has been stated already (§ 145) that the country estates might be of two classes, country-seats for pleasure and farms for profit. In the first case the

location of the house (*vīlla urbāna*, or *pseudourbāna*), the
arrangement of the rooms and the courts, their number and
decoration, would depend entirely upon the taste and means
of the master. Remains of such houses in most varied styles
and plans have been found in various parts of the Roman
world, and accounts of others in more or less detail have come

Fig. 291
A SEASIDE VILLA
From a Pompeian fresco.

down to us in literature, particularly the descriptions of two
of his villas given by Pliny the Younger. Some villas were set
in the hills for coolness, and some near the water. In the
latter case rooms might be built overhanging the water, and
at Baiae, the fashionable seaside resort, villas were actually
built on piles so as to extend from the shore out over the
sea. Cicero, who did not consider himself a rich man, had
at least six villas in different localities. The number is less
surprising when one remembers that there were nowhere the
seaside or mountain hotels so common now, so that it was
necessary to stay in a private house, one's own or another's,
when one sought to escape from the city for change or rest.

449. Vitruvius says that in the country house the peristyle

usually came next the front door. Next was the atrium, surrounded by colonnades opening on the palaestra and walks.
Such houses were equipped with rooms of all sorts for all
occasions and seasons, with baths, libraries, covered walks,
gardens, everything that could make for convenience or
pleasure. Rooms and colonnades for use in hot weather faced
the north; those for winter were planned to catch the sun.
Attractive views were taken into account in arranging the
rooms and their windows.

450. Gardens. At the beginning of our era complaint of
the extent of the pleasure grounds of the great estates and of
the amount of land thus withdrawn from cultivation (§ 145)
had become a literary commonplace. Gardens were an important part of these estates. They were architectural in
character, that is, they were carefully laid out in straight
lines or regular curves. The *xystus* was a parterre of trim
flowerbeds in geometrical designs, edged with clipped box or
rosemary. The favorite flowers were the rose (*rosa*)—the
cabbage rose, the damask, and a few others—lilies (*lilia*) and
violets (*violae*), though *violae* seems to have included stocks,
wallflowers, and perhaps sweet rocket as well.

451. There were the *hippodromus* for driving or riding, and
the *gestātiōnēs* for walking or for an airing in the *lectīca*. The
plane was a favorite shade tree (§ 295). Colonnades or
clipped hedges provided shelter from sun or wind. Garden
houses commanded favorite views and might include *trīclīnia*
(§ 204). If the water supply permitted there were pools,
fountains, and canals, and the terraced hillside gardens gave
opportunity for effective use of water as it fell from level to
level. Vines were trained on trellises or arbors (*pergulae*).
Ivy was trained on trellises, walls, or trees by the *topiā-
rius*, who had to be an expert in clipping the hedges of box,
myrtle, or cypress and in trimming box into the symmetrical
or fantastic shapes that we still call topiary work.

452. If these gardens afforded less color in summer, or less variety of flower and shrub in their season than ours do now, they were much more effective the year round from their careful design and use of evergreen foliage, water, statuary, and permanent architectural features.   During the Renaissance the Roman garden was revived.   It may be studied now, much as the Romans themselves once knew it, in the gardens of the famous Italian villas which landscape gardeners and architects try to reproduce for us today.

Fig. 292
CYPRESSES IN THE VILLA D'ESTE AT TIVOLI

453. Country Life. Little is known of the life of the small farmer.   Ancient as well as modern poets have written charmingly idyllic pictures of the farm and the life upon it, where people still lived and worked as in the brave days of old.   The farmer probably worked hard for seven days and went to town on the market days (*nūndinae*) to sell his produce, see his friends, and hear the news.   His wife looked after the house and the family, supervising the slaves who did the actual work.   The rural festivals added color to the farmer's life, for the old religion kept its force longest in the country, even as it began there.

454. Literature tells us more of the landlord of the large estate. Cato lists the duties of the owner on arrival at the farm. After saluting his household gods, he is to go over the farm himself before calling for the *vīlicus* to make his report. After discussing this and giving further orders, he should go over the accounts and make plans for selling produce on hand and any superfluous stock (§ 159). Pliny the Younger laments the amount of time that has to be given to accounts and the affairs of his tenants, to the hindrance of his literary work. Though the busy city man fled to the country to escape the social duties of the city (§ 426) as well as to rest from his work there, there was no lack of social life among the villas, and the interruptions from this source were sometimes an annoyance too. Exercise, bath, and dinner formed part of the day's routine, as in town. In addition to the exercise of the palaestra one might walk, ride, or drive over the estate. There were hunting and fishing, too, for the sporting landlord and his guests. The guests were numerous, because the lack of good inns made hospitality a constant duty (§ 388).

Fig. 293
A BOAR HUNT
A mosaic found in Rome.

CHAPTER XIII

TOWN LIFE

REFERENCES: Dill, 196-250; Reid, 436-522; Abbott, *Society and Politics*, 3-21; Abbott, *The Common People*, 145-204; Mau-Kelsey, 485-508; Friedländer, *Town Life;* Abbott and Johnson, 56-68, 138-151, 197-231.

455. Little is told us in literature about the life of the country towns (*mūnicipia*). This is the more remarkable because most of the great writers were not Roman-born but

FIG. 294
THE FORUM AT POMPEII
To the north is Vesuvius.

came from the *mūnicipia* of Italy or the provinces. Most of our information is derived from the inscriptions that the citizens of these towns have left behind them, and from the excavations. These remains, dating chiefly from the Imperial

367

Age, may be studied not merely in Italy but in all the provinces.

456. City Government. The towns were for the most part self-governing. The charters of some of them have been found. The magistrates were elected by popular vote, and the election notices painted on the walls at Pompeii show that all classes took a lively interest in the elections. This does not mean that the spirit of the municipalities was demo-

FIG. 295
EXCAVATIONS AT POMPEII
A general view of part of the excavations on each side of one street.

cratic. The classes were divided by clearly-drawn lines. The candidates for office must come from those who were eligible for membership in the town council (*cūria*); for this there was a property qualification. They must be free-born and of good reputation and not engaged in any disreputable business. No salaries were attached to the offices, however. Indeed, each magistrate was expected to pay a fee (*honōrārium*) on his election, and to make substantial gifts for the benefit of the citizens and the beautifying of the town. Like the great magistrates at Rome they were entitled to the *toga praetexta*, the curule chair, the attendance of lictors, and special seats at the games.

457. Town Council. The *cūria*, or town council, usually consisted of one hundred members (*decuriōnēs*), including the ex-magistrates. They had to be of a certain age, at least twenty-five; they had to possess the required amount of property, and be free-born. They were entitled to the best places at the games and to the *bisellia* (§ 355). Apparently they used the city water free of charge, and at any public entertainment or distribution of money they were entitled to

FIG. 296
THE TEMPLE OF JUPITER
This temple is in the main part of the Forum of Pompeii. To the north is Vesuvius.

a larger share than the common people. Each probably paid a fee on his admission to the *cūria* and was expected to make generous gifts of some sort for the benefit of his city.

458. Equitēs. Members of the equestrian order made up the aristocracy of the *mūnicipia* as the "nobles" did at Rome. Conspicuous among them were the retired army officers, occasionally tribunes, but more often the centurions who were sometimes retired with equestrian rank, particularly the *prīmipīlāriī*, or men who had attained the chief centurionship of their legions. Such a man might come back to cut a big figure in his home town (*patria*), or might settle in the province where he had seen service (§ 416). In either case inscriptions often survive to tell us of his war record and his benefactions to his native town.

459. Augustālēs. Below and apart from these were rated the wealthy freedmen. Ineligible for office and council as they were, a special distinction and an opportunity for service and generosity were provided for them in the institution of the *Augustālēs*, a college of priests in charge first of the worship of Augustus and then of the following emperors. Each year

Fig. 297
RUINS OF BATHS AT OSTIA

the *decuriōnēs* selected a board of six (*sēvirī*) to act for that year. At the public ceremonies of which they were in charge they were entitled to wear a gold ring like that of the *equitēs* and the bordered toga. They paid a fee on election, provided the necessary sacrifices, and proudly rivaled the *decuriōnēs* in gifts to the community.

460. Plēbs. Then came the *plēbs*, the citizens not entitled to serve in the council, and below them the poor freedmen. These were the men who kept or worked in the small shops and made up the membership of the many guilds of which we find traces at Pompeii and which must have been very much the same in other cities (§ 420). However hard their work and simple their fare, they could not have found their life mere drudgery. They expected the magistrates to see to it that bread and oil, the two great necessities of life, were abundant and cheap in the markets. They also expected them to furnish entertainment in the shape of games in the amphitheater and theater and of feasts as well. Even small towns had their public baths, where the fee was always

Fig. 298
THE EXTERIOR OF THE AMPHITHEATER AT VERONA

low, and was sometimes remitted for longer or shorter periods by the generosity of wealthy citizens (§ 372).

461. Public Buildings. In its baths, theater, and amphitheater, *fora*, basilicas, paved streets, bridges, aqueducts, arches, and statues, each town was modeled upon Rome. Domestic architecture varied. The Roman houses in Britain and Africa are not of the type that we find at Pompeii (§ 186). But in public buildings and public works the towns were Roman—as can be easily seen wherever their remains are found. Some of the most striking examples are in Africa, where in the Imperial Age the Romans maintained thriv-

ing towns in regions that are desert now (§ 435). The strong
civic pride of each town and the keen rivalry between neighboring towns expressed itself particularly in handsome
buildings and in public works. It has often been said that
at no other time in the world were there so many beautiful
towns as there were in the Roman Empire during the third
century of our era. Yet this does not mean that municipal

Fig. 299
THE INTERIOR OF THE AMPHITHEATER AT VERONA
The seats have been restored for use in modern times.

taxation was heavy or that the revenues from lands and
other city property paid for all these works. Much was
expected from the generosity of the official class, and much
was received (§§ 456-457). Others, women as well as men,
gave liberally. The amphitheater at Pompeii (§ 353) was
given by two men who had held high office in the city.
A very lively and distinguished old lady, Ummidia Quadra-
tilla, gave a temple and amphitheater at Casinum. Among
the gifts of Pliny the Younger to his native town was a
library with funds for its maintenance (§ 402). The dedica-

tion of such a building was often celebrated by the donor
with a feast for the community, where the citizens shared
according to their rank (§ 456). Inscriptions regularly commemorated such gifts. Sometimes in appreciation of his
generosity the *cūria* voted a cit-
izen a statue of honor; sometimes
he paid for the statue, too!

462. Schools. But the municipalities did not show the large
and elaborate school buildings
conspicuous in our towns now
(§ 120), nor were there likely to
be school taxes. Until a very late
period education remained generally a private matter. There
were occasional endowments from
the wealthy for educational purposes, as, more often, for other
charitable foundations. Elementary schools must have been
established in the Italian towns

and throughout the provinces generally with the spread of
Roman influence. The more advanced schools would naturally be found only in the larger towns and cities. At the
beginning of the second century of our era Pliny the Younger
tells of contributing largely to a fund to open a school in
his native town of Comum, that the boys might not have
to go to Mediolanum (Milan). The arguments he uses for
the education of the boys at home are very much like those
used for the establishment of junior colleges in many of
our towns at present. Some boys were sent to Rome for
the sake of better schools and more famous teachers than the
country and provincial towns afforded. Agricola found the
establishment of schools in Britain a useful aid in strength-
ening the Roman hold on the conquered territory.

463. Town Life and City Life. At all times the man who was Roman-born looked down on the country towns and their people. The satirists indeed contrast the quiet simplicity of the municipality with the turmoil and vice of cosmopolitan Rome. But then, as now, many preferred the complexity and excitement of the great city with all its discomforts to the greater amount of comfort that their incomes would have brought them in a town. Property of course was cheaper and rents were lower in the small town. It was possible to live there in a comfortable house on an income that provided only a cramped lodging in one of the great *insulae* of the city. Tunic and sandals could be worn instead of the heavy and expensive toga (§ 240) and shoes (*calceī:* § 251). The range of interests in the small town was narrower, often intensely local. To the energetic and generous citizen this local interest and civic pride offered an outlet, and that it was a welcome one is shown by the keen competition for local honors until a late period of the Empire.

FIG. 301
A STREET IN OSTIA

CHAPTER XIV

BURIAL PLACES AND FUNERAL CEREMONIES

REFERENCES: Marquardt, 340-385; Becker-Göll, III, 481-547; Friedländer, II, 210-218; Pauly-Wissowa, under *columbārium;* Smith, Harper's, Rich, Walters, Daremberg-Saglio, under *columbārium, fūnus, sepulcrum;* Baumeister, 308-311, 1520-1522; Mau-Kelsey, 405-428; Gusman, 44-54; Egbert, 230-242; Lanciani, *Ancient Rome,* 64-67, 129-133; McDaniel, 186-197; Showerman, 418-433.

464. Importance of Burial. The Romans' view of the future life explains the importance they attached to the ceremonial burial of the dead. The soul, they thought, could find rest only when the body had been duly laid in the grave; until this was done it haunted the home, unhappy itself and bringing unhappiness to others. To perform funeral offices was a solemn religious duty, devolving upon the surviving members of the family (§ 34); the Latin expression for such rites, *iūsta facere,* shows that these marks of respect were looked upon as the right of the dead. In the case of a body lost at sea, or for any other reason unrecovered, the ceremonies were just as piously performed; an empty tomb (*cenotaphium*) was erected sometimes in honor of the dead. Such rites the Roman was bound to perform carefully, if he came anywhere upon the unburied corpse of a citizen, because all men were members of the greater family of the commonwealth. In this case the scattering of three handfuls of dust over the body was sufficient for ceremonial burial and the happiness of the troubled spirit, if for any reason the body could not actually be interred.

465. Interment and Cremation. Burial was the way of disposing of the dead practiced most anciently by the Romans, and, even after cremation came into very general use, it was ceremonially necessary that some small part of the remains, usually the bone of a finger, should be buried in the earth. Burning was practiced before the time of the Twelve Tables (traditional date, 451 B.C.), for it is mentioned in them together with burial, but we do not know how long before. Hygienic reasons had probably something to do with its general adoption; this implies, of course, cities of considerable size. By the time of Augustus it was all but universal, but even in Rome the practice of burial was never entirely discontinued, for cremation was too costly for the very poorest classes, and some of the wealthiest and most aristocratic families held fast to the more ancient custom. The Cornelii, for example, always buried their dead until the great dictator, Cornelius Sulla, required his body to be burned for fear that his bones might be disinterred and dishonored by his enemies, as he had dishonored those of Marius. Children less than forty days old were always buried, and so, too, as a rule, were slaves whose funeral expenses were paid by their masters. After the introduction of Christianity burial came again to be the prevailing use, partly because of the increased expense of burning.

466. Places of Burial. The Twelve Tables forbade the burial or even the burning of the dead within the walls of the city. For the very poor, places of burial were provided in localities outside the walls, corresponding in some degree to the potter's field of modern cities. The well-to-do made their burial places as conspicuous as their means would permit, with the hope that the inscriptions upon the monuments would keep alive the names and virtues of the dead, and with the idea, perhaps, that the dead still had some part in the busy life around them. To this end they lined the great roads on either side for miles out of the cities with rows of tombs of the most elaborate and costly architecture. In the vicinity of Rome the Appian Way, as the oldest road (§ 385), showed the monuments of the noblest and most ancient families, but none of the roads lacked such memorials.

Many of these tombs were standing in the sixteenth century; a few still remain. The custom was followed in the smaller towns, and an idea of the importance of the monuments may be had from the so-called "Street of Tombs" outside of Pompeii (Figs. 302, 313). There were other burial places near the cities, of course, less conspicuous and less expensive, and on the farms and country estates like provision was made for persons of humbler station.

Fig. 302
"THE STREET OF TOMBS," OUTSIDE POMPEII

467. The Tombs. The tombs, whether intended to receive the bodies or merely the ashes, or both, differed widely in size and construction according to the different purposes for which they were erected. Some were for individuals only, but these in most cases were strictly public memorials as distinguished from actual tombs intended to receive the remains of the dead. The larger number of those that lined the roads were family tombs, ample in size for whole generations of descendants and retainers of the family, including *hospitēs* (§§ 183-185), who had died away from their own homes, and freedmen (§ 175). Others were erected on a large scale by speculators who sold at low prices space for a few urns to persons not rich enough to erect tombs of their own and without any claim on a family or clan burying place (§ 19). In imitation of these structures others were erected on the same plan by burial societies formed by persons of the artisan class, and others still by benevolent men, as baths (§ 373) and libraries (§ 402) were erected and maintained for the public good. Something will be said of the tombs of all these kinds after the public burying places have been described.

468. The Potter's Field. During the Republic the Esquiline Hill, or at least the eastern part of it, was the place to which was carted all the refuse of the city that the sewers would not carry away. Here, too, were the grave-pits (*puticulī*) for the pauper class. They were merely holes in the ground, about twelve feet square, without lining of any kind. Into them were thrown the bodies of the friendless poor, and along with them and over them the carcasses of dead animals and the filth and scrapings of the streets. The pits were kept open, uncovered apparently even when filled, and the stench and the disease-breeding pollution made the hill absolutely uninhabitable. Under Augustus the danger to the health of the whole city became so great that the dumping grounds were moved to a greater distance, and the Esquiline, covered over, pits and all, with pure soil to the depth of twenty-five feet, was made a park, known as the *Hortī Maecēnātis*.

469. It is not to be understood, however, that the bodies of Roman citizens were ordinarily disposed of in this revolting way. Faithful freedmen were cared for by their patrons, the industrious poor made provision for themselves in co-operative societies, mentioned elsewhere (§§ 420, 467, 475), and the proletariat class (§ 417) was in general saved from such a fate by clansmen (§ 22), by patrons (§ 179), or by the benevolence of individuals. Only in times of plague and pestilence, it is safe to say, were the bodies of known citizens cast into these pits, as under like circumstances bodies have been burned in heaps in modern cities. The uncounted thousands that peopled the potter's field of Rome were the riffraff from foreign lands, abandoned slaves (§ 156), the victims that perished in the arena (§ 362), outcasts of the criminal class, and the "unidentified" that are buried nowadays at public expense. Criminals put to death by authority were not buried at all; their carcasses were left to birds and beasts of prey at the place of execution near the Esquiline Gate.

470. Plan of Tombs and Grounds. The utmost diversity prevails in the outward form and construction of the tombs, but those of the classical period seem to have been planned with the thought that the tomb was to be a home for the dead and that they were not altogether

Fig. 303
INTERIOR OF A TOMB AT POMPEII

cut off from the living. The tomb, therefore, whether built for one person or for many, was ordinarily a building inclosing a room (*sepulcrum*); this room was the most important part of the tomb. Attention has been called (§ 189) to the fact that even the urns had in ancient times the shape of the house of one room. The floor of the *sepulcrum* was quite commonly below the level of the surrounding grounds and was reached by a short flight of steps. Around the base of the walls ran a slightly elevated platform (*podium:* cf. §§ 337, 357) on which were placed the coffins of those who were buried, while the urns were placed either on the platform or in the niches in the wall. An altar or shrine is often found, at which offerings were made to the *mānēs* of the departed. Lamps are very common and so are other simple articles of furniture, and the walls, floors, and ceilings are decorated in the same style as those of houses (§ 220). Things that the living had liked to have around them, especially things that they used in their ordinary occupations, were placed in the tomb with the dead at the time of burial, or burned with them on the funeral pyre; an effort was made to give an air of life to the chamber of rest. The interior of a tomb at Pompeii is shown in Figure 303.

471. The monument itself was always built upon a plot of ground as spacious as the means of the builders would permit; sometimes it was several acres in extent. In it provision was made for the comfort of surviving members of the family, who were bound to visit the resting place of their dead on certain regularly recurring festivals (§ 483). If the grounds were small, there would be at least a seat, perhaps a bench. On more extensive grounds there were places of shelter, arbors, or summer houses. Dining-rooms, too, in which were celebrated the anniversary feasts, and private *ustrīnae* (places for the burning of bodies) are frequently mentioned. Often the grounds were laid out as gardens or parks, with trees and flowers, wells, cisterns or fountains, and even a house, and other buildings perhaps, for the accommodation of the slaves or freedmen who were in charge. A plan of such a garden is shown in Figure 304. In the middle of the garden is placed the *ārea*, that is, the plot of ground set aside for the tomb, with several buildings upon it, one of which is a storehouse or granary (*horreum*); around the tomb itself are beds of roses and violets, used in festivals (§ 483); around them in turn are grapes trained on trellises (*vīneolae*). In front is a terrace (*sōlārium:* cf. § 207), and in the rear two pools (*piscīnae*) connected with the *ārea* by a little canal, while at

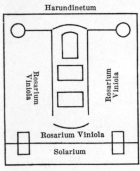

FIG. 304
PLAN OF GROUNDS
AROUND A TOMB

the back is a thicket of shrubbery (*harundinētum*). The
purpose of the granary is not clear, as no grain seems to
have been raised on the lot, but it may have been left where
it stood before the ground was consecrated. A tomb surrounded by grounds of some extent was called a *cēpotaphium*.

472. Exterior of the Tombs. An idea of the exterior appearance of monuments of the better sort may be had from
Figures 302, 305, 312, 313. The forms are many. Monu-

FIG. 305
TOMB OF CECILIA METELLA ON THE APPIAN WAY, NEAR ROME

ments shaped like altars and temples are most common, perhaps, but memorial arches and niches are often found. At
Pompeii the semicircular bench that was used for conversation out of doors occurs several times, covered and uncovered.
Not all the tombs have the sepulchral chamber; the remains
were sometimes deposited in the earth beneath the monument. In such cases a tube or pipe of lead ran from the
receptacle to the surface, through which offerings of wine
and milk could be poured (§§ 474, 483).

In the northern part of the *Campus Mārtius*, Augustus
built a mausoleum for himself and family in 28 B.C. This was
a great circular structure of concrete with marble or stucco

facing.   Above was a mound of earth planted with trees and flowers, on the summit of which stood a statue of Augustus. On each side of the entrance were the famous bronze tablets inscribed with the *Rēs Gestae*, the record of his work.   The ashes of the young Marcellus were the first placed here, in 28 B.C., and those of the Emperor Nerva the last, in 98

FIG. 306
COLUMBĀRIUM IN THE VIGNA CODINI, ON THE APPIAN WAY, ROME

A.D.   The mausoleum was plundered by Alaric in 419 A.D.   In medieval times it became a fortress of the Colonna.   About 1550 the Soderini made it into hanging gardens.   It has been a bull ring and a circus, and is now a concert hall.   The most imposing of all the tombs was the Mausoleum of Hadrian (Fig. 312) at Rome, now the Castle of St. Angelo.

473. The *Columbāria*.   From the family tombs were developed the immense structures mentioned in § 467, structures which were intended to receive great numbers of urns.

They began to be erected in the time of Augustus, when the high price of land made the purchase of private burial grounds impossible for the poorer classes. An idea of their interior arrangement may be had from the ruins (Fig. 306) of one erected on the Appian Way and of one at Ostia (Fig. 310). From their resemblance to a dovecote or pigeon house they were called *columbāria*. They are us-

Fig. 307
SARCOPHAGUS OF SCĪPIŌ BARBĀTUS
This sarcophagus and bust were found in the tomb of the Scipios on the Appian Way.
Now in the Vatican Museum, Rome.

ually partly underground, rectangular in form, with great numbers of the niches (also called *columbāria*) running in regular rows horizontally (*gradūs*) and vertically (*ōrdinēs*). In the larger *columbāria* provision was made for as many as a thousand urns. Around the walls at the base was a *podium*, on which were placed the sarcophagi of those whose remains had not been burned, and sometimes chambers were excavated beneath the floor for the same purpose. In the *podium* were also niches, that no space might be lost. If the height of the building was great enough to warrant it, wooden galleries ran around the walls. Access to the room was given by a stairway in which were niches, too; light was furnished by small windows near the ceiling, and walls and floors were handsomely finished and decorated.

474. The niches were sometimes rectangular in form, but more commonly half round, as shown in Figures 306 and 310.

FIG. 308
AEDICULA

Some of the *columbāria* have the lower rows rectangular, those above arched. They contained ordinarily two urns (*ōllae, ōllae ossuāriae*) each, arranged side by side, that they could be visible from the front. Occasionally the niches were made deep enough for two sets of urns, those behind being elevated a little over those in front. Above or below each niche was fastened to the wall a piece of marble (*titulus*) on which was cut the name of the owner. If a person required for his family a group of four or six niches, it was customary to mark them off from the others by wall decorations to show that they made a unit; a very common way was to erect pillars at the sides so as to give the appearance of the front of a temple (Fig. 308). Such groups were called *aediculae*. The value of the places depended upon their position; those in the higher rows (*gradūs*) were less expensive than those near the floor; those under the stairway were the least desirable of all. The urns themselves were of various materials and were usually cemented to the bottom of the niches. The tops could be removed, but they, too, were sealed after the ashes had been placed in them; small openings were left through which offerings of milk and wine could be poured (§ 472). On the urns, or their tops, were painted the names of the dead, with sometimes the day and the month of death. The year is rarely found. Over the door of such a *columbārium* on the outside was cut an inscription giving the names of the owners, the date of erection, and other particulars.

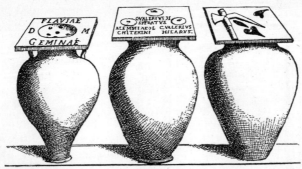

Fig. 309
CINERARY URNS

475. The Burial Societies. Early in the Empire, associations were formed for the purpose of meeting the funeral expenses of their members, whether the remains were to be buried or cremated, or for the purpose of building *columbāria*, or for both. These co-operative associations (*collēgia fūnerātīcia*) started originally among members of the same guild (§ 420) or among persons of the same occupation. They called themselves by many names, *cultōrēs* of this deity or that, *collēgia salūtāria, collēgia iuvenum*, etc., but their objects and methods were practically the same. If the members had provided places for the disposal of their bodies

after death, they now provided for the necessary funeral
expenses by paying into the common fund weekly a small
fixed sum, easily within the reach of the poorest of them.
When a member died, a stated sum was drawn from the
treasury for his funeral, a committee saw that the rites were
decently performed, and at the proper seasons (§ 483) the
society made corporate offerings to the dead. If the purpose

Fig. 310
COLUMBĀRIUM AT OSTIA

of the society was the building of a *columbārium*, the cost
was first determined and the sum total divided into what we
should call shares (*sortēs virīlēs*), each member taking as many
as he could afford and paying their value into the treasury.
Sometimes a benevolent person would contribute toward
the expense of the undertaking, and then such a person would
be made an honorary member of the society with the title
of *patrōnus* or *patrōna*. The erection of the building was
intrusted to a number of *cūrātōrēs*, chosen by ballot, naturally

the largest shareholders and most influential men. They let the contracts and superintended the construction, rendering account of all the money expended. The office of the *cūrātōrēs* was considered very honorable, especially as their names appeared on the inscription outside the building, and they often showed their appreciation of the honor done them by providing at their own expense for the decoration of the interior, or by furnishing all or a part of the *titulī*, *ōllae*, etc., or by erecting on the surrounding grounds places of shelter and dining-rooms for the use of the members.

476. After the completion of the building the *cūrātōrēs* allotted the niches to the individual members. The niches were either numbered consecutively throughout or their position was fixed by the number of the *ōrdō* and *gradus* (§ 473) in which they were situated. Because they were not all equally desirable, as has been explained, the *cūrātōrēs* divided them into sections as fairly as possible and then assigned the sections (*locī*) by lot to the shareholders. If a man held several shares of stock, he received a corresponding number of *locī*, though they might be in widely different parts of the building. The members were allowed freely to dispose of their holdings by exchange, sale, or gift, and many of the larger stockholders probably engaged in the enterprise for the sake of the profits to be made in this way. After the division was made, the owners had their names cut upon the *titulī*, and might put up columns to mark the *aediculae* (§ 474), set up statues, etc., if they pleased. Some of the *titulī* give, besides the name of the owner, the number and position of his *locī* or *ōllae*. Sometimes they record the purchase

L · ABVCIVS · HERMES · IN · HOC
ORDINE · AB · IMO · AD · SVMMVM
COLVMBARIA · IX · OLLAE · XVIII
SIBI · POSTERISQVE · SVIS[1]

---

[1] Titulus in Columbarium: "Lucius Abucius Hermes [has acquired] in this row, running from the lowest tier to the highest, nine niches with eighteen urns for [the ashes of] himself and his descendants."

of *ōllae*, giving the number bought and the name of the previous owner. Sometimes the names on the *ōllae* do not correspond with that over the niche, showing that the owner had sold a part only of his holdings, or that the purchaser had not taken the trouble to replace the *titulus*. The expenses of maintenance were probably paid from the weekly dues of the members, as were the funeral benefits.

477. Funeral Ceremonies. The detailed accounts of funeral ceremonies that have come down to us relate almost exclusively to those of persons of high position, and the information gleaned from other sources (§ 11) is so scattered that there is great danger of confusing usages of widely different times. It is quite certain, however, that, at all times, very young children were buried simply and quietly (*fūnus acerbum*), that no ceremonies at all attended the burial of slaves (§ 465) when conducted by their masters (nothing is known of the forms used by the burial societies mentioned in § 475), and that citizens of the lowest class were laid to rest without public parade (*fūnus plēbēium*). It is also known that burials took place by night except during the last century of the Republic and the first two centuries of the Empire, and it is natural to suppose that, even in the case of persons of high position, there was ordinarily much less of pomp and parade than on occasions that the Roman writers thought it worth while to describe. This was found true in the matter of wedding festivities (§ 79).

478. At the House. When the Roman died at home surrounded by his family, it was the duty of his oldest son to bend over the body and call him by name, as if with the hope of recalling him to life. The formal performance of this act (*conclāmātiō*) he announced immediately with the words *conclāmātum est*. The eyes of the dead were then closed, the body was washed with warm water and anointed, the limbs were straightened, and, if the deceased had held a curule office, a wax impression of his features was taken (§§ 200, 230). The body was then dressed in the toga (§ 240) with all the insignia of rank that the dead had been entitled to wear in life, and was placed upon the funeral couch (*lectus fūnebris*) in the *ātrium* (§ 198), with the feet to the door, to lie in state until the time of the funeral. The couch was surrounded with flowers, and incense was burned about it.

Fig. 311
MOURNERS BESIDE A FUNERARY COUCH
From a relief now in the Museo Laterano, Rome.

Before the door of the house were set branches of pine or cypress as a warning that the house was polluted by death. The simple offices that have been described were performed in humble life by the relatives and slaves, in other cases by professional undertakers (*libitīnāriī*), who also embalmed the body and superintended all the rest of the ceremonies. Reference is made occasionally to the kissing of the dying person as he breathed his last, as if this last breath was to be caught in the mouth of the living; and in very early and very late times it was undoubtedly the custom to put a small coin between the teeth of the dead with which to pay his passage across the Styx in Charon's boat. Neither of these formalities seems to have obtained generally in classical times.

479. The Funeral Procession.   The funeral procession of the ordinary citizen was simple enough.   Notice was given to neighbors and friends.   Surrounded by them and by the family, carried on the shoulders of the sons or other near relatives, with perhaps a band of musicians in the lead, the body was borne to the tomb.   The procession of one of the mighty, on the other hand, was marshaled with all possible display and ostentation.   It occurred as soon after death as the necessary preparations could be made, as there was no fixed intervening time.   Notice was given by a public crier in the ancient words of style: *Ollus Quiris lētō datus.   Exsequiās, quibus est commodum, īre iam tempus est.   Ollus ex aedibus effertur.*[1]   Questions of order and precedence were settled by an undertaker (*dēsignātor*).   At the head of the procession went a band of musicians, followed, at least occasionally, by persons singing dirges in praise of the dead, and by bands of buffoons and jesters, who made merry with the bystanders and imitated even the dead man himself.   Then came the imposing part of the display.   The wax masks of the dead man's ancestors had been taken from their place in the *ālae* (§ 200) and assumed by actors in the dress appropriate to the time and station of the worthies they represented.   It must have seemed as if the ancient dead had returned to earth to guide their descendant to his place among them. Servius tells us that six hundred *imāginēs* were displayed at the funeral of the young Marcellus, the nephew of Augustus. Then followed the memorials of the great deeds of the deceased, if he had been a general, as in a triumphal procession, and then the dead man himself, carried with face uncovered on a lofty couch.   Then came the family, including freedmen (especially those made free by the testament of their master) and slaves, and next the friends, all in mourning garb (§§ 246, 253), and all freely giving expression to the emotion

---

[1] "This citizen has been surrendered to death.   For those who find it convenient, it is now time to attend the funeral.   He is being brought from his house."

Fig. 312
HADRIAN'S TOMB

that we try to suppress on such occasions.   Torchbearers
attended the train, even by day, as a remembrance of the
older custom of burial by night.

480. The Funeral Oration.   The procession passed from
the house directly to the place of interment, unless the deceased was a person of sufficient consequence to be honored
by public authority with a funeral oration (*laudātiō*) in the
Forum.   In this case the funeral couch was placed before the
rōstra, the men in the masks took their places on curule
chairs (§ 225) around it, the general crowd was massed in a
semicircle behind, and a son or other near relative delivered
the address.   It recited the virtues and achievements of the
dead and recounted the history of the family to which he
belonged.   Like such addresses in more recent times it

contained much that was false and more that was exaggerated. The honor of the *laudātiō* was freely given in later times, especially to members of the Imperial family, including women. Under the Republic it was less common and more highly prized; so far as we know the only women so honored belonged to the *gēns Iūlia*. It will be remembered that it was Caesar's address on the occasion of the funeral of his aunt, the widow of Marius, that pointed him out to the opponents of Sulla as a future leader. When the address in the Forum was not authorized, one was sometimes given more privately at the grave or at the house.

481. At the Tomb. When the procession reached the place of burial, the proceedings varied according to the time, but all provided for the three things ceremonially necessary: the consecration of the resting place, the casting of earth upon the remains, and the purification of all polluted by the death. In ancient times the body, if buried, was lowered into the grave either upon the couch on which it had been brought to the spot, or in a coffin of burnt clay or stone. If the body was to be burned, a shallow grave was dug and filled with dry wood, upon which the couch and body were placed. The pile was then fired and, when wood and body had been consumed, earth was heaped over the ashes into a mound (*tumulus*). Such a grave in which the body was burned was called *bustum*, and was consecrated as a regular *sepulcrum* by the ceremonies mentioned below. In later times the body, if not to be burned, was placed in a sarcophagus (Fig. 307) already prepared in the tomb (§ 470). If the remains were to be burned, they were taken to the *ustrīna* (§ 471), which was not regarded as a part of the *sepulcrum*, and placed upon the pile of wood (*rogus*). Spices and perfumes were thrown upon them, together with gifts (§ 470) and tokens from the persons present. The pyre was then lighted with a torch by a relative, who kept his face averted during the act. After the fire had burned out, the embers were extinguished with water or wine and those present called a last farewell to the dead. The water of purification was then thrice sprinkled over those present, and all except the immediate family left the place. The ashes were then collected in a cloth to be dried, and the ceremonial bone (§ 465), called *os resectum*, was buried. A sacrifice of a pig was then offered, by which the place of burial was made sacred ground, and food (*silicernium*) was eaten together by the mourners. They then re-

Fig. 313
TOMBS AT POMPEII

turned to the house, which was purified by an offering to the *Larēs*, and the funeral rites were over.

482. Subsequent Ceremonies. With the day of the burial or burning of the remains began the "Nine Days of Sorrow," solemnly observed by the immediate family. Some time during this period, when the ashes had had time to dry thoroughly, members of the family went privately to the *ustrīna*, removed the ashes from the cloth, put them in an *ōlla* (Fig. 309) of earthenware, glass, alabaster, bronze, or other material, and with bare feet and loosened girdles carried them into the *sepulcrum* (§ 470). At the end of the nine days the *sacrificium novendiāle* was offered to the dead and the *cēna novendiālis* took place at the house. On this day, too,

the heirs formally entered upon their inheritance and the
funeral games (§ 344) were originally given. The period of
mourning, however, was not concluded on the ninth day.
For husband or wife, ascendants, and grown descendants
mourning was worn for ten months, the ancient year, for
other adult relatives, eight months, for children between
the ages of three and ten years, for as many months as they
were years old.

483. Memorial Festivals. The memory of the dead was
kept alive by regularly recurring "days of obligation" of both
public and private character. To the former belong the
Parentālia, or *diēs parentālēs* (§ 75), lasting from the thir-
teenth to the twenty-first of February, the final day being
especially distinguished as the *Fērālia*. To the latter belong
the annual celebration of the birthday (or the burial day) of
the person commemorated, and the festivals of violets and
roses (*Violāria, Rosāria*), about the end of March and May
respectively, when violets and roses were distributed among
the relatives and laid upon the graves or heaped over the
urns. On all these occasions offerings were made in the
temples to the gods and at the tombs to the *mānēs* of the
dead, and the lamps were lighted in the tombs (§ 470), and
at the tombs the relatives feasted together and offered food
to their dead (§ 471).

Fig. 314
ROMAN ARCH OF TRIUMPH
This monument is south of
Saint-Remy, France.

CHAPTER XV

THE ROMAN RELIGION

REFERENCES: Fowler, Social Life, 319-352; Fowler, *Religious Experience;* Fowler, *Festivals;* Carter, *Religion;* Carter, *Religious Life;* Halliday; Dill, 443-626; Sandys, *Companion,* 150-165; Cagnat-Chapot, I, 137-171, II, 161-203; Jones, 267-303; Mau-Kelsey, 233-236, 268-273; Bailey, *Legacy,* 237-264; Bailey, *Religion;* McDaniel, 101-105; Showerman, 280-298.

484. The religion of the Romans was originally a simple animism, that is, a belief in spirits or powers (*nūmina*) associated with all things about man and with all man's acts. These spirits were not personified and were not conceived of as human in form. There were no temples and no statues of gods. Rites were clean and simple, performed with a scrupulous exactness felt as pleasing to the gods, who were friendly when thus worshiped. It was the religion of a simple agricultural people. Study of the calendars that have come down to us shows that the older festivals that kept their places in such calendars were marked by larger letters. These were rural festivals, marking the year of the country people. But as the Romans came in contact with other peoples and their religions, and as they developed from a small Italian community to an imperialistic nation, their religion inevitably changed. Gods of conquered communities were brought in. In times of stress gods were imported to meet the emergency. It is believed that the Etruscan kings built the first temples and set up the first statues of gods. Contact with the Greeks led to the introduction of Greek gods and Greek ritual and to the identification of the old Roman gods with Greek gods that seemed most like them. The exactness in the performance of the proper rites led naturally to a deadening formalism; hence, before the end of the Republic, the educated classes were turning instead to philosophy. Others turned to the mystical or orgiastic cults of Greece and the Orient, naturally, as the native stock was more and more displaced by Orientals (§ 129). Under the Empire the Oriental religions became more firmly established, while the cult of the emperors came to be the distinguishing feature of the state religion, until finally both made way for Christianity.

Fig. 315
BRONZE STATUETTE OF CYBELE ON HER CAR
Cybele represents the first Oriental cult at Rome.
Now in the Metropolitan Museum of Art, New York.

485. The Work of Numa. Roman tradition ascribed to Numa, second of the seven kings, the organization of the worship and the assignment to the calendar of the proper festivals in due order. Whether or not we choose to believe that a great priest-king left his personal impress on ritual and calendar, "the religion of Numa" is a convenient phrase by which to designate the religion of the early State. Numa was supposed to have organized the first priestly colleges and to have appointed the first *flāminēs*, or priests of special

gods. The most important of these were the *Flāmen Diālis*,
or priest of Jupiter, and the *flāminēs* of Mars and Quirinus.

486. When the kingship was abolished, the office of *rēx
sacrōrum* was instituted to carry on the rites once in
the charge of the king. He,
the three *flāminēs* mentioned
above, and the college of the
pontificēs, with the *Pontifex
Maximus* at its head, constituted the body controlling and
guiding the state religion. Under the Empire the emperor
was regularly *Pontifex Maximus.*

487. Priestly Colleges. The
Saliī, or dancing priests, were
priests of an old and famous
college who worshiped Mars,
the god of war. A similar college, the *Saliī Collīnī*, was in

Fig. 316
THE TEMPLE OF VESTA IN
THE FORUM
From a relief now in the Uffizi
Gallery, Florence.

charge of the worship of Quirinus. The *pontificēs* (§ 486) were
in charge of the calendar. The *augurēs* interpreted the will of
the gods as shown when the auspices were taken by the
magistrates before any public occasion or action. Among
other official colleges were the *quīndecemvirī*, in charge of the
famous Sibylline Books. Unofficial or private associations or
colleges carried on the worship of various gods. In this connection might be mentioned the burial societies (§ 475),
ostensibly organized to further the worship of some god.

488. One of the oldest and most famous colleges was that
of Vesta, whose worship was in care of the six *Virginēs
Vestālēs*. The sacred fire upon the altar of the *Aedēs Vestae*
symbolized the continuity of the life of the State. There
was no statue of the goddess in the temple. The temple
itself was round and had a pointed roof, and even in its

latest development of marble and bronze had not gone far in shape and size from the round hut of poles and clay and

FIG. 317
A CHIEF VESTAL
A statue found in Rome, now in the Museo Nazionale, Rome.

thatch in which village girls had tended the fire whose maintenance was necessary for the primitive community. To light a fire then had been a toilsome business of rubbing wood on wood, or later striking flint on steel to get the precious spark. But the modern invention of flint and steel was never used to rekindle the sacred fire. Ritual demanded the use of friction.

489. Each Vestal must serve thirty years. Any vacancy in the Order must be filled promptly by the appointment of a girl of suitable family, not less than six years old nor more than ten, physically perfect, of unblemished character, and with both parents living. Ten years were spent by the Vestals in learning their duties, ten in performing those duties, and ten in training the younger Vestals. In addition to the care of the fire the Vestals had a part in most of the festivals of the old calendar. They lived in the *Ātrium Vestae* beside the temple of Vesta in the Forum. At the end of her service a Vestal might return to private life, but such were the privileges and the dignity of the Order that this rarely occurred. A Vestal was freed from her father's *potestās* (§ 29).

FIG. 318
ROMAN MATRON AS PRIESTESS
Statue from Pompeii, in the Museo Nazionale, Naples.

490. The Religion of the Family. The *pater familiās* was the household priest and in charge of the family worship; he was assisted by his wife and children (§§ 34-35). The *Lar Familiāris* was the protecting spirit of the household in town and country. In the country, too, the *Larēs* were the guardian spirits of the fields and were worshiped at the crossroads (*compita*) by the owners and tenants of the lands that met there. In town, too, the *Larēs Compitālēs* were worshiped at street-corner shrines in the various *vīcī* or precincts. For the single *Lar* of the Republican period we later find two. Pompeian household shrines (§ 207) show frequent examples of this. They are represented as boys dressed in belted tunics, stepping lightly as if in dance, a bowl in the right hand, a jug upraised in the left. In place of the old Penates, the protecting spirits of the store-closet, these shrines

Fig. 319
A LAR
Bronze statuette now in the
Metropolitan Museum of Art,
New York.

show images of such of the great gods as each family chose to honor in its private devotions. The *Genius* of the *pater familiās* (§ 96) may be represented in such shrines as a man with the toga drawn over his head as for worship. Often, however, at Pompeii the *Genius* is represented by a serpent. In such shrines we find two, one bearded, for the *Genius* of the father, the other for the *Iūnō* (§ 96) of the wife. Vesta was worshiped at the hearth as the spirit of the fire that was necessary for man's existence.

491. The shrine, originally in the atrium when that was the room where the household lived and worked, followed the hearth to the separate kitchen (§ 203), though examples of shrines are found in the garden or peristyle and occasionally in the atrium or other rooms.

492. The devout prayed and sacrificed every morning, but the usual time for the family devotions was the pause at the *cēna* before the *secunda mēnsa*, when offerings to the household gods were made (§ 311). The Kalends, Nones, and Ides were sacred to the *Larēs*. On these days garlands were hung over the hearth, the *Larēs* were crowned with garlands, and simple offerings were made. Incense and wine were usual offerings; a pig was sacrificed when possible. Horace has a pretty picture of the "rustic Phidyle" who crowns her little *Larēs* with rosemary and myrtle, and offers incense, new grain, and a "greedy pig." The family were also bound to keep up the rites in honor of the dead (§§ 34-35, 483). All family occasions from birth to death were accompanied by the proper rites. Strong religious feeling clung to the family rites and country festivals even when the state religion had stiffened into formalism and many Romans were reaching after strange gods.

FIG. 320
A HOUSEHOLD SHRINE IN POMPEII

493. The *gēns* or clan of which the family formed a part had its own rites (§ 19). The maintenance of these *sacra* was considered necessary not merely for the clan itself, but for the welfare of the State, which might suffer from the god's displeasure if the rites should be neglected.

494. The Religion of the State. Of the early gods,

Jupiter (*Iuppiter*), *Diovis Pater*, was the light-father, worshiped on hilltops, whom men called to witness their agreements. Saturn was a god of the crops, and Venus had to do with gardens. Mars was worshiped in connection with agriculture and with war, for the farmer was fighter, too. Vesta was the spirit of the hearth. There were others of whom we know little. The first temple at Rome was built by the Etruscans on the Capitoline Hill, for Jupiter, Juno, and Minerva. Minerva had come in from Falerii as patron

FIG. 321
THE SUOVETAURILIA
From a relief now in the Louvre, Paris.

of craftsmen and their guilds, and had also her own temple on the Aventine. Diana was a wood-spirit from Aricia. Hercules came from Tibur as a god of commerce, and Castor from Tusculum. Mercury, god of commerce, as his name shows, came from Cumae. These last three were of Greek origin, naturalized in Italy. Because of the famine in 493 B.C., the Sibylline oracle at Cumae advised bringing in Bacchus, Ceres, and Proserpina. Apollo came from Cumae as god of healing, and his temple was built in 432 B.C. In 293 B.C. Aesculapius was brought from Epidaurus to the island in the Tiber, which is still the site of a hospital.

495. The *Magna Māter* was brought by the State from

Phrygia in 205 B.C., during the Second Punic War, but, when
the orgiastic nature of the cult became known, it was ordained that her priests should never be Romans.   However,
this was the beginning of the movement toward the Oriental
religions.

496. Naturally, new modes of worship came in with new
gods.   More and more Greek gods came in and were identified with the older gods.   Greek craftsmen built temples
and made statues of gods like those of Greece. Acquaintance

Fig. 322
RUINS OF THE TEMPLE OF APOLLO, POMPEII

with Greek mythology, literature, and art finally made the
identification complete.

497. The study of Greek philosophy supplanted the old
religion among the upper classes, as has been said (§ 484). As
interest waned in the old religion, some forms and ceremonies
and even priesthoods were discarded, especially during the
troublous times of the Civil Wars. When Augustus restored
order, as part of his constructive policy he stressed a religious
revival, repairing and rebuilding temples and reviving old
priesthoods.

498. Religion in the Imperial Age. The cult of the emperors developed naturally enough from the time of the deification of Julius Caesar. The movement for this deification was of Oriental origin. The *Genius* of the emperor was worshiped as the *Genius* of the father had been worshiped in the household (§ 490). The cult, beginning in the East, was then established in the western provinces and finally in Italy. It was under the care of the *sēvirī Augustālēs* (§ 459) in the municipalities. The worship of the emperor in his lifetime was not permitted at Rome, but spread through the provinces, taking the place of the old state religion. It was this that caused the opposition to Christianity, for the refusal of the Christians to take part was treasonable. Their offense was political, not religious (§ 420, note 1).

Fig. 323
ALTAR DEDICATED TO THE LARS
OF AUGUSTUS

499. The weakening of the old stock (§ 129) and the constantly increasing number of Orientals in the West, along with the campaigns of the armies in the East naturally encouraged the introduction of eastern cults and the spread of their influence. The cult of the *Magna Māter* found a reviving interest among the people from her part of the world (§ 495). The mystery religions gained strength, with their rites of purification and assurance of happiness after death. Among them the worship of Isis had come from

Alexandria with the Egyptians and spread among the lower classes. Mithraism came in from the eastern campaigns with the captives, and later with the troops that had served or had been enlisted in the East. It established itself in Rome and in other cities and followed the army from camp to camp. There were many Jews in Rome, and their religion made some progress. Christianity appeared at Rome first among the lower classes, particularly the Orientals, and finally made its way upward.

Fig. 324
TEMPLE OF JUPITER THE THUNDERER ON
THE CAPITOLINE HILL
(A restoration.)

CHAPTER XVI

THE WATER SUPPLY OF ROME

REFERENCES: *Encyclopaedia Britannica*, fourteenth edition, II, 160-161; Lanciani, *Ruins*, 47-58; Herschel; Cagnat-Chapot, I, 85-110; Mau-Kelsey, 230-233; Jones, 141-154; Smith, under *aquae ductus;* Smith, under *Aquaeductus;* Harper's, Daremberg-Saglio, etc., under *aqua,* and other Latin words in the text of this book; Bailey, *Legacy,* 465-472; Gest, 62-107.

500. The site of Rome itself was well supplied with water. Springs were abundant, and wells could be sunk to find water at no great depth. Rain water was collected in cisterns, and the water from the Tiber was used. But these sources came to be inadequate, and in 312 B.C. the first of the great aqueducts (*aquae*) was built by the famous censor, Appius Claudius, and named for him the *Aqua Appia*. It was eleven miles long, of which all but three hundred feet was underground. This and the *Aniō Vetus*, built forty years later, supplied the lower levels of the city. The first high-level aqueduct, the *Mārcia*, was built by Quintus Marcius Rex, to bring water to the top of the Capitoline Hill, in 140 B.C. Its water was and still is particularly cold and good. The *Tepula*, named from the temperature of its waters, and completed in 125 B.C., was the last built during the Republic. Under Augustus three more were built, the *Jūlia* and the *Virgō* by Agrippa, and the *Alsietīna* by Augustus, for his *naumachia* (§ 364). The *Claudia* (Fig. 2), whose ruined arches are still a magnificent sight near Rome, and the *Aniō Novus* were begun by Caligula and finished by Claudius. The *Trāiāna* was built by Trajan in 109 A.D., and the last, the *Alexandrīna*, by Alexander Severus. Eleven aqueducts then served ancient Rome. Modern Rome is considered unusually well supplied with water from four, using the sources and occasionally the channels of as many

405

of the ancient ones. The *Virgō*, now *Acqua Vergine*, was first restored by Pius V in 1570. The springs of the *Alexandrīna* supply the *Acqua Felice*, built in 1585. The *Aqua Trāiāna* was restored as the *Acqua Paola* in 1611. The

FIG. 325
THE ARCH OF DRUSUS AT ROME
The Arch of Drusus carried a branch of the *Aqua Mārcia* across the Appian Way to the Baths of Caracalla.

famous *Mārcia* was reconstructed in 1870 as the *Acqua Pia*, or *Marcia-Pia*.

501. The channels of the aqueducts were generally built of masonry, for lack of sufficiently strong pipes. Cast-iron pipes the Romans did not have, lead was rarely used for large pipes, and bronze would have been too expensive. Because of this lack, and not because they did not understand the principle of the siphon, high pressure aqueducts were less commonly constructed. To avoid high pressure, the aqueducts that supplied Rome with water, and many others, were built at a very easy slope and frequently carried around hills and valleys, though tunnels and bridges were sometimes used to save distance. The great arches, so impressive in their ruins, were used for comparatively short distances, as most of the channels were underground.

502. In the cities the water was carried into distributing reservoirs (*castella*), from which ran the street mains. Lead pipes (*fistulae*) carried the water into the houses. These pipes were made of strips of sheet lead with the edges folded together and welded at the joining, thus being pear-shaped rather than round. As these pipes were stamped with the name of the owner and user, the finding of many at Rome in our own time has made it possible to locate the sites of the residences of many distinguished Romans. In Pompeii these pipes can be seen easily now, for in that mild climate they were often laid on the ground close to the house, not buried as in most parts of this country.

The poor must have carried the water that they used from the public fountains that were placed at frequent intervals in the streets, where the water ran constantly for all comers.

Fig. 326
THE PONT DU GARD, A ROMAN AQUEDUCT NEAR NÎMES

BOOKS ON ROME AND ROMAN LIFE[1]

ABBOTT, FRANK FROST, *The Common People of Ancient Rome* (New York, Scribner's, 1911). [Abbott, *The Common People*.]

ABBOTT, FRANK FROST, *A Short History of Rome* (Chicago, Scott, Foresman and Company, 1906). [Abbott, *History of Rome*.]

ABBOTT, FRANK FROST, *A History and Description of Roman Political Institutions*, third edition (Boston, Ginn, 1911). [Abbott, *Roman Political Institutions*.]

ABBOTT, FRANK FROST, *Roman Politics*, in the Series entitled "Our Debt to Greece and Rome" (Boston, Marshall Jones Company, 1923; now published by Longmans, New York). [Abbott, *Roman Politics*.]

ABBOTT, FRANK FROST, *Society and Politics in Ancient Rome* (New York, Scribner's, 1909). [Abbott, *Society and Politics*.]

ABBOTT, FRANK FROST, and JOHNSON, ALLEN CHESTER, *Municipal Administration in the Roman Empire* (Princeton University Press, 1926). [Abbott and Johnson.]

BAILEY, CYRIL, *The Legacy of Rome* (Oxford: At the Clarendon Press, 1923). [Bailey, *Legacy*.]

BAILEY, CYRIL, *The Religion of Ancient Rome* (London, Constable, 1921). [Bailey, *Religion*.]

BAUMEISTER: *see* page 25.

BECKER-GÖLL: *see* page 23.

BLÜMNER (two works): *see* pages 23 and 24.

BOAK, A. E. R., *A History of Rome to 565 A. D.*, second edition (New York, Macmillan, 1929). [Boak.]

CAGNAT, RENÉ: *Cours d'epigraphie Latine*, fourth edition (Paris, Fontemoing, 1914). [Cagnat, *Cours d'epigraphie Latine*.]

CAGNAT-CHAPOT: *see* page 24.

CALZA: *see* page 26.

CARTER, JESSE BENEDICT, *The Religion of Numa* (London, Macmillan, 1906). [Carter, *Religion*.]

CARTER, JESSE BENEDICT, *The Religious Life of Ancient Rome* (Boston, Houghton Mifflin, 1911). [Carter, *Religious Life*.]

---

[1]This list includes all works named or cited in this book. At the close of each item will be given in square brackets [ ] the abbreviation by which the particular work will be named in references to it in this book.

CHARLESWORTH, MARTIN PERCIVAL, *Trade-Routes and Commerce of the Roman Empire*, second edition (Cambridge: At the University Press, 1926). [Charlesworth.]

CICERO, *Selected Orations and Letters of Cicero*, edited by Harold Whetstone Johnston, revised by Hugh Macmaster Kingery (Chicago, Scott, Foresman and Company, 1910). [Johnston-Kingery.]

DAREMBERG-SAGLIO: *see* page 25.

DAVIS, WILLIAM STEARNS, *The Influence of Wealth in Imperial Rome* (New York, Macmillan, 1910). [Davis.]

DILL, SAMUEL, *Roman Society from Nero to Marcus Aurelius* (London, Macmillan, 1904). [Dill.]

DUFF, A. M., *Freedmen in the Early Roman Empire* (Oxford: At the Clarendon Press, 1928). [Duff.]

EGBERT, JAMES C., JR., *Introduction to the Study of Latin Inscriptions* (New York, American Book Company, 1896). [Egbert.]

ENGELMANN: *see* page 26.

FOWLER, W. WARDE, *The Roman Festivals of the Period of the Republic* (London, Macmillan, 1899). [Fowler, *Festivals.*]

FOWLER, W. WARDE, *The Religious Experience of the Roman People from the Earliest Times to the Age of Augustus* (London, Macmillan, 1911). [Fowler, *Religious Experience.*]

FOWLER, W. WARDE, *Social Life at Rome in the Age of Cicero* (London, Macmillan, 1909). [Fowler, *Social Life.*]

FRANK, TENNEY, *An Economic History of Rome to the End of the Republic*, second edition (Baltimore, The Johns Hopkins Press, 1927). [Frank, *An Economic History.*]

FRANK, TENNEY, *A History of Rome* (New York, Holt, 1923). [Frank, *History of Rome.*]

FRIEDLÄNDER, *Roman Life and Manners*, etc.: *see* pages 23-24.

FRIEDLÄNDER, LUDWIG, *Städtewesen im Italien im Ersten Jahrhundert*, translated by William E. Waters, under the title *Town Life in Ancient Italy* (Boston, Sanborn, 1902). The English translation is the work referred to in this book. [Friedländer-Waters.]

GEST, ALEXANDER PURVES, *Engineering*, in the Series entitled "Our Debt to Greece and Rome" (New York, Longmans, 1930). [Gest.]

GRANRUD, JOHN E., *Roman Constitutional History* (Boston, Allyn and Bacon, 1902). [Granrud.]

GREENIDGE, A. H. J., *Roman Public Life* (London, Macmillan, 1901). [Greenidge.]

GUSMAN: *see* page 26.

GWYNN, AUBREY, *Roman Education from Cicero to Quintilian* (Oxford: At the Clarendon Press, 1926). [Gwynn.]

HALL, F. W., *A Companion to Classical Texts* (Oxford: At the Clarendon Press, 1913). [Hall.]

HALLIDAY, WILLIAM REGINALD, *Lectures on the History of Roman Religion* (Liverpool, The University Press of Liverpool; London, Hodder and Stoughton, 1922). [Halliday.]

HARPER'S: *see* page 25.

HEITLAND, W. E., *Agricola: A Study of Agriculture and Rustic Life in the Graeco-Roman World from the Point of View of Labour* (Cambridge: At the University Press, 1921). [Heitland.]

HERSCHEL, CLEMENS, *The Two Books on the Water Supply of the City of Rome of Sextus Julius Frontinus, Water Commissioner of the City of Rome* A.D. *97*, second edition (New York, Longmans, 1913). Frontinus's work on aqueducts was translated also by Bennett, Charles E., as part of a volume on Frontinus in *The Loeb Classical Library* (London, Heinemann—New York, Putnam's, 1925). [Herschel.]

JOHNSTON, HAROLD WHETSTONE, *Latin Manuscripts* (Chicago, Scott, Foresman and Company, 1897). [Johnston, *Latin Manuscripts*.]

JOHNSTON-KINGERY: *see* page 410, under *Cicero*.

JONES, H. STUART: *see* page 24.

LANCIANI, RODOLFO, *Ancient Rome in the Light of Recent Discoveries* (Boston, Houghton Mifflin, 1889). [Lanciani, *Ancient Rome*.]

LANCIANI, RODOLFO, *The Ruins and Excavations of Ancient Rome. A Companion Book for Students and Travelers* (Boston, Houghton Mifflin, 1897). [Lanciani, *Ruins*.]

MCDANIEL, WALTON BROOKS, *Roman Private Life*, etc.: *see* page 24.

MCDANIEL, WALTON BROOKS, *Guide for the Study of English Books on Roman Private Life* (New York, The Service Bureau for Classical Teachers, 1926). [McDaniel, *Guide*.]

MARQUARDT, *Das Privatleben der Römer: see* page 23.

MARQUARDT, JOACHIM, *Römische Staatsverwaltung*, second edition, in three volumes (Leipzig, Hirzel, 1881, 1884, 1888). The second volume was revised by H. Dessau and A. v. Domaszewski, the third by G. Wissowa). [Marquardt, *Staatsverwaltung*.]

MAU-KELSEY: *see* page 26.

MIDDLETON, J. HENRY, *The Remains of Ancient Rome*, two volumes (London and Edinburgh, Black, 1892). [Middleton.]

OVERBECK: *see* page 26.

PAULY-WISSOWA: *see* pages 24-25.

REID, JAMES S., *The Municipalities of the Roman Empire* (Cambridge: At the University Press, 1913). [Reid.]

RICH: *see* page 25.

RITSCHL, FRIEDRICH, *Priscae Latinitatis Monumenta Epigraphica ad Archetyporum Fidem Exemplis Lithographis Repraesentata* (Berlin, 1862).

Roman Farm Management. The Treatises of Cato and Varro, Done into English with Notes of Modern Instances, by a Virginia Farmer (New York, Macmillan, 1913). The "Virginia Farmer" was Fairfax Harrison. [*Roman Farm Management.*]

ROSTOVTZEFF, MICHAEL, *The Social and Economic History of the Roman Empire* (Oxford: At the Clarendon Press, 1926). [Rostovtzeff.]

SANDYS, *A Companion,* etc.: *see* page 24.

SANDYS, SIR JOHN EDWIN, *Latin Epigraphy: An Introduction to the Study of Latin Inscriptions,* second edition, revised by S. G. Campbell (Cambridge: At the University Press, 1927). [Sandys, *Latin Inscriptions.*]

SCHREIBER: *see* page 25.

SHERMAN, CHARLES PHINEAS, *Roman Law in the Modern World,* three volumes (Boston, The Boston Book Company, 1917). [Sherman.]

SHOWERMAN, GRANT, *Rome and the Romans* (New York, Macmillan, 1931). [Showerman.]

SMITH: *see* page 25.

TANZER, HELEN H., *The Villas of Pliny the Younger* (New York, Columbia University Press, 1924). [Tanzer.]

WALTERS: *see* page 25.

WALTZING, JEAN PIERRE, *Étude historique sur les corporations professionelles chez les Romains, depuis les origines jusqu'à à la chute de l'empire d'occident,* four volumes (Louvain, 1895-1900). [Waltzing.]

WILSON, LILLIAN M., *The Roman Toga* (Baltimore, The Johns Hopkins Press, 1924). [Wilson.]

INDEX

413

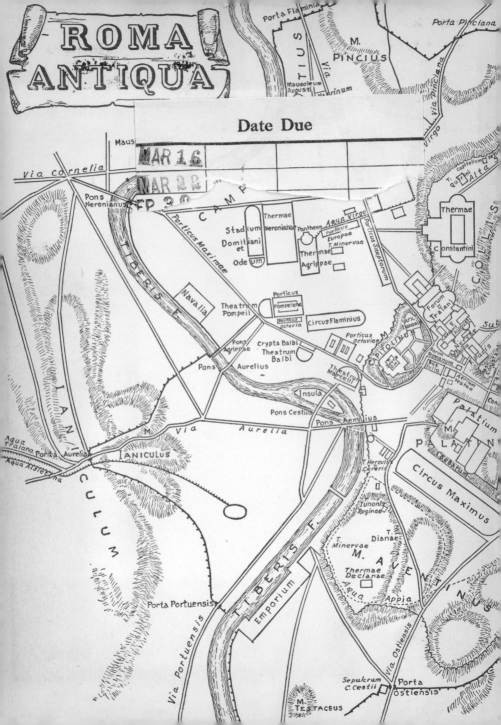